LOVE IS A
BURNING THING

LOVE IS A BURNING THING

A Memoir

NINA ST. PIERRE

DUTTON

DUTTON

An imprint of Penguin Random House LLC
penguinrandomhouse.com

Copyright © 2024 by Nina St. Pierre
Penguin Random House supports copyright. Copyright fuels creativity,
encourages diverse voices, promotes free speech, and creates a vibrant culture.
Thank you for buying an authorized edition of this book and for complying with
copyright laws by not reproducing, scanning, or distributing any part of it in
any form without permission. You are supporting writers and allowing Penguin
Random House to continue to publish books for every reader.

DUTTON and the D colophon are registered trademarks of
Penguin Random House LLC.

Photographs on page 286 (top) courtesy of the author;
(bottom) by Elizabeth W. Lary

LIBRARY OF CONGRESS CATALOGING-IN-PUBLICATION DATA

Names: St. Pierre, Nina, author.
Title: Love is a burning thing: a memoir / Nina St. Pierre.
Description: [New York]: Dutton, [2024]
Identifiers: LCCN 2023050416 | ISBN 9780593473825 (hardcover) |
ISBN 9780593473832 (ebook)
Subjects: LCSH: Mothers and daughters–Psychology. |
Parent and child–Psychology. | Family–Psychology.
Classification: LCC HQ755.85 S72 2024 | DDC 306.874/3–dc23/eng/20240213
LC record available at https://lccn.loc.gov/2023050416

Printed in the United States of America
1st Printing

BOOK DESIGN BY SHANNON NICOLE PLUNKETT

Penguin Random House is committed to publishing works of quality
and integrity. In that spirit, we are proud to offer this book to our readers;
however, the story, the experiences, and the words are the author's alone.
Some names and identifying characteristics have been changed to
protect the privacy of the individuals involved.

Some people have concrete stories.

The holes poked in them are all fun. A drunk uncle at Christmas revising your mother's version while everyone laughs. The spouse who fills in essential details she conveniently left out. There is little at stake, really. The truth may be novel, but it is of minor consequence.

But for those left piecing together shards—for the stock of the dispirited, the heirs of fragmentation—this story is for you.

LOVE IS A
BURNING THING

AUTHOR'S NOTE

I started writing this book in 2011. It's taken many forms since, tracking my development as human, writer, and thinker, as much as recounting what happened. Like the story it tells, its construction is an imperfect collage. A record of what I don't know as much as of what I do.

Memoir is not autobiography. It is a curated work of memory. And mine, while vivid in places, can be only sparsely confirmed. Most of the people who could correct me or help fill in blanks were dead at the book's inception or died in the long course of its writing. For others, I did what I could to honor their perceptions and fact-check where possible. Some names or identifying details have been changed. No characters have been composited, but in certain instances, for the sake of economy, time has been compressed or expanded. In some places, particularly with my mother and her recurring stories, I chose one moment in time to illustrate ongoingness. Often, I had to reconstitute from what scraps I had.

There remains much that isn't mine to tell.

As in any family, mine lived the quotidian slog—mundane moments at the laundromat, sitting around watching TV, endless immemorable meals; we had laughter and joy and inside jokes. The goal of this project was never to capture us in totality.

Instead, scenes and moments were curated, winnowed down in an attempt to answer the question that has haunted me: What was happening with my mother, and why didn't, or couldn't, I understand?

Quiet, Inanna, the ways of
the underworld are perfect.
They may not be questioned.

—*THE DESCENT OF INANNA*, 1900–1600 BCE

Bound by wild desire,
I fell into a ring of fire.

—JOHNNY CASH, "RING OF FIRE," 1963

A fire has four stages:

ignition, growth, free burn, and decay.

PART I

Ignition

I.

could tell you a lot about fire.

How its color depends on what it eats. How wood and fabric and gas and skin all burn different shades. How the symbols we have for fire and danger and stop are red, but red is just the beginning. Red burns between 950 and 1,800 degrees. After that, fire turns orange, then yellow, then at 2,400 degrees, white. White of purity, virginity, cleansing. White, closest to god. Around 2,600 degrees, fire turns the blue of water and sky and cool breezes. Of baby-boy rooms. It is blue that can eat through bone.

I could tell you how human limbs burn like branches. First the epidermis—the top layer of skin—peels back and chars, then the deeper dermis layers split and fizzle, releasing subcutaneous fat, which can melt and seep into clothing. A clothed human body is like an inside-out candle. If it can develop enough of a "wick," that is, if there is enough fat soaked into the fabric to use as fuel, it can burn for up to seven hours.

My mother wanted to be cremated. That's all I knew. After all that fire, in the end, we had to pay a professional to do it. I wish I could have laughed at the irony.

Charmaine drove me to pick up her remains at Dignity Memorial in Redding, California. After I signed a stack of paperwork and folded the "permit to transport human remains" into my purse, a man handed me an emerald-green felt bag with a silky drawstring. Inside, my mother's ashes were sealed in a cheap plastic box. She'd always looked good in that shade of green. Verdant against her chestnut-colored hair and eyes. Forested against her olive skin. Maybe we were always going to arrive here, me cradling what was left of my mother in the crook of my arm. Charmaine and I walked silent and somber over the hot asphalt of the funeral home parking lot, the late-winter sun bearing down on us.

She grabbed my sweaty palm in hers and squeezed tight.

"You all right?" she asked.

I looked at her and shrugged. "I mean."

"Yeah, I know. Just figured I should say . . . something?"

I could tell you that flames look like tears because of gravity and the upward motion of air molecules. That in space, at zero G, a piece of paper doesn't burn skyward in a hungry rising, but horizontally from side to side.

But just as the facts of my mother's death explain little about her story, facts about fire reveal little of what it wants. Of its hunger and complexity. In some ways, it's simple chemistry, a perfect collision of elements ignited by a spark. But it moves in other ways, too; ways that are human, unpredictable, vengeful. It nurtures and destroys. Sustains life and ashes it.

And in my family, it was always there—waiting.

I wouldn't be able to see all the ways that it blazed through our lives until it was over—until everything was gone.

The first night in our new house on Morris Street, my mom, my little brother, Chris, and I slept in a row on the floor of the attic bedroom. It was 1992, when winters in Northern California still meant blizzards and black ice. The propane tank hadn't been filled yet, so Chris and I burrowed deep into the new Garfield sleeping bags that Mom had splurged on at Walmart. She propped up a tiny space heater by our feet. In the middle of the night, it fell and the carpet burst into flames.

We woke to her rolling us away from the fire like logs. She screamed as she slapped it down with an old T-shirt. It burned through the carpet and foam underneath, leaving a topographic crater ringed with nubby singed bits. Mom threw a cheap rug over the hole and we moved my things in.

A year later, my brother and I sat in the same spot, smoking fake cigarettes—strips of college-ruled paper that I'd rolled into skinny tubes. I was twelve; he was four. When we lit the tubes, they flamed, then faded quickly into an electric red line that quietly ate the paper. Smoke curled a wispy dome around our heads, but it wasn't concentrated enough to inhale. We weren't smoking, really. It was the burn that held us. Its tiny, contained danger.

"Guys?" Mom called as she started up the staircase. In one super motion, I snatched the matches from Chris's hands, scooped up the crumpled paper scraps, and shoved it all into the top drawer of my dresser. As she scaled the final stair to the landing, I spied a half-empty water glass across the room and sprinted to it. I crammed the lit "cigarette" into the water and listened to it hiss, then pirouetted around to flash a smile at Mom. She sniffed the air and narrowed her eyes at my brother, who was busy wiping match sulfur onto his jeans.

"What're you up to, Neen?"

"Nothing," I said. "Just listening to music." I reached across the bed to turn up the boombox on my milk-crate nightstand.

"Were you burning something?"

My face was blank. She looked to Chris, her silence weighted.

"What were you burning, Chrissy?"

"Nothing," he mumbled. His eyes fell to his hands, answering her without meaning to.

"Neen!" she said, sounding more weary than angry.

"Sorry," I whispered. And I was. Not just because she'd caught me "smoking" or because I was a bad influence on my little brother, but because I knew what fire was capable of. And that should have been enough.

I could tell you a lot about fire, and all of it I know because of her.

———————————————————————

Ten years before I was born, at 4:40 on the morning of November 10, 1971, my mother and a woman named Raelle Weinstein sat "yogi-style" on the floor of an Ann Arbor, Michigan, kitchen and lit themselves on fire. Raelle was twenty-six. My mother had just turned twenty. They were just blocks from the University of Michigan campus, where my mother had been a student. Police tracked the smell of burning hair to find them sitting on the floor, facing each other, screaming.

"They weren't doing anything to put the fire out," Police Chief Walter Krasny told *The Ann Arbor News* in his official statement. "We have no idea why they would do something like this. They didn't use gasoline or anything. We presume they were fully clothed in street clothing and just set themselves on fire."

Firemen smothered the flames and cut remnants of clothing from the women's bodies, rolled them into wool blankets, and rushed them into the ambulance. As the siren screamed its make-way to the UM Burn Center, the women held hands. "It's lovely to die together," whispered one. That's what news reports would say. *One of the girls.* Maybe they were burned too badly to tell which. Or maybe it didn't matter, because it was all just background, scene-setting for an era of protest, student unrest, spiritual awakening, cultism.

As days passed, hospital staff reported that the women continued to act strange and refused to make a statement to police.

Raelle died a month after the fire, just before Christmas.

My mother spent six months total in the burn center, most of them wrapped in gauze and high on morphine, undergoing numerous blood transfusions, skin grafts, and surgeries. She incurred third-degree burns over most of her body. As she healed, her upper legs, torso, back, and neck were left covered in flat, ropy scars and small spongy patches where the grafts had taken. She lost her outer ears, or the spirally part we think of as ears, entirely, and her right elbow was burned down to bone; the tendons never fully healed, leaving her hand forever stuck half-open, clawed. By miracle or luck, the fire halted right at her jawline and above her knees, leaving her face and lower legs untouched, so that as long as she dressed in a particular way, from a distance, no one could ever tell. My entire life she wore pants or long skirts or knee-length shorts, to cover her legs, and up top, a turtleneck. Every single day, she wore one: turtlenecks under her T-shirts, button-downs, even dresses.

There was a nurse in the burn unit who wheeled Mom to daily whirlpool baths, where, as she healed, dead skin was pulled from her body like strands of egg in egg-drop soup. The nurse was a teacher of Transcendental Meditation (TM), a trademarked technique brought to the US by an Indian man called Maharishi Mahesh Yogi. Learning TM might help Mom in her recovery, the nurse thought. It might offer relief during a period of profound physical and psychic pain. I wonder if she intuited that my mother was searching for something "more."

Normally, it takes three days to be initiated into TM. The ritual is structured and precise, which I know because at ten years old, I sat sweaty and cross-legged in a carpeted room in Austin, Texas, for three days with Kathy, a woman with mousy chin-length hair and a soothing voice, as she chanted in Sanskrit, burned incense, and built an altar under a photo of Guru Dev, the northern Indian monk who was Maharishi's guru and taught him the technique he would later bring to the US. Following Kathy's instructions, my father helped me gather a small bundle of lilies, two pieces of whole fruit, and a brand-new white handkerchief, to place at the altar. A longtime TM practitioner and devotee, who found Maharishi around the same time as my mother, Dad was eager for me to receive my adult mantra as soon as it was allowed. He waited outside the door every day for three days while the ceremony and instruction took place. I don't remember much besides the sense of ritual—an initiation through sound and smoke.

In the burn unit, Mom and her nurse must have improvised. Maybe they used the hospital chapel. There wouldn't have been incense, but perhaps they plucked a few flowers from a bouquet that Mom's father, Lou, left on a visit, a get-well token from a neighbor back home in Livonia. Maybe they pillaged the hospital cafeteria, pocketing a bruised apple to offer at Guru Dev's photo. Small details like that wouldn't have mattered. Not to my mother, anyhow. Her devotion was never meant to be dogmatic. To be confined by effigies or inelastic rituals. She erected altars wherever she went.

A turquoise silk scarf laid over a cardboard box.

A thrifted blanket draped over a plastic patio chair.

Throwaway nothings refashioned into something sacred.

I can see the rooms she prayed in so clearly. Trios of veladoras, Catholic prayer candles, burned low in their votives. Patron saint cards lined the windowsills. Her mother's glass rosary, one of her few family keepsakes, snaked between laminated images of St. Francis, the Virgin de Guadalupe, and Joan of Arc, with Archangel Michael at the center. God's chief angel, Michael, was no soft, cooing thing but a winged warrior. It was said that in the end times, he would wield his sword and slay demons. *The Satan slayer*, Mom called him. "Now that is one angel you don't want to fuck with!" she'd hoot. Those unafraid to draw blood in the name of justice inspired my mother's greatest loyalty.

As a girl she'd attended Catholic school in Detroit, where nuns rapped their knuckles with rulers and sins were absolved with a string of Hail Marys. Long defected by the time I was born, she clung to personal relationships with the saints, carrying a sense of sacrifice and mysticism into her adult life. But it was that day in the hospital chapel, staring at the photo of Guru Dev, that her true devotion bloomed.

"Something in his eyes, Neen," she'd tell me later, recounting her initiation into TM. "That was it. That was what I'd been looking for my whole life." She never said what *that* was, exactly. But I would spend my young life by her side as she lost and found and lost it again—its pursuit propelling her ever forward. That day in the hospital, her scars still forming, she must have been desperate for something unkillable.

Something like faith.

II.

Hey, dickhead!" Rick Mann's voice echoed through the hall. Shira spun around to face him. Skimming six feet with the shoulders of a weight lifter, Shira wore a teetering blond beehive that I was always waiting to see slide off her head like butter off a corncob. Rick called Shira a drag queen, but I knew her as my neighbor and mother of my friend Aradonus, a stocky white boy a few years older than me with a fade and a stoic German countenance. The worn wooden floors creaked under Shira's feet as she stomped down the hall.

"Listen, Rick," she said. "I'm about up to here with yer bullshit." She shot a hand above her head as if to mark a high-water line. She looked like she could crush him, but Rick just smiled. Shira didn't understand that the angrier she got, the more fun he had. He pushed people's buttons for sport. He liked to see how far they would go. Where their limits were. If they had any.

Rick had only a few inches on Mom, who was five feet two, but his presence was outsize. A stocky dark-skinned Black man with a white skunk stripe running through his short, tight curls, he couldn't have been more different from my father, a soft-spoken white man whose once-sturdy swimmer's frame had gone willowy from years of meditation and macrobiotic meals. Rick was a social worker and a provocateur, which squared if you understood life in the 1980s in the Tenderloin. San Francisco's poorest neighborhood, it was a triangle of welfare services, soup kitchens, and free clinics. Rick spoke the lingua franca of the streets but was savvy enough to wrestle with bureaucrats. A natural conduit between worlds, he helped people navigate arcane social service systems. And talked trash while doing it. Shit-talking was his love language.

"Anita!" Shira yelled, exasperated. "You better get your man."

Mom stepped into the hall where I was watching the showdown from the top step. She passed me my backpack and coat. "Not my problem," she said, putting up her good hand in protest. "I have to get her to school. We're about to be late."

Rick cackled. "What's new?"

Mom zipped her coat first, then leaned down to button mine. She smelled like Suave and baby powder. "Okay, Bird. We gotta hustle if we're gonna make the train." She smiled like it was a game, her long teeth flashing. Her eyes crinkled softly at the edges. "Ready to hustle?"

Ready, I nodded.

She clenched my hand in hers, and together, we flew down three flights of stairs. The carpet squished under my feet, releasing poofs of stale smoke. My free hand surfed the railing. Its worn wood was slick against my palm.

"Anita!" Shira shouted down as we cleared the last step.

In the lobby, I waved to our landlord, Rainbow, who sat all day behind a big glass wall like a teller in a bank, then we stepped out into the San Francisco morning, which like every San Francisco morning, was overcast and alive. It was a grimy Technicolor universe. Boomboxes blared. Smells of piss and garbage were heavy. We rushed past an emaciated couple smoking on the corner, arguing over who owed who what from last night, from last week, forever.

Debts unpayable.

Memories dip-dyed in a haze of drugs.

Our territory was only about five blocks in any direction, but it felt pulsing and vertical. A brokedown kingdom of brick buildings with zigzagging fire escapes. Though no one called it that, the Tenderloin's official nickname was Hotel City, after the rows and rows of hotels that had housed thousands of people at the turn of the century and had since been converted into single-room occupancies, or SROs—studios with shared bathrooms in the hall. Some buildings, like ours, had kitchenettes, but many forbade cooking altogether. Most of the neighborhood lived on food stamps, which you couldn't use to purchase prepared foods. People got by on whatever they could store in mini fridges and cook in microwaves.

Everyone was poor-poor, on the edge of survival. Older folks skimmed by on Social Security or disability, and single parents like Mom managed an ever-shifting matrix of meager child-support and welfare checks. Those who were physically or mentally able to work busted ass to make ends meet with whatever part-time jobs they could piece together. People shot up on street corners. Many lived there, too.

Life in the Tenderloin was less a story than a cast of characters. A band of outcasts. Storytellers and survivors. Misfits and drag queens and ex-cons. Gender benders and make-doers. A tableau of dirty neon and laughter. Screams of "Free lunch! Free lunch!"

We struggled and strived together—waited in line at St. Anthony's for hot cafeteria lunches, took home holiday food boxes from the Self-Help Center where our friend Treat worked. On special occasions, we gathered in each other's studios for meals cooked with illegal hot plates and Crockpots. We clapped and hallelujahed on Sundays at Glide Church. We became family in the particular way that only those with nothing left to lose can do.

───────────────────────────

Mom was released from the burn unit in the spring of 1972. She was turning twenty-one, and spent that year becoming a certified TM teacher. Afterward, she traveled to Paris, Colombia, and what was then called the Panama Canal Zone, initiating new meditators.

TM was exploding in popularity. By the mid-'70s, more than forty thousand people around the world were paying to learn every month.

Aunt Fern, her mom's sister, lived in a tiny pink house in North Miami and invited Mom to come stay with her. She took the offer and dove headfirst into helping run the Miami TM Center. It was in Miami that she met my father, the son of a renowned local surgeon. A self-made man from Depression-era Kentucky with an army-funded medical education, my dad's dad was the poster boy for bootstrapping. He could do anything. A champion collegiate diver and pilot, he was also an inventor with dozens of patents to his name, some of which made his family, eventually, *very comfortable*, as people with money like to say. My grandmother on my dad's side was a Northwestern sorority girl, and the daughter of a bank president. My father's parents were attuned to hard work, traditional American values, and material achievement. They didn't get him at all. The second boy of four all-American blond athletes, he was a swimmer and the most introspective of his brothers. Growing up, he had abundant material comforts. Boats and planes, nice clothes all a given. And yet.

In the long shadow of his father's accomplishments, he wondered what any of it mattered—the achievements or accolades or wealth—if we couldn't achieve world peace.

After high school, he went west to the University of Colorado Boulder, where he dabbled in mind-altering substances. His second semester, he attended a talk about Transcendental Meditation and was struck by its potential. Drugs were fleeting bliss; transcendence, its stable version. In TM, he saw the opportunity to make a lasting difference. For himself. For all of us. Like my mother, he found what he'd been searching for.

Inspired by the egalitarian visions of Buckminster Fuller, and a chance meeting with Paolo Soleri, the Italian futurist architect who'd built Arcosanti in the desert Southwest, he decided to study what many creative spirits in high-achieving families do—architecture. He was initiated into TM, dropped out of Boulder, and went back home to Miami to take architecture prerequisites at the local community college. He got a job at Sherwin-Williams and was mixing a can of house paint one day when my mom came in to hang flyers for a local TM rally. Her fervor convinced him to come along.

"She was a true believer," Dad would recall years later. To be a *true believer* was his highest compliment. Though Maharishi insisted that TM was not a religion, my father took to it like a zealot.

After a year together, my parents married—not to satisfy their families, or even because they were particularly infatuated with each other, but because Maharishi said his followers should either be married or be celibate. They exchanged vows in the grotto of a Coral Gables church. Mom wore a crown of baby's breath and carried a bouquet of yellow roses and ferns. Her father, Lou, walked her down the aisle, and her older brother and only sibling, Dan, was there. Her mother, my grandmother Rodolpha, or Rod, as they called her for short, had already been dead for fourteen years.

In the faded sepia wedding photos, my parents are twinning in shaggy bangs and silly grins. Dad is mod in a slim-fit baby-blue suit, while Mom exudes bohemian minimalism in a simple white-lace dress with a collar that covers the burn scars on her neck. Her right hand claws as she shoves a slice of cake into Dad's mouth. In the background, my three grandparents stand in a row, heads tilted, hands crossed at their waists, politely grinning. *It's not the life I had envisioned for her,* Grandpa Lou wrote in a journal I'd find after my mother's death. *But she married a nice young man, and is now an expert in consciousness.*

What I don't think any of my grandparents understood was that, for my parents, and for the thousands of others who devoted their young lives to Maharishi in the 1960s, '70s, and '80s, TM was more than a stress-relief technique or a hippie-dippie spiritual fad. It was a movement, an infusion of peace and harmony after the suppressive 1950s cocktail-and-pills culture that preceded the Vietnam War. They were responding to a generation more concerned with material security than addressing the pain that American imperialism had wrought on the nation's psyche.

In an era of wartime hypocrisy and institutional cover-ups, their contribution was sitting silently with their eyes closed for twenty minutes, twice a day, and repeating the secret Sanskrit mantra they'd been granted at initiation. They treated meditation as their job, a seriousness that Maharishi encouraged, even capitalized on. In my mother's diaries, she wrote that during the Iran-Contra scandal, Maharishi told young meditators that if they overslept and didn't show up for a morning meditation, a hostage might not be set free. My father refutes this. "Maybe hearsay," he says.

But he doesn't argue that Maharishi used to say of his devotees: "Young bodies, old souls."

TM was going to be a ripple effect. By raising their individual consciousness through daily meditation, my parents would help raise the collective consciousness and, eventually, as more and more meditators joined, push the planet toward the ultimate goal: Unity Consciousness. The highest realm of enlightenment. A state I picture as Neo cracking the Matrix and experiencing singularity in binary form. The moment when we realize *we are all one* and have access to a shared "field" of information, or what theoretical physicists call the unified field.

With everyone functioning on that higher plane, there would be no urge or need to steal, rape, murder, incite war, or enact any of the violent transgressions that have kept human beings in turmoil for millennia. We would not repress or abuse or enslave others. We would willingly redistribute wealth and resources.

Something like utopia, I suppose. Heaven on earth.

After my parents married, they moved to Fairfield, Iowa, the unlikely heart of America's growing TM movement. Maharishi had purchased an old college campus to create Maharishi International University, an accredited school focused on "consciousness-based education." Overnight, the typical midwestern small town became home to thousands of TM practitioners draped in flaxen shawls and subsisting on rice and dal and veggie curries. The 'rus (short for "gurus"), as the townspeople called them, coexisted with local Iowans—a nucleus of god consciousness in the middle of forever cornfields.

My parents, who were in their late twenties and had both dropped out—Mom because of the fire, Dad because architecture turned out to be not for him—wanted to finish school. Like any college student, they went to class, wrote papers, and worked jobs on and off campus. But twice a day, they stopped what they were doing and climbed a hill at the edge of town, with hundreds of other bright-eyed believers, to meditate in giant golden domes—one for men and another for women. You could only meditate in the domes if you'd become a Sidha, which required taking the Sidhis, Maharishi's advanced course. In Sanskrit, *siddhi* means, loosely, "spiritual gifts and attainments from yoga." It implies magical or supernatural powers such as clairvoyance, invisibility, flight, and other skills most often assigned, in Western culture, to superhero(ines). The idea being that if you practiced what they called yogic flying long enough, one day you might be able to levitate.

My parents didn't have much in the way of material wealth or support in Iowa. They'd relinquished comfortable lives to pursue enlightenment. Daily choices on what to eat, wear, and study evolved based on guidance issued from their guru, which trickled down and was reinforced via movement administration. It was a small price to pay for the greater good. For a life that inched the planet closer to harmony.

The only thing my mother did want was a baby.

She was almost thirty, but Dad wasn't ready. He wanted to get his master's degree. To become a TM teacher, too. He'd never really imagined himself as a father. Also, they were broke. But that would never stop my mom from doing anything. To hear my father tell it, her will was stronger than his ambivalence. After she broke down crying in the parking lot of a bank one night, he agreed to try.

She got pregnant that summer. In the winter of '81, a month away from giving birth, she fell on the ice and broke her "good" arm. It was still in a sling when I was born; still in a sling a week later, when my dad's youngest brother, Brett, died unexpectedly, and he had to fly to Kentucky for the burial. Mom's dad, Lou, had come from Michigan to meet me, and told my dad that he'd stay with us. But something came up and Lou had to go, leaving my mom alone with one half-working arm and a newborn. When Dad came home from burying his brother, she wasn't there to greet him and mourn his tragic loss. Instead, she'd moved out of their apartment and rented another upstairs for the two of us. She didn't give my father a key. They'd been together three years by then. I suppose that was her way of saying it was over. She was like that.

If you could feel the end coming, it was already too late.

"It was like talking to a brick wall," she'd bitch about my father years later, offering little to no other concrete information about why they'd split up. As for him, he seemed baffled by her. Still does. What happened after that is fuzzy, but what is exceedingly clear is that I was going to be *her* child.

For the next few years, they were estranged co-parents, which according to Dad consisted of Mom's constantly "taking off" with me, and his trying to track us down. Without warning, she'd bus us to Detroit to visit her father. Or to Massachusetts, where Maharishi had another TM center. For a while, when I was two, we all left Iowa together to do "urban outreach" for Maharishi in Washington, DC. My dad got a job managing a laundry facility and scraping by, but my mom, once again, "took off for parts unknown." Finally Dad got a call from his mother, saying that we were in Miami. My grandparents had tried to talk her into staying. *Get a job and put Nina in day care*, they urged. But that was not her idea of mothering—it never would be. She was going to raise her kid herself. When we went back to DC months later, Dad says I didn't recognize him. "Mommy, who's that man?" I asked.

"That's your daddy," she said.

Dad tells me all of this once my mother is long gone and I'm trying to piece together my life before memory. As he shares these stories, something sparks. A sense of splitting. Of constant motion and upheaval. Of Mother as center, with no checks or balances. He tells me the stories, but not how they made him feel.

After a while, Maharishi summoned his followers back to Iowa, to participate in the Taste of Utopia Course. If the square root of 1 percent of the world's population meditated together in the same place at the same time, Maharishi said, it would raise the consciousness of the planet and decrease global violence. It was 1984 and the population was roughly 4.9 billion, so they needed 7,000 people. For years afterward, studies trickled out measuring what the movement called the extended super radiance effect, or the Maharishi Effect. Global violence had decreased by up to 30 percent during the time of the course.

We drove back to Iowa in a Volvo in a winter storm as Christmas approached. My mother piloted the car through waves of white as my father huddled in the back, a Florida boy, certain that we were done for. Mom had grown up in Detroit and balked at anyone afraid to drive in a blizzard. When she needed to go, she needed to go. No storm—of man or nature—could stop her.

Back in Iowa, Dad started dating Beth, the woman he would later marry. It was Beth who picked up the phone when Mom called to say that she was going to California and needed to leave me with them for a while. I was about to turn four. Dad and Beth met her at the bus stop for the handoff.

In my thirties when I first heard this, I had a romantic image of my estranged parents meeting. Snowflakes lightly dusting our faces, a halo from the streetlamp warping our reflections—the three of us together for the last time. A snow-globe family portrait. I imagined Mom kissing my forehead, whispering, *See you soon, Bird,* before disappearing onto the bus.

Dad tells me what she said when she called was: "Come pick her up or I'm taking her to an orphanage." I laugh in disbelief, my mouth agape. Not because it's such a terrible thought—every parent must want to drop their kid at an orphanage at some point. It's funny in a way I'm not sure how to reconcile. The idea of a mother who'd had her fill is simply not the mother I knew. The woman who raised me, who trekked up and down the long spine of California with me, and later, my brother, in tow—she clung to her children like we were sun, and she, earth.

Mom spoke rarely of those early years. On leaving my father, she said little. On leaving the TM movement, a bit more. As a teacher, she'd been expected to maintain certain standards of dress and behavior. Maharishi warned that if TM was mixed with other spiritual modalities, its efficacy could not be guaranteed, nor measured. But she'd started to dabble in other esoteric practices of the time, like reading tarot cards and channeling—when a human allows a spirit, either dead or deistic, to speak through them. The administration frowned on her actions and tried to squelch them. And in that, they lost her. Even the practice that had saved her life was not enough to demand total allegiance.

No matter how captivated my mother ever became with a person, place, or practice, she would always, eventually, choose freedom.

When Mom called that fall and said she was ready for me, Beth, who was going to visit her family in California, drove me 2,000 miles cross-country in her VW Bug, from Iowa to the rugged coast of Humboldt County, California, where Mom was living with a man named Bob, a kindly, bearded lumberjack type, in a log cabin in Trinidad, a coastal village deep in the redwood forest. My arrival there is a carousel of images: faded stills pierced by new scents, flavors, and sensations on the skin.

The soft red bark of the *Sequoia sempervirens* surrounding our cabin. Salty morning fog that left tiny crystals lingering on the face. Sweet vanilla and soggy sugar cones from a soft-serve shack along the highway. The cold smooth of the agate-studded beach where we ran from icy morning waves in rolled-up jeans and bare feet. Handfuls of seashells dotting our windowsills.

My real memory, though, begins in motion. Miles of pocked road beneath the slick of wet tires, as the two-lane highway became a six-lane freeway, and then, the streets narrowed, again and again, until there was no room for a car, and we were on foot, in the Tenderloin, navigating a maze of streets cluttered with soup kitchens and kids jumping double Dutch in alleyways.

I was a kindergartner. We were on our way to school.

Somewhere behind us, three flights up, Rick and Shira were still getting into it.

Ding ding ding! The trolley car rolled past, and we leaned back, bracing ourselves against the vertiginous decline of Powell Street. At the bottom of the hill, we were sucked into a mass of people rushing to work, winding and bending around one another like a flock of birds. Mom yanked me past tourists snapping pictures of homeless men peeing in storm drains, past the trolley turnaround, and down again into the BART station. A rush of hot wind blew back our hair and Mom scrambled to hold hers down, careful never to reveal the scars on her neck. We boarded the first train of two on our daily hour-long journey to White Pony, a private elementary school in the lily-white suburb of Lafayette that Mom had somehow gotten me into. Maybe Dad's parents were paying.

White Pony was another universe. A gentle sunlit place. Citrus trees dotted the orderly campus. A sprawling playground ran up to a grassy hillside where we sat at snack time to eat whole pomegranates, unearthing veins of bloody seeds from tissue-paper skins. Our tiny fingers were stained for days. Later, I'd learn that the school was run by a group called Sufism Reoriented, a vague American rebranding of mystical Islam founded by Meher Baba in the early 1950s, which many now consider a cult. But then, I basked in the quiet order of the teachers, who spoke in low calm tones—nothing like the clatter and chaos of the Tenderloin.

As I traveled between two worlds each morning, shifting from the hard, bright urgency of the city to the serenity of White Pony, I began to sense that one did not translate to the other. That they never would, exactly, and that no one from either world could be expected to understand. Little by little, I tucked these disparate ways of being, moving, speaking, into me.

III.

We moved into the Mission District studio that Rick shared with his sixteen-year-old son, Rick Jr., whom we called Brother Rick. Mom and Rick fought. A lot. When it got bad, Brother Rick would take me out with him to roam the streets. Through a sonic curtain of squad car wails, he'd replay his action-packed adventures. Like how he and his friends had jacked a payload of TVs from the back of a parked van.

"Easy," he'd say, flashing an impish grin as we swerved around garbage trucks and street sweeps. The smells were different in the Mission—fresh tortillas, stewy pork. Brother Rick was going to be a DJ. He'd bring along his boombox and play me cassettes of early Too Short or Timex Social Club's "Rumors," which, a decade later, I would dance to a sample of at house parties reborn as Master P's "Stop Hatin."

Mom fell asleep early and easy every night, while I lay awake, covers to my chin, watching the screen flicker against the walls as Rick watched late-night horror movie marathons. He loved the classics and watched them like they were slapstick. Campy stuff like *Night of the Living Dead* and *Nightmare on Elm Street*. "Ya, ya, get 'em!" He'd clap and holler. He tried to make me watch, too, determined to show me how fake it was, how it couldn't hurt me. "Don't you see?" he'd say. "That head, exploding right there? Bam! Rubber." He was trying to teach me how real other dangers were in comparison, but I was always more scared of make-believe than real life—more afraid of imagined horror than the threats that existed outside. Something about the shifting terrain of the fictional, the ways rules could be bent and rewritten, terrified me. As if every story had its own reality and you never knew what the terms were until it was too late.

Their fighting got worse. I hated the sound. The sense that something bad was about to happen. One day, I slipped away to the bathroom and shut the door quietly behind me, hoping no one would hear the metallic click. Fully clothed, I lay down in the empty clawfoot tub. The porcelain a cool salve against my neck. The shouting grew distant, garbled, underwater. I must have fallen asleep, because I was startled awake. It was quiet. Too quiet. Something was wrong.

Just then Mom yanked open the door and snapped me up. "Neen," she said, grinning. She had that look in her eyes. The one that meant *go*. "You ready to blow this joint?"

"Where we going?" I whispered, rubbing the sleep from my eyes.

"To a pretty place up north. Wayyyy north. With lots of trees. There's a special mountain there, my friend told me. A *cosmic* mountain. Now, doesn't *that* sound cool?"

I shrugged. I was young enough and had moved enough in those first six years that leaving and staying were sort of the same thing. People slipped in and out of our lives like water. It was all an adventure still. Leaving, just a part of the game. I hadn't yet learned that, to my mother, home itself was a movable thing.

Three months pregnant, Mom packed our bags to leave.

Her friend must have told her to take Interstate 5 so far north that we couldn't possibly be in California anymore. To drive until civilization seemed long gone. To drive until it was. *There you'll find the light workers*, he must have said, *the spirit seekers, the indigo kids. There you'll find what you're looking for.*

In the mythology of my childhood, my mother leaving my father and the Midwest and TM were signs of her indefatigable independence. Her refusal to be claimed or hemmed in. She was a woman on the run—a neon flash if you blinked.

She had to *split this town.*

Blow this joint.

Get the hell outta Dodge.

But if I could have telescoped back in time to the moment when my father was mourning his brother and she moved out with me, still a newborn, swaddled against her chest, I might have seen something that would help me understand what came later. I might have seen how she took her kids and ran. How "The Man," as a structural force of oppression, and individual men, even those she chose, pined for, and obsessed over, would become antagonists in a great sinister play, from whose final act we were always fleeing. I would have seen that initial departure as one in a continuum, designed to protect what she valued most: her autonomy and her children. Or rather, her right to parent us. It wasn't just the patriarchy we were sloughing off. There was something more complex at play. Something that like the rules of imagined realms, I wouldn't understand until it was too late.

IV.

It made sense that we wound up in California: land of dreamers, of reinvention. It was the only place big enough in miles and possibility to corral my mother. A place where we could drive for hours, moving through new landscapes, new states of mind, and remain within state lines. In California, we could thrive in ellipses.

What made less sense was landing in Siskiyou County.

Halfway between San Francisco and Portland, this was *wayyyy* north.

Not Bay Area north. Not even Sacramento north. But true north.

Middle-of-fucking-nowhere north.

Terrain of obsidian and sage, of pine, and scarlet-skinned manzanita, here you could drive the entire length of the county on mountainous back roads, winding past hidden alpine lakes with names like Hart, Castle, China, and Gumboot. Winter blizzards melted into icy summer swimming creeks so cold they burned. And every night when darkness fell, the sky was the inkiest black you'd ever seen; the stars, endless layers of pinhole lights. New ones born each time you blinked. It was the birthplace of the Sacramento River, which pumped aqueous transmissions through the arteries of the north counties before dropping down to water the farmlands of the Central Valley.

It was home to nature lovers and activists and multigenerational timber families. To ranchers and hunters and retired railroaders eking by on meager pensions. To Native families and New Age renegades. To light seekers and SSIers and court mediators; to early bird specials and redneck good ol' boys. To mythmakers and meth users and high school dropouts; beer bellies and never-will-bes.

It was a place where many valued gun rights and autonomy more than higher education; where *stewarding the land* could mean harvesting it or fighting to preserve it. A region whose settler identity was shaped by industries of extraction: Railroad. Water. Timber. Gold. In the 1940s, a group of citizens attempted to secede from California and create a new northern state to reflect what they called *rural values.* Their vision for the "State of Jefferson" was an ersatz Wild West, with no sales, income, or liquor tax; its government financed by mining and timber royalties. Labor strikes would be outlawed and slot machines banned as unfair competition to the booming stud-poker industry. Holdouts still claim that if Pearl Harbor hadn't been bombed and shifted the nation's political attentions, "Jefferson" would have become the forty-ninth state. By the time we arrived in 1988, the secession movement had gone dormant, but its libertarian undercurrent and *don't tread on me* ethos were alive and kicking. Siskiyou was, and remains, one of the few counties that consistently votes red in the forever-blue Golden State.

"Lonely as God, and white as a winter moon," wrote poet and explorer Joaquin Miller when he first glimpsed Mount Shasta. As we approached from the south, the mountain rose sudden and luminous from a thick sea of pine. Her ridges were long swoops of meringue, her summit crowned by saucer-shaped lenticular clouds.

Shasta was the crown jewel of Siskiyou County. The size of Rhode Island and Delaware combined, with fewer than fifty thousand people, the county was an evergreen nowhereland. Nothing but trees. Interstate 5 cut through the heart of the county. At its farthest reaches were tiny hamlets like Montague and Etna, Scott Valley, Tulelake and Modoc. But most of the county's residents lived in a string of towns just off of the freeway: Dunsmuir, Mount Shasta City, McCloud, Weed, Yreka. Most were single-stoplight towns, former industry boomtowns, none with populations larger than three thousand. To those passing through, they were pit stops—there was little to distinguish one town from the next. But to those who called this place home, each was a distinct universe, its intricacies and politics hard to understand from the outside. Everything embedded with family histories and subcultures, with long lineages of alliances and grudges. When you don't have much, every detail matters.

While its settler roots were overwhelmingly conservative, there was a long history of seekers, mystics, and charlatans flocking to the area. People came from around the world to bask in the otherworldly power of Mount Shasta, a mountain that meant many things to many people. To the United States Geological Survey, she was a potentially active volcano, with high threat of eruption. To those in esoteric circuits, she was the root chakra of the world— a cosmic portal to divine knowledge. And to Native communities who'd lived in the region, some for nine thousand years, and many of whom still did, Mount Shasta, or Buliyum Puyuuk, as the Winnemem Wintu call it, was central to spiritual practices and creation stories. Physically, she marked the convergence of ancestral territories of Shasta, Achomawi, Wintu, Karuk, and other Native communities.

White mystics who settled the region told tales of a secret city hidden inside the mountain populated by Lemurians, an enlightened civilization of extremely tall blond people. They led secret tours up its flanks to hunt for the entrance, while many Native people visited the mountain only in times of ceremony or healing. It was too powerful, some myths said. If you stayed too long, you might go crazy. Tourists took no heed. And seekers like Mom arrived in waves, spurred by word of mouth, hungry for a chance to glimpse the sublime.

It was a place of contradiction. Of ideologically opposed factions living in community, if not communion. At the base of the mountain was Mount Shasta City, the most touristy and monied town in the county. Its main street housed more crystal shops than dry cleaners, and the sight of white women in dream catcher earrings was as common as tobacco-chewing bubbas gunning their mud-streaked trucks through town.

At every gas station, the same postcard hung on a crooked wire rack near the register. Over a photo of the mountain backlit by a deep-plum sunset, in Comic Sans lettering, it said:

Mount Shasta
Where Heaven and Earth Meet

We landed first at the Pufferbilly Apartments in Dunsmuir, a tree-choked canyon ten minutes south of Mount Shasta City. Pufferbilly was across from the Amtrak station on Sacramento Avenue, which had been Dunsmuir's main drag in its railroad heyday. By the time we arrived, it was a string of abandoned storefronts and dilapidated buildings. But compared to our cramped San Francisco studio, the apartment was an oasis. Mom gave me the bedroom, where tall old-fashioned windows opened into a brick air shaft that I could holler down and hear my voice bounce back. Time was marked by the whistle of departures and arrivals, a sound both urgent and comforting.

I'd missed a chunk of first grade in the move, but started fresh in second at Dunsmuir Elementary, where I made fast friends with Carra, a willowy chitchatty white girl, who asked me to play on the bars at recess my first day and that was that. Her parents, Tom and Sue, were Deadheads with matching skull tattoos instead of wedding rings and took her to shows with them. When I was striking through the streets of the Tenderloin with Mom, she'd been sitting on her dad's shoulders, bouncing to the beat of "Sugar Magnolia." Tom rode a Harley, built his own trucks, and had a mammoth collection of classic rock albums, which he blasted at five in the morning, ready to greet the day with multiple shots of espresso—a holdover from his time as a long-haul trucker. My mom had grown up on Motown and show tunes, and weaned me on the same. Tom was the only reason I knew anything about rock and roll.

People asked if Carra and I were sisters, often. We had the same dark brown hair and eyes, but that wasn't it. It was that we *seemed* the same. We shared the same frenetic, loping Valley Girl shorthand and bonded over an unarticulated attachment to being cute, fun, "normal" girls, raised by parents who were anything but. We understood instinctively where the other had come from, and where we were hoping to go. She was already close with Charmaine, a stocky, even-keeled blond girl who lived across the railroad tracks. On weekends when the weather was nice, I'd invite them over for tea parties on our tin roof overlooking the train station. We'd climb up the back of the couch and pull ourselves through a high window, then sit cross-legged in a circle, sipping invisible tea and squinting against the blaring reflection. Tin Roof Sundays. I lived for the small-town sophistication.

If, for my mother, moving way north was a compromise between the mystical and the affordable—a place where she could find like-minded New Age friends while comfortably paying her bills—for me, it was grounding. I embraced the empty fields of dry grass and grunting men in Carhartt and work boots. Pickups with flat tires slumped in gravel yards, and dogs on thick ropes charged passing cars as neighbors eyed each other through sagging chain-link fences—all of which brought me a strange comfort. Being broke was not easy, but it was familiar.

My father was living in Texas by then. He'd married Beth and moved to another intentional TM community in Austin's Hill Country, where a group of meditators pooled their money to buy ranch land and take a crack at subdivision-as-utopia. Every summer, I flew solo from California to stay with them for a month. They lived in a humble two-story townhouse. It was immaculate—the north pole to Mom's south. My time there was the closest I'd ever get to a middle-class suburban existence. The residents owned the roads, and each family had their own home, but every night, the parents met to do their evening meditation, or "program," together in a giant golden dome near the community mailboxes. Everyone, including most of the kids, meditated twice a day, every day.

Once I was old enough, I'd stay home while Dad and Beth walked to the dome. Most nights, I didn't meditate at all, but ate as many gingersnaps as I could from the cookie jar without making an obvious dent, and binged *Golden Girls*, a favorite of Mom's and mine, which Beth thought was too adult. If she knew what I'd already seen, she'd have understood how tame four seniors cracking dirty jokes was. In Hill Country, I learned not only how to meditate but how to fold myself into the shape that they wanted. One always striving toward purity and order.

After a month at my father's, I'd fly to his parents' house in Miami, where, for two weeks, I lived a life of quiet luxury. Upon my arrival at their peach split-level, my grandmother immediately ferried me to the salon to doctor my cheap haircut or to the mall for a shopping spree at the Limited, which might as well have been Prada. We spent weekend afternoons on their sailboat in Biscayne Bay, dined on fresh lobster, and from time to time, flew to their property in the Bahamas. It was an annual summer vacation from being broke. A journey into alternate lives, which like the world of White Pony, I could never fully inhabit or take home with me.

While each place became part of me, they were disparate, with restrictions and expectations all their own. In Texas, I was expected to be more spiritual and disciplined. And in Miami, no matter how hard my mother tried, I never arrived polished enough. With my dad's family, there were mantras to be upheld, chores to be perfected, selves to be coiffed, impressions to be made. Striving takes many forms, but it is striving all the same. Always a betterment.

In Siskiyou, just as I had in the shit-and-piss streets of San Francisco, I felt accepted as is.

There was something communal about the desolation. We all shopped at the only mall within an hour's drive. No one teased me for wearing knockoff Keds like they did at bougie Miami summer camps. Everyone there was like us—just getting by.

One night, I woke to deep groans coming from the living room and rolled out of bed to find Mom cross-legged on the couch, holding her belly, Lamaze breathing. "*Hee-hee-hooooo. Hee-hee-hooooooo.* Bird, be my big girl and call Lourdes, okay? Heeeee heeeee *heeeeeeeee.* Pick up the phone. Her number's on the phone book. Yep, there, right there on the floor."

Fifteen minutes later, Lourdes, her midwife, pulled up in an old Volvo. We loaded Mom into the back and drove to the hospital in Mount Shasta, where she was whisked away on a gurney, and I was led to the waiting room, where's Mom's friend Kim was waiting to watch over me. A tall woman with thin salt-and-pepper hair and a Romanesque nose, Kim had big energy. She wore plum velvet shirts and occasionally burst into vocal scales in public, which she did that day, her high soprano trilling out a strange aria of *Welcome, Welcome,* as my mother's bloody screams echoed through the antiseptic halls. Early that morning, in the only hospital for thirty miles in any direction, my brother arrived, healthy, happy, and enormous. She named him Christopher. I like to think that it was after St. Christopher, the patron saint of travelers.

We called him Chris.

And, with him, we were three.

―――――――――――――――――

We had no family around. Rick and Mom had gone through an off-and-on custody battle, exchanging nasty letters, before finally settling on weekend and holiday visitations. Both he and my father sent monthly child support, though it was meager, according to my mother. She had no steady partner or boyfriend and, when she left the Midwest, seemed to have left her family behind for good. Her father died just before Chris was born, and she spoke of him rarely. Her brother had disappeared years ago, leaving no forwarding address. Her aunt Fern was the only one we heard from; every year on our birthdays, she sent a sentimental Hallmark card with a crisp five-dollar bill inside.

We got by with the support of a small network of women. Mostly white single moms who pooled their resources to purchase brown rice and miso paste in bulk from a mail-order co-op, and who casually, while waiting in line at the bakery, discussed their experiences with the "Greys," sinister aliens said to abduct people, render them unconscious, and conduct scientific experiments on their bodies, often sexual in nature.

Over watery coffee, they chitchatted about the reincarnation of Saint Germain and esoteric ideas like ascension and universal love and indigo kids. They reflected on Nostradamus's predictions that California would one day crack off like brittle and sink into the Pacific. About how, at the top levels, Freemasons were actually Satanists; Bill Clinton was a clone; and the government was being run by a reptile race. They were spiritual, proto-woke women whose politics skirted appropriation and appreciation. Women whose praxis on class and race was often wrapped in far-flung conspiracy and cosmic rhetoric. They were saying many of the things, with different intonation and intention, that decades later would emerge as conspirituality—a hybrid belief system that combines conspiracy theory (or the belief that the world is controlled by a secret order of individuals) and the New Age credo that we are entering a "new paradigm."

There was Evelyn, Mom's first friend up north and, comparatively, one of the most grounded. A silver-haired poet, she, like many of the mystical women there, had left a conservative family of origin in the Midwest to come to California and live on her own terms. Evelyn was "walking the red road," which from what I could tell meant adorning her apartment with pictures of Native people and gnarled wooden walking sticks draped in feathers. Her fingers were stacked with silver and turquoise rings, her hair pinned back with handmade feather clips. I didn't know then that the red road was not something she could set out on but a path for Native people, another appropriation of the area's Indigenous spiritualities.

Then there was Kim, the waiting-room soprano.

And, later, Tammy, a shit-talking, chain-smoking East Coast hippie who named her daughter after the goddess Radha.

And Sita Ram, whose birth name was something like Ann but who'd adopted the moniker of not only one Hindu god, Sita, but also her spousal deity, Rama.

And, finally, Marge, the senior of the group, a seventysomething former navy woman who called everyone "dear heart" and sang her words after one glass of cheap merlot.

In the Tenderloin, our friends had been street-smart and hard-knock. They were white, Black, Eastern European, Asian, gay, queer, straight. They were drag queens and ex-cons. Some were religious, while others believed in nothing but that which had saved them—their own two hands. They all had to contend with close-to-the-bone city living, which lent a sharpness to any notions of divinity. Whatever spiritual ideas our friends in the Bay held were tempered by the relentless grind of staying alive. But in Siskiyou

County, even the poorest were buffered from the pace of city life. There, in the forest said to be populated by fairies, they reinvented themselves via reworkings of Eastern or Indigenous traditions or joined new movements started by seekers who'd landed in Shasta before them.

V.

The most visible homegrown religion was the I AM movement. Started by a guy named Guy, who came to Mount Shasta from Chicago in the 1930s, I AM was a reference to Exodus 3:14, when Moses encounters the burning bush and is charged with leading the Israelites out of Egypt. Moses asks the fire who he should say gave the order.

God-as-fire replies, "I am who I am. This is what you are to say to the Israelites: '*I am* has sent me to you.'"

In the I AM origin story, its founder, Guy Ballard, was hiking on the mountain when he encountered a divine being named Saint Germain, who shared generic messages of peace and love. Ballard, like Moses on Mount Horeb, was told to share these messages with others, which he did; soon, followers flocked to him.

The I AMers had a building on Mount Shasta Boulevard, and their images were plastered around town. Pictures of beatific blond people bathed in golden light and surrounded by lavender auras—a pastel version of Catholic saint portraits. Their theology centered around a spiritual council of "Ascended Masters" who Ballard claimed were working behind the scenes to guide human destiny. These Masters were mostly repurposed or reincarnated versions of historic gurus or deities from other world religions: Jesus, Kwan Yin, the Buddhist goddess of compassion, and other vaguely mythological creations unique to the movement itself, like Lady Portia, a mash-up of Mother Mary and Lady Justice. All of these masters had conveniently chosen Guy, and later his wife, Edna, as human channels to issue what they called decrees. There were decrees for opulence, to remove pride, and to balance the body. In a secular space, they might be called manifestations, or affirmations: *I am the Presence producing abundance wherever I choose to use it.* Reciting decrees, it was said, could alter states of being or situations by harnessing creative fire or god energy—the "I Am."

Soon Mom was weaving them into her daily spiritual practice.

Ballard and his ilk created a mystical economy for the area. His theology went down easy with locals, as it built upon existing New Age mythology around the mountain. Bowling Green State sociologist Madeline Duntley, who has studied the area's spiritual tourism in depth, calls I AM and its successors "frontier esotericism." By tapping the mountain as a wellspring of new syncretic religions, they occupied psychic space already home to Native spiritualities, saying *ours now.* Or, at best, ours, too.

They were, as Duntley puts it, spiritual prospectors.

A 2018 Pew research study isolated four core beliefs that define "New Age" thinking: belief in psychics, reincarnation, and astrology, and the belief that spiritual energy can be located in physical things. Sixty percent of Americans, Christians included, Pew found, hold at least one of these beliefs, though many would be hard-pressed to explain what New Ageism is. And for good reason. It's a slippery term. While it conjures images of crystal shops and floaty people in linen pants, it's actually part of a broader Western esoteric tradition, which views earth as a series of levels, or realms, that represent ascending states of consciousness. It's not a religion, exactly, but a decentralized web of beliefs. A way of seeing the world. A lens.

New Ageism, which exploded in the US around the time my

parents were getting into TM, was one of several spiritual branches of thinking spawned from Theosophy, a chopped-and-screwed nineteenth-century mix of global mythologies repackaged and introduced to the West by Russian noblewoman Helena Blavatsky in the late 1800s. Theosophy is a nondenominational set of "truths" underlying religion, philosophy, and science. Truths that Blavatksy said had already been arrived at by ancient world civilizations but had been forgotten or lost to attrition, until she rediscovered them, synthesized them, and put them into writing. By reintroducing this universal knowledge to Americans through dozens of self-published pamphlets and books, Blavatsky positioned herself not as a prophet or direct channel à la Ballard but as a cosmic archaeologist of sorts—an excavator of essential universal truths.

Theosophy had no defined moral code or dogma, but it tapped Eastern concepts, like the oneness of all, universal brotherhood, and reincarnation. As most nineteenth-century Westerners were poorly educated on religious traditions of the East and basic Buddhist tenets, Theosophy offered a microdose of Orientalism. It was "ancient wisdom" light. Stripped of spiritual rigor or cultural context, its teachings were much like how yoga in the US has been decontextualized and mutated into Justin Timberlake–scored power hours and tech-bro flexibility Olympics.

Blavatsky insisted that it was not a religion, but *a religious transmission*—information being channeled—that could help the ordinary person prepare themselves for a "new age" of peace and love. This idea, *the unlocking of ancient secrets* to access new knowledge, is the foundation of New Age thinking, a framing first introduced by independent theosophist David Spangler in the 1970s, who stated that the cosmos—what we might call "the universe" today—was set to undergo a metamorphosis in the coming generation, and that shift would make a powerful amount of spiritual energy available to the average person. Spiritual energy that, if they could learn to properly access and utilize it, would bring about a global transformation in humanity. A shift in *consciousness*. New Age practices were not oriented toward heaven, but allowed people on earth to become spiritually refined enough to unlock new levels of consciousness, which would in turn create peace and harmony. It was a new "ascension narrative." Instead of leaving earth to arrive at heaven, they could use knowledge to create heaven on earth. Again, something like *utopia*.

In times when public trust in institutions is low, esoteric beliefs and practices often grow in popularity. Many of the alternative spiritual practices popularized as my parents' generation came into itself pointed toward the same thing—shifting human consciousness via core universal truths. Truths that were already at the center of most world religions: love, peace, kindness, harmony, justice. But in the New Age, it had been almost video-gamified, tiered into levels and realms; ascending states to be unlocked. It was the accrual of wisdom or knowledge, not strength or bravery or riches, that would advance you. Practices including prayer, chanting, altar making, divination, and astrology pointed one back to the self. Whereas traditional religion asked followers to earn their place in a congregation or the afterlife, New Age practices were simply tools to unlock existing knowledge.

In the 1970s, Americans' trust in the government was at an all-time low. It wasn't just Vietnam. Theories about COINTELPRO were circulating, as were whispers that the CIA was responsible for killing Black Panther Party founder Huey P. Newton and Martin Luther King Jr.

New Age spirituality broke down traditional religious power structures, giving the ordinary person power. Not only did it grant them access to the divine, but it allowed them to pick and choose what they liked from any belief system and mash it together with another.

It wasn't just a cultural reset; it provided a framework to an entire generation of people with no language to address the trauma of war, mental illness, or the fallout of poverty—financial or spiritual. It was not about being saved or redeemed but about *finding your own way*, which resonated further with the American ideal of self-sufficiency. It called to the nonconformist and the individualist, as it allowed for "reinvention."

Spangler's "next generation"—children like me whose parents devoted their lives to the expansion of consciousness—were born into the belief that enlightenment was within our reach and that we should strive toward it. But many of us didn't have the real-world structural or organizational support to integrate these ideas. Lacking the stability of tradition that our parents had sprung loose from, we were already floating. While our parents believed in justice and universal love, many of the spiritual principles we inherited didn't reckon on a practical, structural level with the issues of their time or ours.

In a way, a consciousness-based approach belies the impossible strictures of the world we have created. It becomes a sort of super(natural) solution to problems we find unfixable. While it may be a path to true expansion and connection, it's also a bypass because it depends on the individual awakening to seed change. The buck keeps passing. Every utopia is a failed experiment because the dissonance between life in the bubble and on the outside is too great. Its pressure deflates even the most idealistic.

All those women who'd left the Midwest and rebirthed themselves where the land met the sea, who baptized themselves in the possibility of the West and the names of gods whose languages they didn't speak; what they didn't fully grasp was that wherever you go, there you are. In this life or any other. Reinvention is not the same as reincarnation. Enlightenment is the long game. Not something you could skip over by moving to California and naming yourself Sita Ram.

I imagine Mom and her friends, the early TM acolytes, the rough-and-tumble street congregations of the Bay, the single moms of Shasta, all climbing the rungs of consciousness together. There they are colorful bohemian avatars meeting challenges (karma); slaying enemies (shadows, demons, fears); gaining tools (vague wisdom).

For those just passing through, Mount Shasta's signature postcard—*Where Heaven and Earth Meet*—was a novelty. A souvenir they might buy and send home, scrawling benign missives on the back from their vacation to the literal middle of nowhere. But as I would soon come to understand, for my mother and those like her, the tag line was literal. The mountain was a threshold: a portal between this world and all they imagined lay beyond.

VI.

Chris was a joyful, potbellied baby, always giggling, like those little statues of Buddha in the windows or gardens of Mom's friends' houses. I adored my brother and was only slightly jealous of his newborn freedom. Our age gap was too big for any true sibling rivalry, and I quickly assumed a hybrid role as big sister/second parent, which only increased as Rick's quarterly visitations eventually petered out. If Mom needed a break, I fed or helped bathe him. I hardly remember him crying at all.

Those first few years in Dunsmuir were tranquil. We moved around to a few different apartments, but otherwise, life was simple and slow. Mom was working as an assistant at a day care, so she took Chris with her while I was at school. The rest of the time, we read books, played Barbies, or sat at the laundromat, waiting on slow, shoddy dryers that ate our quarters like candy, while Mom drilled me on spelling words and geography facts. In third grade, I won the school geography bee and made it to the finals for spelling, where I lost on the word *eclipse*. I pushed Chris around town in his stroller, held meetings for the Peace Club that Carra and I had started in the wake of the Gulf War, and hiked into the woods above town, where I was building a tree house with a group of older neighborhood kids.

We didn't have much, but everyone knew our names. Mom made sure of that—making family wherever we were. Our first Christmas there, Dad and Beth came to visit and took me sledding on the mountain. Mom got a tree and let me drench it in silvery tinsel—the good, old-fashioned kind that came in little rectangular boxes with cellophane windows. I threw it over the branches in handfuls and let them rain down. We added garlands, too. Shimmery red, royal blue, tacky gold. Our trees were always a bit crooked, but like drunken washed-up divas, still they glimmered.

"You know, we weren't allowed to hang tinsel," Mom would say, attaching wire hooks to the ornaments. "My brother and me. Our mom insisted on hanging it one strand at a time. It had to be perfect. We would have just messed it up. That's what she said." I nodded. She'd told me before. For much of my life, it was one of the few characterizing details I knew about my grandmother Rod, who'd died when my mother was thirteen, and was everything that my mother was not.

What I knew about my grandmother could fit in a paragraph: The youngest of three French-Canadian Catholic schoolgirls from a small town outside Quebec, along the St. Lawrence River, Rod was the consummate 1950s housewife. Curvy, vivacious, and four feet eleven, she made a killer hors d'oeuvre platter, which she served at bombastic parties that ended with her martini-drunk and dancing on the table to Herb Alpert & the Tijuana Brass. She was a woman who'd rented a pony and full Western regalia for my mom's fourth birthday. A woman who raged at her husband in Québécois so the kids wouldn't understand. A woman whose spirit like so many in her time was squashed by the quiet oppression of suburban conformity.

At least, that's how Mom told it, implying that things were not as they seemed. That domestic perfection was hollow. Sometimes, as she told the tinsel story, she'd laugh at its absurdity. Other times, her mouth pulled into a thin line, her eyes growing distant and cloudy.

I guess our trees were her middle finger to all that.

A fuck-you to aesthetics over authenticity, image over joy.

Joy took precedence wherever possible. We were always broke, so our adventures were low-budget. When Mom got antsy, we'd jump in the car and go for a drive. Sometimes we'd follow Everitt Memorial Highway, the road that spiraled up the flank of Mount Shasta, ending at Old Ski Bowl, the highest point you could reach by car. We'd get out and walk around. In the summers, it smelled like cooked earth, and from that close up, the mountain looked less like a postcard and more like the imposing volcano it was. It was our place to talk and think. A cathedral of magma and pine.

Later, when things got bad, we'd visit Ski Bowl often.

It always reminded Mom of why we'd come north.

Other days, we drove farther. She'd wake us early, still crusty-eyed: "Hey, guys, let's blow this joint!" As she warmed up the car, I'd throw a change of clothes in a bag just in case. Still in pj's, Chris would drag his sleeping bag and pillow to the back seat and lie down, while Mom called the school to excuse me. She hated lying and chose her words carefully to avoid any untruth. *Nina won't be attending today,* she'd say, winking at me. *It's a family matter.* And it was.

We'd drive an hour north just over the Oregon border into Medford and spend the day walking around the Rogue Valley Mall. Or the same distance south to Redding, to hunt for deals on dented cans and generic bagged cereal at Grocery Outlet, or "Canned Foods," as we called it. Or to Chuck E. Cheese, where Chris and I had mastered the art of stretching twenty dollars into hours of play. I'd identified which games would release extra tickets if you pulled slowly enough at just the right angle. If Mom was extra antsy, we might drive the three-plus hours to Sacramento for an overnight. Halfway there, Chris would launch his campaign. "Train museum! Train museum!" he'd chant. In Old Town, there was a museum with an extensive, and incredibly boring, exhibit on the history and importance of trains in the region. In Dunsmuir, train whistles blew so many times a day that you stopped hearing them at all. Chris was obsessed. He'd wander for hours, watching the model trains chug along looping tracks, memorizing their names and engine types and reciting them to us later, unprompted, in our room at a Motel 6, where we'd order a large cheese pizza—half off with a coupon from the front desk—and stay up late watching HBO and jumping on the beds, leaping from one to the next, squealing as we flew past each other.

If things were really bad or really good—sometimes it was hard to tell the difference—we'd keep driving to San Francisco, just to listen to the sea lions bark at Pier 39. Or to Santa Cruz to wander the boardwalk and take a single ride on the rickety old roller coaster. A couple times a year, Mom really got *a wild hair up her ass,* and we'd drive twelve hours to San Diego and go to Mission Beach or wander around Seaport Village or hit a second-run movie theater. Then there were the days that we left California altogether, crossing the logjammed border into Baja, where she'd discovered a Mexican Chuck E. Cheese–style arcade called Imagina Tu Diversión.

Like most single parents, she needed escape. Because she couldn't afford, and didn't really trust, babysitters, everywhere she went, we went. She didn't get girls' nights out. Or date, really. Instead, she curated a rotating cast of destinations where diversion for us was free or cheap, the people-watching exciting, and the energy high enough to give her a jolt of life force and inspiration. Chris and I window-shopped or played arcade games and sometimes bought a small cheap thing to eat or drink that we could nurse while she scribbled plans in her drugstore notebooks.

To-do lists, how-to-pay-the-bills lists.

All her plans for *more*—a labyrinth of hopes and dreams, shifting balances and credit-card advances, attempts at clarification and reconciliation—were in those pages. Mom moving money around on paper was the white noise of our youth.

We never got souvenirs. The saltwater taffy. The old-timey photos in Western saloon-wear. The live oysters that might contain a
pearl. Chris was little still, so he might beg for an overpriced hot
dog at the boardwalk. But I didn't even want touristy things. By
then, I knew the true cost of each small luxury. What I coveted was
the ease that I imagined came with a life in which you could afford
throwaway tchotchkes. A life in which you could spend money on
frivolous things, or even things that mattered, without worrying
about what came next. A life in which pleasure didn't mean a
hard time coming. In which every treat didn't have a trapdoor.
More than craving momentary pleasure, I grew to anticipate its
fallout.

After our trips, in the weeks to follow, there would be a deficit
somewhere. An unpaid phone bill. A lag in kerosene. And we'd be
waiting, again. For the next check. The next trip. Mom might
snap, resentful of what she'd splurged on. In the meantime, she'd
turn on the oven and open it to warm the house. Ask my father to
cover a bill. Haggle with bill collectors, and set up new payment
plans with incrementally smaller payments, which would rack up
interest that she'd chip away at forever, barely making a dent. Because I knew what moments of freedom cost, I tried to slow time
and savor each treat, each ride, the sounds and smells of people
and sea; I clung to moments of levity; to my brother and me jumping
gleefully on motel beds, the swish of air as his body flew past mine.

Partway through fifth grade, Mom moved us again. This time,
into a room at the Alpenrose, a Bavarian-themed motel in Mount
Shasta. We'd been there about three weeks and Mom kept saying it
was temporary, but it felt like she was saying something else, because wasn't that the whole point of a motel? *Temporary.* Everything
at the Alpenrose was a prop for home: the stiff curtains screeching
along rusted metal rails, the pressboard dining table that bubbled

under the sweat of Mom's Coke cans. Even the bedspreads with their oversize flowers and scratchy polyester linings.

It'd been a few years since I changed schools last, and it seemed like there were rules now. From what I could tell, coolness hinged on having poufy bangs or boobs or boyfriends. It was hard to isolate a single factor because Meghan, the most popular girl at Sisson Elementary, had all three. Lithe and bony, I was years from developing anything resembling a figure. My long, stick-straight hair would not, with any amount of Aqua Net, approach a respectable wavy bang. And boys looked right through me. Despite all this, Meghan hadn't yet determined that I was uncool. As the new kid, you have a fleeting window of power in which you can be anyone. But mine was bound to collapse when my classmates found out that I was living in room number 5 of a Bavarian-themed motel with my mom and three-year-old brother.

Every time we moved, I had to present myself to a new group of kids and hope for acceptance. As an outsider in a rural area, where most families had lived for generations, I had no stored social capital. There was no big sister to part the sea for me; no family name to lean on. We were thousands of miles from anyone who shared our DNA. With no family around, friends meant more.

Pipes screeched and the hum of running water went silent. For a moment, room number 5 had a heartbeat. Mom stepped out of the bathroom. Milky clouds of steam coiled up around her as she twisted a ratty motel towel around her hair. Another, tucked around her body, barely covered her cheeks.

"I've got to get this crown fixed," she muttered, picking at her teeth in the pocked bathroom mirror. "A trip down south soon."

Down south was Tijuana, where you could get ninety-nine-dollar root canals.

"Whatcha watching, Bird?" She craned her neck to catch a glimpse from across the room. "Oooh, my show."

"Every episode is the same." I sighed, kicking my legs out from under the scratchy duvet. "You already know what's going to happen."

"I just like the legal stuff." She shrugged. "You know, I should have been a lawyer."

She plopped down on the bed. "Scooch over, bb."

"Ohhhh, there he is," she cooed, her body bending toward the screen. Her fingers were water-soaked prunes; her feet pink and fresh-scrubbed. "My maaaan! Mr. Logan. Turn it up, will you?"

I groaned. Because she'd lost her outer ears in the fire, the part that funnels sound to the eardrum, Chris and I had to listen to her shows—*JAG*, *Law & Order*, *Kojak*—at high volume. The TV blared as she unwrapped her hair and pulled a pick through it with her good hand. Droplets of water flung off her ends, landing in little splats on my cheek. I watched her comb out the tangles, my eyes drawn to her elbow. The rest of her scars were old, but the elbow always seemed freshly wounded. The skin over it was stretched thin, like the purply flesh at the end of a chicken bone. If she bumped it too hard, it bled.

During the commercial, she turned to face me.

"I'm gonna get us a real place, you know," she said quietly. Her eyes were soft and watery. I rolled mine. "I know, Mom," I said, stuffing down my growing resentment of our motel life.

"Things got bad for a bit there, babe," she said, looking deep in reverie. "I haven't been well."

I thought things had been okay. Besides moving to the Alpenrose, I thought we'd been fine.

"But she's gonna help us do better."

"She?"

"She wasn't taking good care of you and Chrissy," she said, cupping my cheek with a soggy hand.

I flinched, swallowing an eerie feeling. The air was choked with humidity.

"Who is she?" I asked, looking at her without making eye contact. She pulled a frayed corner of her towel over the V where her legs met.

"Bird," she said, taking my hand in hers. "I'm what they call a walk-in."

I'd seen that word before. On a clinic window. A hair salon.

"Walk-ins don't need appointments, right?" I said.

"Right." She laughed. She seemed almost charmed. "They just walk right in!"

Something was off about her smile, her tone. I glanced at my brother, who was deep asleep on the other bed, wrapped in a tangle of sheets, tiny snores slipping from his open mouth like beads.

I hesitated. "What are you walking *into*?"

"It's not exactly like that." Her voice cracked. "You see. Someone is walking into me."

The hair on my arms went vertical. I was overwhelmed with the sudden urge to bolt out of the room. To run to the front desk and report a missing person. To ask for help. My mother's voice remained steady, its warm husky tone unchanged, but I couldn't calm the energy shuttling through my veins. My body hummed with nerves. I flipped through channels.

Mom took the remote from my hand and grabbed an empty Coke can from the other table.

"So, there's Anita One," she said, wiggling the remote. "And there's Anita Two." She tapped the can.

"Anita Two is a Coke can?" I snapped. I was starting to feel really weird.

She laughed. "No, babe. Pretend these are souls. You know

about souls, right?" A rhetorical question, but I nodded. I understood the soul to be your inside-you. The essence of who you were.

"There are many versions of us," she went on. "Before I was born, I made a deal with a new version of my soul to swoop in and spiff me up when I got tired. See, you're supposed to get better as you go along. For some of us, when the first version has done all that it can, the next one steps in."

That made sense. Seemed logical, almost. But the hot prickle of my skin said otherwise. She wasn't talking about self-improvement. About the natural evolution of things. This was something etheric. Supernatural. Something I couldn't name or see had taken over her body.

"I'm still me, Bird!" she said, doing a little bounce on the bed. *Anita Two knew my nickname.* She was so close I could feel the dew of her skin. I scooted away.

"I'm still Mom," she said.

But I didn't believe her.

"I'm just new and improved."

I cursed every time I'd wished for a new and improved mom, every time I'd wished that we would stop moving, or that I could buy name-brand clothes. If I could have asked my mother for anything then, it would be to stay with me.

The mother I knew. *Anita One.*

Snatching back the remote, I flew through the channels. A commercial for Sunny Delight came on. I pictured Florida, brightness, oranges, vitamin C, palm trees, my grandparents' pool. Anywhere but here.

"It's better this way, really," said Anita Two, pulling me to her chest. The fake-sweet of Suave and dusty motel soap lingered between us. She even smelled like my mom.

From the corner of my eye, I scanned her face, one of the few places free of scars. We shared the same deep-set brown eyes and olive skin that tanned with ease, but my mother's features were more angular and extreme. Handsome almost. Steep, regal cheek-bones and a hooked nose. Her broad forehead was permanently furrowed, deep lines plowed across her brow. Most days, she swept dramatic fuchsia Wet n Wild onto her lips, then dabbed the same onto her cheeks, rubbing it in tiny circles with her fingers until it softened and bloomed into a clownish blush. She lined her eyes with black-brown pencil, which she said accentuated dark eyes like ours better than jet-black—her singular beauty tip. One that I would return to later, when I started to cover myself, too, to show the world the version of me, of us, that I wanted it to see.

Quiet tears carved channels down my cheeks.

"You're still Anita?" I whispered.

"Yes, babe."

Anita Two ran her hand up and down my back, nodding like she knew how I felt. My heart was all bass. How could she leave without saying goodbye? And how could I trust this new person? I brushed away tears with the back of my hand, trying not to make a sound. I pulled away from my mother's strange embrace and tucked myself into the tight envelope of the motel sheets. As the TV blared, I closed my eyes and traveled over my mother in my mind, looking for something to cling to, but all I could see was skin. Where mine was peach-fuzz smooth, hers was jagged, full of ridges and caverns. Spiderwebbed burn scars spread across her chest and belly and back, spun halfway down her arms and legs. I pretended to be asleep for what seemed like an hour, tracing its crevices in my mind, searching for the moment I lost Anita One, and wondering what, if anything, her scars had to do with leaving.

Her skin became something else that day. Not a covering for muscle and bone and blood but something foreign to travel, like terrain—a map I was missing the legend to. I knew every contour of her body, but for the first time in my life, I didn't know my mother.

VII.

"You may know a walk-in," begins *Strangers Among Us*, Ruth Montgomery's seminal 1980s book on the phenomenon. "You may even be one. They are high-minded entities permitted to take over the bodies of human beings who wish to depart this life. Their mission is to lead us into an astonishing new age." Most walk-ins, Montgomery writes, have a pre-agreed-upon contract before their body is born. Just as my mother had told me, the original soul, "the walk-out," agrees to use the body to fulfill a particular duty or learn a certain lesson, then vacate it at a set time so the next soul, the walk-in, can use its physical form to learn its own karmic lessons. It wasn't just a personal metamorphosis, then. Like Spangler's theory of the New Age, walk-ins were here to help usher in collective awakening.

My parents were seekers, their lives oriented toward spiritual pursuits—my father with his daily practice of TM and adoption of the Bahá'í religion shortly before I was born, and my mother with her bushwhacking mash-up of Catholicism and everything under the New Age umbrella. What they didn't school me on directly osmosed into me the way a musician's child might clock a missing note or an athlete's kid inherit their good arm. Mom chatted freely about books she was reading and ideas she was puzzling through. One week it was I AM decrees; the next, readings from *A Course in Miracles*. As she went, she'd incorporate what resonated from each practice or teaching, and leave the rest, collaging together a roving, bespoke doctrine.

Because she didn't use sin-based logic or demand that I believe what she shared, her journey felt like an invitation. The ideas were there, swirling. I knew what she believed the same way I knew what was in her bank account—she told me.

Until that night at the Alpenrose, her beliefs had been fascinating possibilities. Jesus turning water to wine seemed like an impressive party trick. Hindu deities meditating for five thousand years was funny in the way that unfathomable numbers are when you're little—*I love you a gazillion million*. Time isn't linear: kids get it. Even when she told me how Christian Science founder Mary Baker Eddy, a woman she quoted often, didn't believe in illness or the doctors need to treat it, it was little more than trivia.

I'd absorbed these stories without fear of their possibilities. They were interesting, but I didn't think they were real, exactly. And they certainly weren't a threat. While I was starting to resent all the moving and lack of structure in our lives, I had never been afraid.

Not until Mom said she was a walk-in.

In *The Myth of Normal: Trauma, Illness & Healing in a Toxic Culture*, Dr. Gabor Maté explores trauma as a loss of connection to ourselves and the world around us. "As the lost connection gets internalized, it forges our view of reality: we come to believe in a world that we see through its cracked lens." My mother hadn't left. She was right there. She was loving and present. She fed and clothed us. Supported our interests. But her soul, her inside-you—the one I had trusted and known and loved—was gone. Which meant not only that the essence of the mother I'd known was missing but that there was a whole other realm in which I could lose someone. There was loss in places I didn't even know existed. An otherworld that could impact the one we lived in. That conversation upended the reality I had taken for granted. It cracked my lens; blew out the bounds of my already-vast world.

World-building has rules. Including rules about how to move from one world to the next. Even in horror. I'm thinking of the scene from *Buffy the Vampire Slayer*, the film, when Benny, a vampire, floats outside his human friend Pike's window, begging to be let in so he can feed. "You're floating, man," Pike says, shaking his head. "I'm hungry!" screams Benny, baring his fangs. Vampires couldn't come in without being invited. As long as we understood the logic of a world, we could avoid its dangers. Just like Rick had tried to tell me. Trauma is not the abandonment itself, Maté writes, but the wound it leaves you with.

Our conversation that day in room number 5 was the first deep schism between my mother's experience and what I had perceived as reality. She might have opened herself to adjacent otherworlds, but I didn't have to. I would figure out how to erect my own barriers. Containers. Order.

A few months later, she told me that her father, Lou, who'd died right after Chris was born, had left her some money and that we could maybe buy a house. I was elated. A house was the ultimate container. A place where life was meted out in sitcom scenarios. A house would keep out vampires.

The house she found was in Weed, a dusty lumber town ten miles north of Mount Shasta. It was two stories with peeling forest-green paint and a dead-grass yard. Inside, the walls were wood-paneled, the linoleum grimy, and the lighting left over from the '70s. After the tour, we stood in the gravel drive and Mom asked me if she should buy it. It took everything I had not to scream: *Yes!* For once, I wasn't thinking about our finances or how my egging her on might backfire if she came up short later. All the caution I'd learned to exercise fell away. Nothing was stronger than my urge to live in—to *own*—this home. If a grandfather I barely remembered had left Mom enough to put a down payment on a $40,000 house at 9 percent interest (see also: criminal interest rates for poor people with bad credit), who was I to turn my back on god's will?

The house was on Morris Street, in a neighborhood called Angel Valley, just across from the town mill. It did not matter, or even occur to me, that it was sort of a dump. Like most homes in Angel Valley and neighboring Lincoln Heights, it was on its third generation of grime. Weed had been founded as a timber milling company town in the late 1800s after a man named Abner Weed was traveling through and noted the extremely high winds. Winds ideal for drying lumber. By the 1920s he'd built a huge mill and hundreds of homes surrounding it, to house workers recruited from the South, including many Black families from Mississippi and Louisiana. Those families joined a wave of Italian immigrants, and white and Mexican workers, in running what would become, for a time, one of the world's largest lumber milling complexes. Once deemed the "Sodom and Gomorrah of Siskiyou" by the *Redding Free Press*, at its prime, Weed was a booming timber town with Wild West brawls, whispers of murder, twelve saloons on Main Street, and money to burn.

Over the next several decades, the timber industry declined but the families stayed, making Weed one of the most racially diverse towns north of Sacramento. Which wasn't saying much. But it was anomalous in the sea of rural whiteness that was north-north California. By the time we arrived in 1992, Weed was a pit stop with a slogan: *Weed Like to Welcome You*. People didn't visit anymore. They stopped to pose for photos underneath the Weed Arch, pinching ghost joints between pointer finger and thumb. They bought I HEART WEED shirts and shot glasses, filled their gas tanks, and hit the Taco Bell drive-through. The timber empire had dwindled to one plywood processing facility, which still employed half the town. Our house was just down the street.

Aside from an unobstructed view of Mount Shasta on the horizon, our new neighborhood, Angel Valley, wasn't scenic or angelic. It wasn't even really a valley but an open plateau scattered with homes and vacant lots—sparse of trees. The air was thick with the chemical musk of glue and wet timber. But for me, it was a bright omen. Mom had been talking about angels all my life. And look where we wound up.

The house on Morris Street had stories. Two of them, as in stairs, which meant ascending, *arriving*. Owning meant we no longer rented, which meant we couldn't be moved, which meant we were, finally, officially, *from* somewhere. "We need a home in the psychological sense as much as we need one in the physical: to compensate for a vulnerability," writes philosopher Alain de Botton in *The Architecture of Happiness*. "We need our rooms to align us to desirable versions of ourselves and to keep alive the important, evanescent sides of us."

We were far from middle class, but miraculously, it seemed to me, had achieved one of its markers. I didn't understand yet that we were poor, but not poor-poor. Generationally, there had been money and mobility. On both sides, back to my grandparents, almost everyone in my family was college-educated or had resources. My dad's parents were the surgeon and the Northwestern-educated banker's daughter; and my mother's father, Grandpa Lou, also French Canadian, had been a metallurgical engineer for a steel company that worked with Ford Motor Company.

But out west, with Mom, struggle was all I knew.

We got by on about $1,000 a month. Our living situations were shifting and precarious. She cobbled together jobs in day care and housekeeping, domestic roles, or anything that allowed her to take us along or be there when we got home from school. We'd been off and on welfare most of my life. Our cars, when we had them, were always on the brink of collapse. Eating a single dinner out could break the bank for weeks. Every month, she chose what bills to pay, running through them like a game of roulette. She took paycheck advances and paid their high interest rates.

Mom cut herself away from home, and what I imagine was a more comfortable life, when she became a TM teacher, choosing poverty with purpose over ease. She'd left the Midwest and landed in San Francisco, alone and broke. Anyone who might have helped her—a partner or her father, maybe—she harbored a strange resentment toward.

One year at Christmas, she flipped out when my Miami grandmother, who always included presents for her and Chris, sent her a designer red-leather purse instead of a check. The card said something like: *Just for fun. A little something you wouldn't buy for yourself.* I could picture my grandmother writing the thoughtful note, imagining that if *she* were broke, she'd want a red-leather purse to make her feel better. Telling herself that life was more than just struggle, so why shouldn't my mom live a little and look good doing it? The thing is, my grandmother had never really been broke. Not like us.

Mom pitched the purse across the room into the Christmas tree, which wobbled and jangled, tossing reflective shimmers onto the walls. "Of course I wouldn't buy it for myself," she shouted to no one after reading the card. "Because I would pay the effin' heating bill!" I didn't know who to be more embarrassed for—Mom, my grandma, or me in the middle, at a loss for what to say, and ashamed on both sides.

Moving day, as we shuttled tiny batches of our belongings from car to our new house, we were so close to capital-*F* family that I could taste it. *Family as seen on TV.* With fun-loving holidays and lively dinners. Roaring fireplaces and space to dream. My sense of levity had sprung a slow leak, and the house came just in time to ground me, to help recapture my most "important, evanescent" self, and let the adults figure out the rest. Morris Street would become my island between worlds.

During the early days there, I worried less.

Funded by my Miami grandparents, who were enthusiastic to support anything that might culture me, I'd been taking dance lessons several nights a week at a drafty studio under the direction of a kindhearted Christian woman named Tana. Dance became my sole extracurricular, all-encompassing passion, and future life plan. Other kids prattled on about becoming marine biologists or astronauts or veterinarians. I was going to be a dancer. There was no plan B. I didn't dream of being a ballerina or a Broadway star, but dancing backup for the biggest stars of our time. It was the MTV age. Music videos were peak pop culture. Next to my bed lay a worn copy of *The Magic of Paula Abdul: From Straight Up to Spellbound*, an eighty-eight-page unauthorized biography. Every night, I'd read it, tracing my finger over the facts of Paula until her story became part of me. While my mother soaked in edgy tales on the mystical life of Mother Mary, I read up on my own saints and saviors: Janet, Madonna, and Paula. Every Thursday, I watched *In Living Color*, sitting through an hour of jokes I didn't understand just for the Fly Girls dance breaks, which featured a pre-J.Lo Jennifer Lopez as a young dancer from the Bronx. In a world of bubbly blond protagonists, J.Lo and Paula were something to aspire to. Real dancers. Dark hair, dark eyes, olive skin. Paula and I even shared a signature beauty mark.

Mom made sure I practiced several times a week and brought a carload of my friends to the annual recitals. Afterward, she'd treat us to McDonald's and give my performance her critique first, praise, second. Carra, whose parents had never criticized a thing she'd done, thought that was extremely weird—rude, even. It didn't seem so to me. Criticism meant that Mom took me seriously. That she was not going to coddle me. If that's what it took to be great, *bring it on*. I could take it. I wasn't the most technically gifted dancer, but I worked hard and memorized the routines better than anyone else. I visualized bodies in motion at the first strain of a good song on the radio. Marked beats in my mind while showering. Mouthed 5-6-7-8 as I read the cereal box. Dance was a way to move without leaving. It was departure with a guaranteed landing.

At Weed Elementary, I made fast friends with a group of four. There was Veronica, a goofy Mexican prankster with a tough-girl front; Sam, a sarcastic Chinese girl whose family owned the best, or the only, really, Chinese restaurant in Siskiyou County; Taylor, a white, country blond who threw her entire head back when she laughed; and Kiara, a tall swanlike Black girl who, during weekly class visits to the public library, showed us where the Harlequin section was. We'd huddle in a musty corner and hide a romance novel behind sanctioned reading, scanning quickly for keywords like *rod* and *nipple*.

By some grace, this group accepted me, and even let me talk them into performing the lip-sync routine I'd choreographed to En Vogue's "Free Your Mind" for the school's sixth-grade talent show. And they didn't ditch me after I got us sent to the principal's office for throwing bags of cornstarch into the audience at the line "I'm not out here selling dope." Or when for my twelfth birthday, I begged Mom to rent the 1983 masterpiece *Flashdance* on VHS and forced them to sit quietly and watch on the fuzzy blown-out console TV. They just stuck my training bra in the freezer as punishment after I fell asleep first that night.

My new friends weren't serious about showbiz like me, but there was nothing else to do in Weed, so when I christened us a troupe, they showed up twice a week and subjected themselves to my dictatorial art direction during rigorous rehearsals in my *studio*, aka my attic bedroom.

"Five and six and seven and eight!" I clapped out the beats as Taylor and Kiara squatted low and cranked their elbows.

I like 'em round and big and when I pull up . . .

"No, no, it's elbow, elbow, bing bing bam," I said, turning around to demonstrate the combination. "Here, mirror me."

Taylor rewound the tape and played it again. The interlude hit. *She looks like one of those rap guys' girlfriends.*

"Ayyeeeee," Veronica hollered, throwing her ass to the wall and sticking out her tongue.

"What are you listening to?" Mom shouted up the stairs. "Is that appropriate?"

"Yeah, Mom," I lied. "Tana plays it at dance!"

The girls giggled. *Shh,* I motioned, saying a silent thank-you for Mom's crappy hearing. If a song had a good beat and she couldn't make out crass lyrics, she'd let it fly.

"Okay, focus," I said. "One and two and three, four."

Chris raced up the stairs and plowed through our formation, pumping his arms up and down and shaking his butt. "Oh yeah, oh yeah!"

"Get out!" I cried. "We're rehearsing."

"I can dance, too." He flopped on the ground and attempted the worm, his tiny limbs jerking through the air.

"Aw, Neen, let him stay," Kiara chided, her grin wide.

"Get out of here, now. *Mom!*"

She appeared at the top of the steps. "He just wants to hang with the gals," she said, flashing a pleading smile. "The *cool* gals."

"Oh my god. Fine. But don't get in the way. This is serious."

I was going to take us all the way.

First stop, *Star Search.* Next, world tour.

Morris Street provided me physical space to practice, and as I moved freely through the house, choreographing numbers, my dreams crystallized. Years later, Carra would find a worksheet from an exercise we'd done in school before I moved to Weed. The assignment was to interview each other. "Where do you imagine yourself at fifty?" she'd asked me.

My answer: "As a dancer or model. Living in my mansion."

Something silly that any kid with dreams of stardom might say.

But even then, it wasn't money I'd coveted. A shirt from Contempo Casuals would have made me feel rich. I'd never even seen a mansion, except on *Lifestyles of the Rich and Famous*, but what I yearned for was a bigness of life. I wanted comfort and expansion; normalcy and glamour; freedom and belonging; to stand out and to fit in. As I seesawed between desires, the house on Morris became my pivot point. I absorbed the syncopation of rural life. The daily ride home from Weed Elementary was marked by the thump-thump of tires over rusty railroad tracks. The incessant *ch-ch-ch-ch* of industrial sprinklers spraying down piles of logs became a lullaby, and I nestled close to it like someone who might tuck me in.

Like a father, maybe.

Steady now, steady, Neen, it called. *Almost home.*

VIII.

From my bedroom window, I had a perfectly framed view of the mountain. Summer nights when my room was a sauna, I'd climb out the window and sit on the roof to watch the sunset. Knees to chest, I'd stare past the top of the scraggly neighborhood pines and wait for alpenglow—the moment just after the sun dropped below the horizon, and the sky around the mountain went from tangerine to mauve to a royal purple glow. Those nights, I could imagine why people came from around the world to visit. Why they called the mountain cosmic. But while Mom and Co. fixated on UFOs and the secret Lemurian city, they talked less about the very real and imminent possibility of eruption. In school, we'd learned that Mount Shasta was part of the Ring of Fire, a horseshoe of volcanoes and fault lines stretching all the way from Indonesia to Chile. Most of the world's largest eruptions and earthquakes came from the Ring of Fire.

Mount Shasta typically blew every six hundred to eight hundred years, but it had been three thousand since the last eruption, which meant, technically, that it could happen any day. And when it did, geologists predicted that it would decimate Mount Shasta City and rain down lava and ash on McCloud and Weed.

I imagined a torrent of cinder in our front yard.

Our car, melted. Our house, buried.

Each volcano has its own warning signs. Some spew ash for

days before an eruption. Others balloon with magma, puffing themselves up from the inside until their elevation increases slightly. On Mount Shasta, seismic activity—a ripple of small earthquakes—warned of coming eruption. As I kept my eyes on the horizon, I'd missed what was starting to happen downstairs.

Lingering outside Mom's prayer-room door, I could make out the low hum of her voice on the phone. She'd been doing this more. Having hushed conversations behind closed doors. I pressed my ear closer to listen. "It's a past-life thing," she was saying. Her voice sounded husky and conspiratorial. "I mean, Jesus. He could be my son." The tops of my ears prickled, like antennae picking up a scratchy signal.

When I was sure she'd hung up, I waited a beat, knocked, and walked in. A sliver of space between the bathroom and the stairs to my room, the prayer room was her sanctuary—the only space in the house she'd claimed as her own. She'd given the bedrooms to Chris and me, and slept mostly on the couch. *Moms,* she said. *That's what we do.* Every day she'd slip away, shutting the hollow door to pray or chant or decree or whatever she was into at the time. Some days, she was gone ten minutes, others—days when the lines on her forehead were deep moats—she might be in there for an hour. She was just on the other side of the door, but she was gone. In the place where we couldn't reach her. The one I never fully understood. A place that was hers to return to no matter where we lived or what her account balance was.

That day, she was standing in her walk-in closet getting dressed, her back to me. She muttered while pushing hangers frantically from side to side looking for something to wear. She hadn't heard me come in. I scanned the room for clues as to what she'd been talking about.

Religious texts and thrift-store esoterica were stacked against the walls like cairns. Books she'd schlepped from home to home: the Holy Bible, a cheap paperback King James version, its tissue-paper pages folded over and stained with margin notes; *A Course in Miracles*, a text "channeled" by Helen Schucman—the Columbia University psychologist who claimed Jesus spoke to her—largely constructed around biblical passages focused on love and rewritten in the first person; *Science and Health*, the foundational text of Mary Baker Eddy's controversial belief in mind over matter.

Along the far wall, more books were crammed into cheap Fingerhut bookcases already sagging in the middle. Those were the less read, the ones she was always going to get around to. Suzanne Somers's workout plan, Australian motivational speaker Susan Powter's *Stop the Insanity!* Books on how to improve financial fitness. The occasional biography of a misunderstood starlet. There were no novels or volumes of poetry. Everything was oriented toward growth, expansion, actualization, healing, improvement. Toward change.

After leaving TM, Mom had discarded the idea of a single teacher or guru but was still seeking answers, or constructing them herself, collaging together a theory here, a deity there.

In another life, she might have been a scholar.

In this one, I think she was reading to survive.

In the center of the room was a patio chair draped with an afghan, where she sat to read. Sometimes, if she wasn't there when I passed through on the way up to my room, I'd stop and flip through whatever book was splayed open on her chair. Scanning arcane words she'd underlined—*divine principle, material law, ascension, soul matrix*—I tried to dissect them like a code. To find something that would explain where she went when she stopped talking mid-conversation, her sentences hanging in midair. She was studying the divine, and I was studying her—the scripture of a mother adrift. Trying to see where it might lead, and if I should follow.

I was more concerned with my social life at yet another new school than with parting the veil between worlds, but it felt like a condition of my birth to consider the mystical. To truly understand my mother, I had to entertain that UFOs *might* be hidden inside lenticular clouds. That spirits and angels existed was baseline, and Mom spoke of them often without explaining, unless I stopped to ask, arresting her assumptions with a *what?* A *huh?*

I plopped down in her chair, picked up a book, and ran my hand over its worn cover. *The Magic Presence.*

"What's this?" I asked.

"Saint Germain," she called from the closet. "You know, the I AMers? Ballard goes on some trippy journeys with him. To the sacred spots. Here, of course. And the Tetons. That's a real power center, too."

"What do you mean he *goes* with him?"

"You know, astrally."

She'd never explained what the astral plane was exactly, but I had a vague sense of it as a disembodied realm where everyone was made of light. In astral travel, you could leave your body in this world, but your spirit-light-self could travel elsewhere. It was voluntary. You could teach yourself to do it, though like most of this stuff, it came more naturally to some than to others.

Flipping idly through the book, I glanced out the window, and into the neatly trimmed yard of our neighbors Pam and Bo, solid hometown folks who kept one eye out for us and the other on us. Along the windowsill, Mom's saint cards were lined up. Joan of Arc and Saint Francis, the first Catholic stigmatic. Joan burned at the stake for her people, while Francis experienced spontaneous puncture wounds in his hands, feet, and side, mirroring the places where

Jesus had been nailed to the cross and taken a lance to the torso. Joan's and Francis's bodies had become symbols—instruments of justice and devotion.

Mom's heroes weren't girlboss CEOs or flamboyant artists or extraordinary homemakers. She venerated those who had suffered or were willing to for a larger purpose. Those who'd been misunderstood. Persecuted. Who'd fought for what was true and just—no matter the cost. There was an undercurrent of embattlement in our home. A sense of the fight between good and evil, between justice and corruption, not only in our earthly institutions but in the beyond worlds. It was there in the case file she collected on Rick, saving every letter he wrote, or in her looping screeds on the men in her life and how they and the institutions they represented— academia, a movement, or even the broad umbrella of patriarchy— had tried to control her. She reveled in shows starring detectives and lawyers ferreting out the truth. Fighting for the downtrodden. I wonder where it began. Did the fire change her? Or did it just activate who she'd always been? What did she see in that photo of Guru Dev? A portal to a new life that served a larger, spiritual purpose? Or a life in which her suffering—in which all suffering—had meaning?

"Sooo flipping sick of turtlenecks," Mom said, letting out a weary sigh. I set the book aside and glanced over my shoulder.

"Then don't wear one," I said. She poked her head around the door, her thick brows raised in surprise. I was surprised, too. The way it shot out automatic and defiant, it sounded like something I'd been meaning to say.

"Huh?" she said.

"A turtleneck, I mean." I brought my eyes to meet hers. "Don't wear one."

For a moment, she stared at me, her dark eyes flickering. She'd worn some iteration of a turtleneck every day for as long as I could remember. Her turtlenecks were the seasons. Quarterly intervals of our lives were marked by their color and weight. At Easter, she wore butter yellow, delicate pink, baby blue. Mock turtlenecks with teeny flowers heralded the arrival of spring. Christmas brought out crimson reds and forest greens worn under crudely knit holiday vests. We knew the hot sticky of summer had come when she scrambled morning eggs in dickies—mock turtleneck bibs with neck-only coverage to stay cool.

Turtlenecks were her second skin, an armor for the outside world. She revealed her burnskin only after a shower or sometimes at the end of an exhausting day, when it was just the three of us. She'd plop onto the couch in a ratty tee and underwear, house slippers tucked under her legs like a teen. "Gotta let the skin breathe," she'd say. Even in the wavy heat of August, I'd seen my mother swim freely only a few times, and then only deep in the sea, or at a secluded river bend in the woods.

But watching her reach for a turtleneck that day, something clicked.

"Who cares?" I snapped. And for a minute, I believed it. Selfishly, I wanted her to come clean. Allow herself to be fully seen. If she could, then maybe I could, too.

The air was taut with silence. A knob of fear formed in my chest. I'd crossed a line. There was no way to backpedal. If she exploded, we could move on quickly. But if she took quiet offense, ruminating and letting it ripen, the eruption would be worse.

"Nope." She chuckled, finally pulling a baggy mustard-colored turtleneck over her head. I took a deep breath. "Can't have these people ogling me." She gestured toward the window. "The last thing I need is more attention from these good ol' boys."

When she first started talking about the *good ol' boys*, I took it as a generic descriptor of Siskiyou County's conservative gun-toting culture. But she'd been using the term more often, in a more precise and aggrieved way. Not as a monolith or an ethos, the Greek chorus of rural small-town life, but a specific group of actual people. People who were aware of her. Watching her. Gaining on her.

IX.

I've got five bucks tonight," Mom said, digging a crinkled bill from the pocket of her jean jacket. "Get some quarters, Neen. You dole that out and you guys know the deal. Once you spend them . . ."

". . . they're gone," Chris and I chimed in unison.

"Stretch them out!" she called after us, pulling a mini binder from her ink-stained tote and settling down to her lists. When money was too tight for a road trip, we spent weeknights holed up at Mountain Time, a cavernous pizza parlor where the salad bar was always freshly iced. Mom was juggling a few part-time jobs, working as an assistant at a local day care and cleaning houses. For a few dollars' worth of quarters, she bought herself space to think outside the house.

Back pockets jingling, Chris and I raced each other through the dimly lit dining room. We hung a left at the gumball machines and beelined for RoadBlasters. He was going on five and still too short to reach the wheel, so I propped him on my knee to steer and pressed the gas with my foot.

"Whoo!" he shouted, gleeful as he cruised down the highway, blowing up cars and crashing. I put my hands on the wheel to help him steer.

"Neen, let me. It's my game."

"Okay, okay."

After a few rounds, I set him down to stretch. He dug into my pocket and grabbed a handful of coins, then ran toward the 25-cent machines that doled out tiny bouncy balls or fake tattoos or a handful of Skittles.

"Make it last!" I cried after him. "Make it *last.*"

Fifteen minutes later, we were back at the table to beg for more. But Mom was already shoving books into her tote.

"We're outta here," she muttered without looking up.

My shoulders stiffened.

"I have to make a stop on the way home."

"Where?" I asked, praying she wouldn't say Kim's.

"Just a quick pop-by," she said.

"*Where,* Mom?" Chris parroted.

"We'll just swing by and say hi to Kim."

He groaned. "Do we have to?"

Sensing tension and wanting to get ahead of it, I clamped down gently on his hand.

"Mooooom, Neen's squeezing me."

"Cut it," she said. Her voice was serrated. "Clear the plates while I run to the bathroom."

"Kim's is so boring," Chris whined as she walked away. "She has no good toys."

"I know," I said, giving him a noogie. "We'll make our own fun. Just be good."

We walked into Kim's without knocking. "Bumble bee-ee, bumble bee-ee, bumble bee-ee, *bumble beeeee*!!!" Kim glanced up from the piano, where she was running through vocal warm-ups. "Welcome!" she bellowed. Mom dropped her tote in the entryway on a pile of shoes, sidled up to the piano, and started singing scales. Chris flopped onto the tattered Victorian couch, and I hovered near the kitchen.

Whistling to catch my brother's attention, I nodded toward the garage and walked slowly backward. He tiptoed after me, and just as Mom and Kim burst into a rendition of "Ave Maria," I opened the door to the garage, pushed him through, and shut it quickly behind us. In the center of the room was a mountain of clothing. It had its own topography. I'd never seen anything like it, though later, in my twenties, digging through raw tonnage at Goodwill dumps alongside Portland vintage dealers, I'd often think of that chaotic garage. We flung off our shoes and raced up the sides, clothing crumbling underfoot. Sprinting over cotton peaks and into woolen valleys, we shrieked with laughter as cheap sparkly scarves and tiny pants, holdovers from Kim's four kids, now grown and gone, tangled around our legs, the mass sinking beneath us with each step.

The only rule? We had to keep moving.

I sailed over the top, trilling "Ave Marrrriiiaaaa," in my best operatic impersonation, while Chris grunted, flinging his short, stocky body into the air and trying with little success to slap his palm to the roof.

With him, I was still a silly kid making my own fun.

"My kids need structure, a home base," Mom was saying as we slid back through the garage door into the kitchen. "But I don't how long I can do this."

She and Kim were sitting at the table, sipping lukewarm Folgers.

Chris ran to the piano and started banging out a creaky rendition of "Hot Cross Buns."

"Noooo," I groaned.

He cackled and played harder.

HOT CROSS BUNS! HOT CROSS BUNS!

One ear glued to the kitchen, I pushed aside a pile of books to make room on the couch. Like our house, and most of Mom's friends' houses, really, Kim's was cluttered. And the older I got, the more it stressed me out. Maybe it's because those rooms are where

I first clocked changes in my mother, but clutter came to represent an underlying sense of turmoil that I couldn't put my finger on—an external manifestation of internal chaos. A sticky malaise.

I could just make out snippets of the kitchen-table conversation.

"The other night, I go up to refill my coffee, right?" Mom was saying. "Set my mug on the counter with my bad hand. Made a point of it. He didn't skip a beat, Kim, I swear."

"I mean, hey!" Kim said. "Why couldn't he be hot for you?"

"A preppy dude like that?"

HOT CROSS BUNS!

"For the love of god!" I wailed.

"You better get to the bottom of it. It's like with MY case . . ."

Not *the case*. We were never going to get out of there.

Kim's "case" was a rambling epic that I never fully understood. She'd been suing her former dentist for years, claiming he'd destroyed her teeth or something.

Mom's friends all had a governing nemesis. A recurring beef or wound or antagonist that they gathered to strategize about over boxed zinfandel or watered-down coffee. From my perch, I'd listen quietly, wondering why there was always some cosmic reason that their boyfriends treated them crappy or that they didn't get the job. Maybe the guys were just assholes, I thought. Or getting a job was hard. The systems they railed against were real: patriarchy; organized religion; the power-tripping guru; the illusion of choice in a two-party system; the misogyny, classism, and racism of social services that didn't provide single mothers much choice but to live on welfare or work full-time just to pay for day care.

But they spoke about the relentless grind of poverty as tangential versus root cause. Karmic lessons seemed to supersede material factors. When a past-life regression therapist told Mom's friend Molly that her house was messy because she'd been royalty in a former life, the women nodded knowingly. As if that made more sense than her being disorganized and overwhelmed and too broke for childcare. Through spiritual interpretations of everyday events, they could explain anything away, as if their lives were taking place on a mythological battlefield instead of simply under patriarchy and capitalism, which cared little for poor single mothers.

Of her group, Mom seemed the most street-smart. She'd lived in big cities, where she was constantly hustling to find apartments, getting us into schools, working random jobs. All the moving took energy and organization. The life we lived demanded grit and focus and resourcefulness, especially without much money. But while Mom acknowledged real-life factors that held her down, every earthly struggle had a spiritual counterpart. Everything had double, triple, infinite meaning.

Earth was never the end game.

Since the Alpenrose motel, I'd been watching her closely to see if I could perceive any difference in how she held her coffee or applied her lipstick. But she still woke up and drove me to school. Made sure we ate dinner. Took us on spontaneous road trips. Drank her shitty gas station coffee black and blasted Vandross and Anita Baker and watched detective procedurals way too loud. If Anita Two was different, I couldn't tell. Her personality seemed unchanged. Her body, the same.

But as I lingered at the edge of those rooms, half listening to Mom and her friends, and half trying to figure out what was so unsettling or aggravating about their spiritual framing of injustice, I was closer to the heart of the issue than I ever would be again.

You know how once a story ends, you watch it back with new eyes? All the signs are there. They were there the whole time.

The story of Nathan Laredo was like that. It was Nathan whom Mom had been whispering about. The subject of her hushed prayer-room calls. I can't remember how much of the story I over-heard and stitched together later versus how much she told me di-rectly.

And in a way, it doesn't matter, because soon the story would become larger than the sum of its parts. Each distinct moment or instance would be rendered irrelevant in the way that detail is blurred in impressionist art to create an overall effect. Here is what I knew about the man:

He was twenty years younger than her, which at the time made him about twenty-three to her forty-three. His family worked at Mountain Time, where he tossed pies, took orders, and refilled napkin holders. He'd waited on us many times, but I struggled to recall specific features. Nathan had a fiancée, who also worked at Mountain Time. Mom didn't know he was engaged. When she found out, she was mortified, which I understood to mean that they had been flirting. Or at least that she'd liked him.

To clear up the misunderstanding, she decided to write him a letter. *She thought they'd both been flirting. She had no idea about the fiancée, my god. She would never.* As a sixth grader, the letter sounded like so-cial suicide—but she was fixated on clearing her name. She was already an outsider, she said. That's how she told it, as if people were acutely aware of her difference.

Late one night, Chris and I waited in the idling car while she darted across the parking lot of Mountain Time and tucked the handwrit-ten note under the windshield wipers of Nathan's pickup. She hoped they could be friends, she wrote, which was weird. Had they been friends in the first place? I'd barely seen them talk. He was the guy behind the register who smiled lukewarmly as he rang us up for mini pizzas a few times a month. When did this flirting happen? While Chris and I battled at RoadBlasters?

To say the letter backfired is an understatement.

The staff at Mountain Time, who'd greeted us by name for years, started to ignore Mom when she came to the counter, she claimed. They whispered when she walked by, she said. Gave her the "evil eye." Within weeks, word had spread. And word was that my mother was trying to break up Nathan Laredo's engagement. It wasn't just the staff blackballing her.

"That chick at the bank really copped attitude today," she'd say as we curled up on the couch to watch *Family Matters*. "I wonder if she's in on it?"

After a grocery run to Ray's Food Place, she'd sit in the parking lot with the car running and scan her receipts, adding up the totals again and again. "I think they overcharged me," she'd mumble. "They're doing this on purpose."

People started prank calling our house, she said. Flipping her off on the freeway. Gossiping about her at the gas station. Whispering her name at the bank, the laundromat, the post office, just loud enough so that she couldn't help but overhear.

Who does she think she is?

I saw her driving by just to get a look at him.

She's on the hunt for a man.

He's half her age.

Dirty old lady.

Home-wrecker.

Bitch.

At first I didn't know what to make of it. I was used to a level of mystical melodrama, but this was real-life people doing real-life things. We were in Lifetime/*Afterschool Special* terrain. It didn't seem like the most impossible thing. It was a small town. There wasn't much to do. Everyone knew everyone. People gossiped. But I'd never seen any of it happen—not the flirtation or the fallout. The only thing that I had personally witnessed was my mother putting the letter on the truck.

For a while, I let talk of Nathan and the townspeople float past like Mom's plans to move to Baja or start a holiday gift-basket company. Instead of engaging, I sunk deeper into my own world, into dance—a practice that required control and command as well as letting go. Each step count was a time-based container.

Nights upstairs in my room, homework done, I'd listen to music low and come up with new combinations, jotting down coded notes to self in my journal to remember the steps, or repeating them over and over until they were committed to muscle memory, and I no longer had to think about them. Or about anything really. I could just move.

In her memoir, *Dancing on My Grave*, ballerina Gelsey Kirkland details her meteoric career, resurrection, and the cocaine addiction that both buttressed and destroyed her. "If I was not able to control my social world," Kirkland writes, "I could at least begin to coordinate the movement of my own body."

I was coming to learn how may ways there are to use the body. Where my mother had relinquished control of hers—used it as both tool and vessel—I clung to mine.

X.

Mom salted a plate of fried potatoes and set them on the table in front of Chris and me. She was no cook. In reaction to her mother's domestic perfectionism, she'd swung to the other side of the pendulum. Food was fuel. Most of our meals were unremarkable, my memory of them blurred together, but her potatoes were special. They took effort, grease, and time at the stove.

"You know," she said, "she called the house last night and hung up."

"Who?" I asked, glancing at Chris, who was hunched over his salad bowl, picking out shredded carrots.

"Shawna Laredo. The wife." She rolled her eyes. "Or, *excuse me*, fiancée."

My eyebrows peaked. "Really?"

"Yup. Then her little goon Mary drives by yesterday and flips me off while I'm taking you to dance. To DANCE, people! Taking my daughter to ballet, you freaking weirdos. Dolts."

"Who's Mary?" I asked, squeezing mustard and ketchup onto my plate.

"I've invited them to talk to me," she went on, her voice growing louder over the sizzling oil on the stove, the cloud of smoke getting thicker. "To clear up this whole thing. But they're more concerned with protecting their little princey poo. Freakin' lackeys is what they are. Laredo Lackeys. Ha! I tell you, babe: my honesty always comes back to bite me in the ass."

I tried to think of any cars that might have passed us along the way, imagining this woman, Mary, a vague-faced blond fluffing her hair or checking her makeup in the mirror at the stop sign.

"She flipped you off when I was in the car?" I asked.

Maybe Mary had been scrubbing lipstick from her teeth absentmindedly with her middle finger like Mom did. Maybe Mom had misunderstood. Maybe she was noticing things that weren't there. Taking things personally that she shouldn't.

"Nothing real can be threatened, nothing unreal exists!" Mom said. *"Course in Miracles."*

"MOM!"

"Yeah, Bird?"

"Was I in the car when she, *this lady,* flipped you off?"

"Yep," she said, popping the *p.*

"How am I missing all this? Why haven't I seen it?"

"Ohhhh," she chortled. "Honey, they are too smart for that! They might mess with me, but they *know* not to fuck with my kids."

Tension knocked up my spine. There was truth and untruth and something murky emerging between them. Mom dropped another plate of potatoes on the table—this batch charred—and pulled out a chair to sit down. "So, guys," she said, pouring herself a glass of water from the chipped pitcher. "How was *your* day?"

"Fine," I said, desperate to change the subject. "Just messing with the bats." Warm nights, at dusk, Chris and I would go outside and throw rocks up in the air. Bats dove down after them, thinking they were food.

"They just dive and dive," Chris said, making his hand a bird. "For rocks."

"Sound like real dingbats to me," Mom said, flashing a mischievous smile.

Chris stabbed a hunk of lettuce, eyeing it with reluctance.

"Dingbats," he whispered, smiling.

"Pass the dressing, will you, babe?" Mom said. "What's happening at school?"

I didn't tell her about the Harlequin section—how we'd learned to sneak them off the shelves behind other books. Or about my first boyfriend, Casey. I didn't want to bring up anything that had to do with men, with love—anything that could add to the melodrama already playing out at home.

"Working on my project for the science fair," I said with a tidy nod. "How Many Blinks. I'm researching if people blink more watching TV, eating, talking on the phone, or reading a book."

"What's the method?"

"Just sit and stare at them for five minutes and tally every blink. I make them all the same exact sandwich."

"Of course." She winked. "You must have a controlled environment."

"One thousand nine hundred MILLION ZILLION blinks!" Chris said, chewing and blinking as he jiggled his head.

Mom snorted.

"Stopppp!" I whined, laughing. And for a minute, we were at our best. Goofy, light.

Mom broke first. "You're on dishes tonight, bud," she said, getting up abruptly and walking toward her prayer room.

"Mo-om, I told you," Chris protested. "I always get wet. And I'm too short. And . . ." He never threw full-blown fits, just like he'd never cried much as a baby, but if he felt something was unfair, he'd state his case, loudly, again and again, not letting up until Mom agreed. We both had a secret weapon—mine was silence, while he could wear her down.

"Get the chair, Neen. Set him up!"

"Done?" I asked, stacking his plate onto mine and patting the seat of his chair. He stood on it and I dragged the chair to the sink and turned the water on lukewarm to fill the dish bin.

"Squeeze," I said, handing him a crusty bottle of neon-yellow soap. He squeezed hard, chuckling as the bubbles frothed and expanded into the tub. From under the sink, I pulled out rubber gloves and an apron that I tied around his waist. "You got this," I said, stacking the dirty dishes on the counter next to him. He groaned and I left him to play in the soapy water, then complain about being too wet and leave half the dishes until tomorrow when Mom or I would finish them.

<hr />

As I try to locate the seams of the story, they're simply not there. It's as if I woke up one day and this looping endless narrative about the Laredos had always been with us. At first, I'd laughed when Mom started sarcastically calling Nathan the Prince, or Princey Poo, bitching about how the townspeople worshipped him. How they'd listen to anything he said. Take his word over hers. Then things escalated from cartoonish and campy to sinister. Other characters started to emerge. Ray the Real Estate King. Barbara the Bank Teller Bitch. Alliteration added to the farce of it all. My mother, the home-wrecker, the fortysomething outsider with the hots for the twentysomething hometown hero.

There's a campaign against me now, she'd say. She wrote more letters to counteract the rumors. Letters to local church leaders and politicians. People she thought were morally or municipally obligated to side with the truth. Her language became grandiose. It wasn't fucked up but unjust. She wasn't being gossiped about but persecuted. She'd always spoken of saints and martyrs as if they were family members—a bug of her Catholic childhood—but there was a growing correlation between how much she talked about the Laredos and how often she invoked the language and imagery of spiritual warfare. I tried to keep up, but it had quickly metastasized from small-town bullshit to a biblical standoff between good and evil.

Now I understand what I could only sense for most of my youth: when information is untethered from its source, anything can make sense. Without context, or the containers we create for story, there is no wall to throw things against. No way to judge it. In semantics, the study of how we make meaning, all meaning is contextual—dependent on the factors and environment in which it's experienced and the perspective of the people experiencing it. Everything is relative. Everything is relational.

If my mother placed her struggle in a biblical context, then it meant that she, like Joan of Arc or Saint Francis, was going through a painful spiritual tribulation that would ultimately bring her closer to god. If she was just a broke single mother in America living in a small town, where she had a crush on a younger engaged man, her story was more scandalous. She—her desires, her traumas, her hopes—would be implicated.

Maybe the belief system she crafted was an attempt to explain what existed within her—a slow sputtering of voices and stories that had once drawn her in so deep that when it told her to light a fire, she listened.

PART II

Growth

XI.

I n front of self-immolation, even the most secularized of us have a glimpse into a primordial experience of the sacred," writes Romanian American philosopher and self-immolation scholar Costica Bradatan for *The New Statesman*. "Originally, the sacred is defined as something set apart, cut off from the rest, which remains profane; what we feel towards such a radically different other is precisely a mix of terror and fascination."

No other suicidal act is more intertwined with a narrative of sacrifice than self-immolation. We associate it with monks and political activists; students and civilians raging against corrupt governments or social strictures.

We picture martyrs. Joan of Arc. Widows in Sati.

Thích Quảng Đức ablaze in peaceful rage at a Saigon intersection to protest religious persecution.

But for most of history, self-immolation didn't exclusively imply burning or even, necessarily, death. It signified self-sacrifice, both fatal and non. It was not the method that mattered as much as the intent. Chinese Buddhists, who may have the oldest history of the practice, as early as the fourth century, had a ritualized understanding of self-immolation as yīshēn, "abandoning the body," or shěshēn, "giving up the body." Practices of yīshēn included slicing the skin, drowning, and feeding the self to animals. These were holy acts that didn't always result in death but used the body as an instrument of devotion. For them, self-immolation was an act of service, not martyrdom in the way that we understand the term in the modern West.

In a 1965 letter to Dr. Martin Luther King Jr., Vietnamese monk Thích Nhất Hạnh wrote about how difficult it is for the Western Christian conscience to understand the self-immolation of Vietnamese monks. He explained that, again, the actions were neither suicide nor protest. They were devotional. Nhất Hạnh writes:

> During the ceremony of ordination, as practiced in the Mahayana [Buddhist] tradition, the monk-candidate is required to burn one, or more, small spots on his body in taking the vow to observe the 250 rules of a bhikshu, to live the life of a monk, to attain enlightenment and to devote his life to the salvation of all beings . . . The importance is not to take one's life, but to burn. What he really aims at is the expression of his will and determination, not death.

In the Lotus Sutra, a Buddhist scripture, the Bodhisattva Medicine King swallowed oils and incense, then burned his body to honor the Buddha. His action provided a model for how an average person might become a bodhisattva, a person who is capable of reaching enlightenment but delays it to help their fellow people. Well-read in this history, Quảng Đức, and many Vietnamese monks who immolated themselves after him, chanted the Lotus Sutra every day. But his act was read in the West as political protest, which cemented the colloquial usage, if not the official definition of the term *self-immolation* as we use it today—a term synonymous with both method and intent. Maybe it's semantic to argue between burning as an act of protest and as a devotional act with the power to help others, but the difference is that one is *a message*, the other, an offering.

Martyrdom was in the ether the year that Mom and Raelle burned—1971 marked the end of an eight-year period of Vietnamese Buddhist monks self-immolating following Quảng Đức's burning. With all this swirling in the zeitgeist, it's confounding that Mom and Raelle would choose suicide by fire for the hell of it.

We'd been at Morris Street about a year when Mom told me the story. I was in sixth grade. Outside, two-foot banks of plowed snow lined the road. Their dirty ridges glowed pink as the sun set behind the mountain.

"Sit with me, babe." Mom patted a spot next to her on the couch. "It's time for the whole story."

"Of?" I said, plopping down.

"My burns."

"You were in a fire," I said.

"Right, but . . . it was more than that." She spoke with caution, as if choosing her words from a lineup. I looked down, fiddling with a loose strand of tweed from the couch.

I remember trying to sound casual. "More how?"

"Well, you know I went to University of Michigan. I signed up for Russian literature, yadda yadda. But I had other things on my mind. It was the seventies, *hello!* I mean, who gave a rat's ass about the classics? There was so much going on in the world, Neen. I wanted to do something. To really *do* something. You know?"

I knew nothing about what Russian literature or the classics or *the seventies, hello!* meant, but I nodded.

"School seemed so pointless," she said. "But it was *what you did*! It was what kids like me did, anyway. My father expected that at a minimum. Summer after freshman year, things seemed to be really activating in Colorado."

She went on to say that she and a few friends had decided to take a road trip to Boulder. Two of her friends from the dorms, and another woman, an older woman, "a serious type," named Raelle. Raelle wasn't a student but a woman in her mid-twenties. Mom never said where she came from, why she was in Ann Arbor, or how the group knew her.

Things were *activating* in Colorado, which seemed to mean politics and partying. Rallies and marches. Student protests. Drugs.

Expanding minds. Opening hearts. Chakras and shitty weed and clean mountain air. The same things that had drawn my father to Boulder. Strangely, they were there around the same time but wouldn't meet until later, back in Miami, after he'd already attended the talk about TM that would change his life, and after the fire that would change hers. By the end of summer, one of Mom's friends had fallen in love with some guy she met at a rally and decided to stay. And something weird was going on with Raelle. She'd started to talk about a group of men that was following them. About how they would be killed if they were caught. Mom's other friend freaked out and demanded to be taken back to her parents. But Mom listened. In Colorado, her eyes had been opened to the nation's corruption. She was a young Catholic girl shedding what she'd learned about being a good woman, a good wife, a good American. She was developing her own gauge for justice. Maybe it started to sound feasible to her, Raelle's story. It was unlikely that they were being chased by shadowy men. But it wasn't *impossible*. Maybe she was drawn in, as I would be years later, by the shadow of a doubt.

Mom pulled a blanket from the back of the couch and tucked it tidily around our feet. After they dropped the other girl back home, Mom and Raelle returned to Ann Arbor together. It was almost fall then, but Mom didn't reenroll in school. Things escalated quickly. "Raelle talked incessantly about these men. *Why us?* I kept thinking, but to tell you the truth, Neen, it all happened so fast. She was so sure that it was real that she convinced me. If the men found us, she kept saying, not only would they kill us, but they'd torture us first. I couldn't bear the thought of torture."

I wasn't sure if wanted to hear this story at all. I had the acute sense that if I did, there would be no going back to the *before*. There would be only knowing and not-knowing. But she never asked. Or maybe she did, and I don't remember. Even if she had, the daughter that I was, and the woman I would become, would have said *Go on, of course go on.*

"We were so scared all the time," Mom said, her speech getting choppier, faster. Her hands cut through the air, conducting the scene, as she interrupted herself with bursts of detail that she seemed to remember in the moment. "Raelle talked about ending it," she said. "Saying it would be better to do it ourselves. Everything was getting to me. It was all just getting to me."

As her energy became more frenzied, I felt us shuttling toward a portal. I pulled my hands out from under my legs. The backs of my knees were slick with sweat.

"Raelle said we should stab ourselves," she said. "And that I should go first."

"WHAT?" My fingertips buzzed. Mom paused, looking ahead, and then gave a strange little nod as if she was back in that kitchen convincing herself to do it all over again. Or maybe images had started to play and she was simply narrating what she saw, confirming her memories.

"So, I did it."

"You *did* it!?" I screeched.

"We were staying in someone's house for the night. A small house in Ann Arbor."

"Whose house?" I blurted out. Stupid, *stupid*. I didn't give a shit whose house it was. But I needed questions—questions allowed me to slow time, to breathe, to try and regain some sliver of control. Factual details I could grasp.

"I took a butcher knife from the kitchen drawer and stabbed myself," she said. "In the chest." She pressed a finger to her heart, her face deadpan. Her shoulders drooped like an old sweater hanging loose on a hanger.

I looked down at my mother's hands, with their bony fingers, thick blue veins, and smattering of freckles. The hands that had held Chris and me as babies, that had rubbed my feet when they throbbed after back-to-back dance classes or long rehearsals. I tried to imagine those hands palming a blade and plunging it toward her chest. But in my visualization, it never penetrated. Her hands were clumsy and shaking, the knife she used gummy and fake. Like a toy blade, it retracted as soon as it hit skin. I couldn't conjure such self-violence. Not from her. Not then. I leaned close to my mother and felt her warmth. I must have started crying, because she turned to me, her eyes ringed with sadness. Her skin, usually thick and oily, looked dull. Even her sharp cheekbones seemed to sag.

"She couldn't do it," she said. "Raelle. She couldn't go through with the knife."

"That bitch," I said just loud enough for Mom to hear. But it didn't even register. She went on to say how Raelle found a roll of butcher paper instead, and under her direction, they stood side by side in the kitchen of the strange house, twirled themselves into it, and then lit the paper on fire. When Mom came to, a young firefighter had cut off her clothes and wrapped her in a wool blanket.

"He saved my life," she said, suddenly wistful, as if reporting from a dream, or perhaps, another life.

She pulled my legs into her lap. For a while, we stayed like that. Me breathing in the sticky-crayon smell of her drugstore lipstick, her rubbing my feet. As I tried to absorb what she'd told me, I became a girl divided. One part was fixated on the strange details of the story: Whose house was it? What happened to the knife? Where did Raelle come from? What did her parents say? As if the *what* might help me understand the *why*. That girl didn't know it yet, but she would become a writer, a reporter, an excavator of the subconscious. She would seek facts instead of faith. But the other part of me didn't question a thing that day and wouldn't even think of doing so for another twenty years, accepting this version as complete— as both beginning and end—because it was what my mother said. Not only did I have no reason to doubt her, but there was no source to check her facts against.

For a while after she told me about Ann Arbor, one image replayed in my mind. It wasn't my mother lighting the match or the two girls sitting cross-legged, screaming, their hair burning. Those wouldn't come into focus for years. They were still too foreign, too grisly and impossible to imagine. But I saw the blade, again and again. Silvery and glinting against her skin. I never did get it to pierce through skin. But slowly, the wound came into focus. The wound became the story under the story. A clumsy incision, long forgotten, erased by the fire that followed.

It was not just the gruesomeness of the story that changed me. It was the realization that underneath her visible scars, my mother carried another scar—a deeper, original wound, her first attempt at death. So many layers of pain could be concealed within us. Even underneath the most heinous things, there could be still more. That realization and the anxieties it spawned burrowed deep into my gut, where they stayed, fermenting, expanding into a throb, a nebulous sense that things were not okay. That, really, they never had been and never would be.

For twenty years, I told no one her story. I tucked it into me like a grotesque treasure—a cold gem that I guarded with ferocious pride, uncertain who else knew. Mom and I never talked about it again, and no one, not my father or his parents or any of my mother's friends, ever asked me about the fire or what sense I, as a young girl, had made of it.

When a *Detroit Free Press* reporter asked Ann Arbor police chief Walter Krasny whether Mom and Raelle setting themselves on fire was a ceremonial immolation, he replied simply: "Good guess." Which I take to mean either: *That's my theory, but I'm not allowed to officially state it.* Or: *Who the hell knows, your guess is good as mine.*

Fire is not the most immediate or efficient route to death. Other modes of suicide we understand as means to an end. Pills: a quiet, accessible slip-away. A shotgun to the head: if done right, requires no do-over, and there's something to be said for surety. Hanging: achievable with everyday objects and leaves little mess. But there is nothing quiet or pragmatic about lighting yourself on fire. Statistically, burning is not a common act of suicide. Especially in developed Western countries. Especially in tandem. To endure all that pain, it seems there must be meaning. *Intent.*

If they'd made any mention of dissent, their burning would be situated in a lineage of people who had self-immolated to protest everything from the Vietnam War to repressive political systems in their own countries. Names like Hiroko Hayasaki, Celene Jankowski, Nhất Chi Mai, Yui Chunoshin, Robert Rex Vice, Erik Thoen, Ronald Brazee, Kathy Change, Nguyễn Thị Cơ. If they made any mention of protest, their burning would have been in tidy triangulation with those of Alice Herz and George Winne Jr., two people who had walked and lived the same Detroit streets as my mother. Who burned themselves, too.

But all they ever said were those haunting words: "It's lovely to die together."

XII.

When I was halfway through seventh grade, Mom told us we were moving again. She'd already found renters for the house. I was devastated. I was about to turn thirteen and had lived in almost twenty homes in eight different towns and cities. I'd thought Morris Street was it. We'd been there two years. We were going south this time, she said. Way south. As far south as we could go and still be in California. San Diego. She'd found her brother, Dan, who'd disappeared years ago. Somehow she'd squeezed his address out of the lawyer who had been the executor of my grandfather's will.

"Sorry, babe," she said as we packed up. "I know this is gonna be hard on you, but I have to get out. These people are killing me."

The Laredos had become our phantom family—toxic aunts and uncles, gossiping cousins who sucked up precious oxygen in our lives. One day they were out to get her, then nothing for weeks, and suddenly everyone was kissing her ass. *Was it their way of apologizing without acknowledging what they'd done?* she'd wonder aloud. And if so, maybe she should accept the apology and let it all go. But as soon as she softened, the *whole sick cycle* would start again.

We left at dawn. Mom wanted to get an early start so we could arrive before dark. The drive to San Diego was eight hundred miles. Twelve hours down the I-5 from the top to the bottom of the state. We'd done it before. Broken up by the occasional truck stop, the drive was the least scenic route in a state known for scenery. But it was a straight shot. By then, I had each leg memorized.

From the Cascade Range, where we lived, the freeway dropped into the Shasta Valley Basin, then climbed back out and unrolled into hundreds of miles of dry nothingness. Blasting 80 mph past the parched farmlands of the Central Valley, the bottleneck of Fresno, and finally the monotonous landscape of dry twinned hills outside of Buttonwillow that looked like cleavage. The first one in the car to point and yell out "Butt cuts!" which for some reason, we said instead of *butt crack*, was the winner. After that, more endless fields, the air rich with cow shit and onions, before the slow, steady climb up the switchbacks of the Grapevine, semitrucks blaring past aggressively, then coasting down into Santa Clarita, marking the entrance into Southern California proper. Soon we'd be greeted by the endless tangerine haze of LA traffic, and the beaches of San Diego, with Mexico just an hour beyond. The contours of California snaked through my blood. I could travel them anytime.

That didn't mean I wanted to.

Mom backed the truck out of the gravel drive. I wiped condensation from the passenger window and watched our house recede. Chris was asleep in the middle seat, his head drooped on my shoulder, his face relaxed. As the sun rose behind the mountain, my tears dried into chalky crystals. Motion settled on me like a familiar dust. Eventually, I nodded off to the hum of tires whirring down the freeway. The same sound that had welcomed me to San Francisco, to the West, a decade earlier.

How many times can we begin again? I wonder.

How many times can one person be reborn?

When I woke a couple of hours later, the heat was cotton in my mouth. Warm air ripped through the cab of the truck. My hair flew around my face. We were hauling ass. Pushing 80 in a 70, Mom drove like she was outrunning something, like the forest might swallow us up if she didn't get out quick.

We were just past Sacramento when the engine began to smoke. She steered onto the freeway shoulder and turned off the truck. Chris groaned, wiping sleep from his eyes.

"Where we at?" he grumbled. After letting the truck sit for a minute, Mom turned the key, but instead of starting, it sputtered and died. She tried again, and punched the gas—once, twice, three times. Burnt rubber wafted through the heater vents.

"Pray to Saint Michael!" she hollered.

Technically, Saint Christopher was the traveler's saint, but Mom clung to Michael. Not only was he that angel you didn't want to fuck with, but he was also, for reasons unclear to me, our designated spiritual mechanic. We were careful not to abuse his services, invoking him only as a last-ditch attempt on days that we really, *really*, needed to get somewhere. Our automotive history consisted of a string of $2,000 beaters that Mom drove hard until they gave out, then rigged to squeeze out another month or two. Some started only by popping the clutch. Others had zip-tied mufflers or wiper blades that we had to move manually in snowstorms. I'd requested parking-lot jump starts from more strangers than I could count. Each car's final ride was usually in the middle of nowhere. Somewhere like this. Most days, Saint Michael came through. That time, he didn't.

"Shit!" Mom slammed her palm into the steering wheel. We climbed out and stood on the side of the road. Semis blew past. She popped the hood and peered into the engine, fanning away plumes of gray smoke. Chris bent over, coughing.

"Looks pretty bad," she said. "Think we'll have to walk into town."

Two hundred feet up the freeway, there was an exit sign: LODI.

We locked the car and walked down the exit-ramp shoulder,

kicking away tiny pebbles and chunks of blacktop. When we got to the nearest garage, Chris and I sat in the waiting area, inhaling fumes of oil and paint while Mom chatted and laughed with a scruffy mechanic in a tie-dye LYNYRD SKYNYRD T-shirt. An El Camino was jacked up on hydraulics behind him. I watched through the open door, worried about how we were going to pay for this, about how long it would take, and how many days of seventh grade I'd already missed.

"It could be a couple days," Mom said, stepping into the waiting room. "What can I say, guys? *We're stuck in Lodiiii again.*" I rolled my eyes and sank down in my chair. Life with her was like that: a middle-of-the-night move and suddenly we were living a fucking Creedence Clearwater song. Frankly, it was not as quirky or fun as it sounds or looks onscreen in those bohemian mother-daughter stories. I was cranky and weary. Mom held out her hand and Chris jumped up to grab it.

"All I have is this check," she said. "Miller, that's the mechanic, says there's a bank around here. Let's go try to cash it."

After more waiting at the bank, we got a room at a local motel, where we fell into our standard road-trip itinerary—HBO, bed jumping, pizza.

For a day, we waited. Then another. We were used to it.

So much of being poor is waiting.

Waiting for the bus to come. For the car to get fixed. For the check to clear. For the first of the month. The first of the year. To get the shirts off layaway. To get the heat turned back on. Surviving near the poverty line is a series of trapdoors with long wait times. A monotonous hall whose only reprieves are often instant gratifications—moments of newness, flashes of freedom via a last-minute bus ticket or a new bra from Walmart or a trip to the ice cream store. Ordering a pizza that you can't afford instead of paying the electric bill is at times a necessary illusion. It's make-believe. It's pretending that you have more money than you do, that you can indulge in delivery without sacrificing later. It is bending time to your will, for once. Without money, it's hard to feel light. You're always waiting for a release that doesn't come. By giving yourself a tiny pleasure, you snatch time back. For a moment, you are buoyant. This is why we went on road trips instead of paying the water bill.

The next morning, Miller the mechanic called. "It's toast," said Mom as she hung up. "He says it'll cost more than the car's worth to fix." That night, he picked us up in an old Chevy. We tossed everything we'd brought in the back and squeezed onto the bench seat. He dropped us at the Greyhound station, where Mom bought three one-way tickets. We filed onto the bus and pushed toward the middle. Not too close to the bathroom in the back or the front, where people got off and on and could easily snatch a kid. Chris and I found two seats next to each other and Mom slid into one catty-corner across the aisle. The driver dimmed the lights, and as soon as he heard the hydraulic whoosh of the door closing, Chris pulled a blanket up to his chin. We picked up speed, merging onto the I-5, and soon the whir of the passing world rocked me to sleep, too. We were on our way, again.

XIII.

Mom found us a room at the Corinthian, a Palm Springs–style hotel with monthly rates near San Diego's Balboa Park. It was a five-story peach stucco building with exterior walkways overlooking a courtyard filled with royal palms. From the outside, no one could tell that we shared one tiny motel room and slept on a king-size bed together, or that in the mornings before school, we wolfed down spongy blocks of egg as Mom worked to master scrambling them in the microwave. On balmy nights before bed, I stood at the railing and looked down into the courtyard, giving thanks for what I believed was the hotel's chic facade. As far as I was concerned, the Corinthian was Melrose Place.

Whatever defenses had been softened by country living were reactivated as I remembered how to harden my face and move with enough bravado that no one questioned me. This time it wasn't Mom taking me to White Pony on the bus, but me picking up my little brother. Every day after school, I caught the number 7 across town to Little Italy to get him, then together we rode two more buses uptown, to a pool hall in North Park where Mom was working nights. Chris played Mortal Kombat while I did my French homework. We ate Lay's from behind the register while Mom racked balls and rung up middle-aged men with long faces and smoky auras. It was billiards, not pool, they were quick to correct me, but seemed otherwise amused to have us around. Mom managed an easy banter with the players. She remembered details about their lives—their wives' names; if they had kids—which softened them to her. She almost seemed more in her element with bikers and pool sharks than she had with the New Age ladies. More balanced, anyway. More *here*. She didn't talk about the Laredos at all. Up north, she'd become so enfolded in the mystical. But city life was less alienating and isolating, it demanded a sharpness that kept her focused on the material.

"Today's the day," she said one morning. We were going to find her brother. We bused to an address downtown on B Street. As we stepped off the bus, bachata blared from the open doors of a Cadillac parked nearby. An helado cart rolled down the street. Kids chased each other past chain-link fences tangled with scraggly weeds. Mom's face was serene as we approached a single-level stucco building and stepped down into a small grassy courtyard. "Apartment three," she muttered, checking the crumpled note in her hand. She stopped in front of a screen door. "K, guys, this is it!" she said, looking at us expectantly. We stared back, unsure how to respond. Our uncle was a ghost. Mom hadn't seen him since the day she married my dad fifteen years earlier, and had barely told us anything about him or how they grew up. Hand in hand, the three of us stepped up the stairs. Behind a closed screen door, his apartment door was open. Squinting through dusty crosshairs, I saw posters of Lamborghinis in chintzy frames hanging crookedly on the walls. A worn La-Z-Boy sofa.

"Dan?" my mother called, shielding her eyes.

"Hello?" A deep, throaty voice came from inside the apartment.

"Dan? It's me, Anita."

"Neet?" The voice came closer. Then a face. A hairy hand pushing open the screen. We stepped back. My mom and her brother stared at each other across the threshold. They were identical. Dan had the same hooked nose and deep-set eyes and broad forehead with a protruding brow. He shared her exact olive skin tone and hair color. They even had the same thin lips, but his were hidden by an overhang of mustache. I don't know who was more shocked. Them at seeing each other after all those years, or Chris and me at realizing that there were people in the world who looked and sounded like our mother. Who shared her blood. Our blood. Who'd known her long before we ever had, in a world where once upon a time, they'd been all that each other had.

I looked to my brother. His hair was getting long, framing his face with soft swoops. It always waved until it got long enough to curl. His skin was a dark copper, his summer tone. His cheeks were still chubby with baby fat, and as he smiled up at our uncle, a stranger, I could see all his tiny teeth.

"Neet? Is it really you?" Dan said. His arms shook as they embraced. "I just can't believe I'm looking at you."

"It's me!" Mom said, doing a little shimmy with jazz hands. "And the kids!" She waved us forward. "These are my kids. Your niece and nephew."

Dan teared up as his eyes fell on us. Even his sadness looked familiar.

"Hi, guys," he said, ducking his head shyly. "So nice to meet you." He gave me an awkward hug and Chris a clunky head pat and handshake. "So nice to finally meet you. Well, come in, come in. Now, don't mind the place now. It's just me all these years. Don't mind the place."

We shuffled into the dimly lit living room. A hockey game blared on the big-screen TV. Dan and Mom went into the kitchen. Chris plopped down on the couch and glued himself to the game, while I perched on the arm and did my best to eavesdrop. I couldn't make out much, but the sound of my uncle's voice was raspy and more midwestern than my mom's. Most days, I forgot that she'd been raised in Michigan. By Canadians. That her people were hockey lovers. Labatt Blue and Crown Royal drinkers. French speakers. Party throwers. Staunch Catholics. They were so far from the life I'd known, and I realized then just how alone we had always been. Hearing my uncle's voice gripped me with sudden longing, a molecular-level nostalgia. A yearning to know the flesh-and-blood people that had appeared in our story live as distant tragic characters. I knew only a handful of stories. The tinsel, the parties, the drinking, the nuns wielding their rulers, the music, the dance lessons, the death. Mom hadn't been much older than me when she says she found her mother dead in bed.

Before her freshman year of high school, Lou moved them from Detroit to the suburbs. Mom and Dan had grown up in the city. Their youth was Detroit of the 1950s and '60s. Detroit of Motown. Detroit of American industry. Of thriving Black art and politics. Detroit Motor City. Culture spilled out of playhouses and supper clubs. Rod had thrived there, too. The suburbs turned out be too quiet for her. Too homogeneous. After the move, my grandparents started to have blowout fights, Mom said. Rod would hole up in the bedroom to drink alone, she said.

Rod hadn't come out of the room in two days. Mom begged Lou to go check, and when he wouldn't, she barged in herself and found her mother dead, her face tinged blue and pressed to one side. I wonder how much the terror of that moment colored her memory. I wonder if it was really that gruesome and heartless. I wonder if I'm remembering her story correctly at all. Mostly I wonder because of all the stories she'd told me since; because it's hard to imagine it happening that way. To imagine my family that way. But again, I didn't know much about them.

There was so much that I never would.

Dan was out of the house and married with three kids by the time Rod died. He was twenty-two, eight years older than Mom, almost the same age gap as Chris and me. In 1964, it made sense for him to be married with children already. But Mom implied that it was an escape. *Left home the first chance he got*, she said. I think of how Rod became depressed in the suburbs. How even with the perfect nuclear family, there was something cloying about the expectation that she be fulfilled by domestic life.

It killed her, Mom used to say. *He killed her.*

I'd always assumed she was speaking in metaphor. That my grandmother's spirit had been squelched in the suburbs and Mom blamed her father for the move. But looking back, I can conjure the steely look in her eyes, the way her jaw squared when she spoke of her father, and I think that, maybe, she meant it literally. That dysfunction had chiggered itself so deep into her psyche that even when her mother's death certificate stated aneurysm as the cause, she was certain its true root was despair.

Was that the story she told herself over the next three decades—that if her family had stayed in Detroit, Rod would be alive? I wonder if that kept her up at night.

Later, after my mother is gone, I'll do the same thing—assign different causes to her death than what is written on the official piece of paper. I'll collapse all her suffering and square it against cause of death. I'll be looking for ways to say, *no, it wasn't that, no, there was more*. What she was trying to say is that there were emotional and mental problems that no one could or would name. That even if her mother's body had shut down, that was simply the outcome, not the root. Families do this.

We pass these malformed ideas on mindlessly, endlessly, like heirlooms.

Our grotesque little treasures, guarded at all cost.

That first visit to Uncle Dan's, we didn't stay long. As we waved goodbye, he and Mom stared at each other in what, at first, seemed like awe. But when I looked closer, I couldn't tell if my uncle was happy to be found or if he was figuring out how to run again.

XIV.

Finding her brother must have made Mom nostalgic for the rituals of her childhood. We'd never been to a Catholic mass in our lives, but she started taking us every Sunday to Our Lady of the Rosary, a small congregation founded by Italian immigrants. She was adamant that I receive Communion, which meant that, at twelve going on thirteen, I had to be baptized, then complete catechism—a series of educational classes on the theology of the Church. Most kids started catechism when they were seven, which Catholics used to call the Age of Discretion. It was the age at which they believed a child was conscious enough to know right from wrong and could willingly choose god.

Compared to New Age practices, Catholicism, with its regalia and incense, its "stand up, sit down, kneel" choreography, felt pageantlike. There was something soothing about its cadence. Something theatrical and transportive about being enveloped in thick spicy clouds of frankincense. It brought me back to the stage. To a place where I could blank out, where the body took over. Where I didn't have to puzzle through things but simply move, executing the steps we'd learned. Its dogma, which Mom had spent her life actively avoiding, gave me something clear to mark and measure my own beliefs against, to agree or disagree with. Its metaphors were more concrete. Even when they skewed fantastical, they were rooted in real people. We became friendly with a gentle priest at Our Lady named Father Franco. He agreed to baptize me.

Uncle Dan had slowly become part of our lives. He took Chris to baseball games, watched hockey with him, and let him hang in the garage as Dan meticulously applied racing stripes to the collection of Mazda RX-7s that he'd rehabbed. Occasionally, Mom convinced him to meet us at Balboa Park or the zoo. But for the most part, he lived a solitary, frugal life, getting by on SSI, a federal disability program, and later, his portion of Grandpa Lou's inheritance. Mostly we went over to his place, spending summer afternoons in the cool cave of his living room. I sensed a sad armor around my uncle. A dividing line between him and the past that we were not to approach under any circumstances. I didn't know then that he was sick. That even though he'd been sober for years, his liver was shot, after working as a traveling salesman in the '80s, where heavy drinking was part of the gig.

Dan didn't attend mass anymore, but he came to my baptism and stood to my right as Father Franco dribbled water from his fingertips onto my forehead. I should have been a baby, then, cradled in my mother's arms, her kissing my soft, powdery forehead. I imagined the droplets turning back time, power washing the grime from our lives. It was grounding to know that my grandparents, my mother, even my uncle had once done the same. In the church, at least our roots were clear. I'd spent my life so disconnected from Mom's family or our history that being looped back into generations of Catholics was reparative. It seemed to settle Mom, too. Maybe she'd been looking for a way to return. To stitch us back into her family after so many years away.

After baptism, I sped through catechism, where I was shocked to learn that the teacher wanted me to interpret the Bible literally. To receive first Communion, we had to accept the Eucharistic wafer and wine as the body and blood of Christ, sacrificed to wash away our sins. Again, not as gesture or metaphor but as actual flesh and blood, which if you thought about it—and *I did*—was very fucking weird. I was going into eighth grade and virginal. Never even been kissed. No minor sins of mine could have necessitated a man being nailed to a cross, not to mention cannibalization. Mom and I rode the city bus to Macy's anyway, to search for the perfect Communion dress—something cheap, white, elegant. I found a tiny pearl tiara and a simple long-sleeved lace dress, not so different from the one my mother had worn the day she married my father.

When we gathered in the pews for the ceremony, I towered over the others. The rest of the girls, none older than nine, were weighed down by huge frilly gowns, looking like angels from one angle and cheap wedding-cake toppers from another. None of them seemed old enough to make this choice. To think critically about what they—what we—were being asked to do.

Take, eat; this is my body.

In a photo from that day, I stand in front of the pulpit, my hands pressed together in prayer, surrounded by a sea of white lace and ruffle. A simple gold cross hangs at my chest, and my face is earnest, pious even. I am open to receiving the spiritual connection that I've watched my mother chase with ferocity. Sometimes I thought maybe I felt it. Flashes of bliss that coursed through my body, needling my skin. Every cell ringing with something pure and true. Buoyant. Transcendent. It rarely happened in church; instead, it washed over me on the city bus or walking from one class to another. Maybe while reading a book under a tree. At the laundromat. And, more than any other time, while dancing. Suspended in midair. Turning.

Her nostalgia was short-lived. Before I could be confirmed in the Catholic Church and choose my saint name, Mom moved us *again*, this time to Oceanside, a seaside military town forty minutes north of San Diego. We moved into Hillside Gardens on Greenbrier Street, an open-air apartment complex where she took a job as the property manager in exchange for free rent. The residents were mostly young Black and Latino families, and a few other white single parents. There were drug busts and late-night parking lot throw-downs. The courtyard pool was coated in a thin green film and confettied with rotting leaves. On Saturdays, Mom would wake us early, and we'd walk to get donuts, which we ate on the way to the public golf course next door. Chipper blond instructors in khaki shorts offered free lessons on how to hold a club and drive a ball, which Chris and I learned and promptly forgot.

Mom had applied for and gotten me into a performing arts magnet school, where I started to thrive artistically and settle socially along the fringes of the inner circle. A solid mid-level social standing. Good enough for me. The stars of the arts program were in a traveling show choir, which I auditioned for and didn't make, placed instead in the B-rated catchall girls' choir. I donned my velvet dress with puffy blue sleeves and sang with enthusiastic mediocrity. I tried out for the cheerleading squad and made it in the very last round.

Toward the end of the year, things took a turn when I was chosen for a traveling group that visited local schools to perform a lyrical dance number to Céline Dion's "The Power of Love." That must have bumped me up in the eyes of the administrators, because soon after, I usurped the reigning class diva to snag a starring role in a musical medley of songs from *South Pacific*. My rendition of "I'm Gonna Wash That Man Right Outa My Hair," the lyrics of which I understood only in the most innocent, campy sense, felt like a real turning point for my future on the stage.

I didn't go to my dad's that summer. Instead, my grandmother sent me on a two-week tour of Europe under the supervision of a high school English teacher she knew. I traveled to London, Paris, Rome, and Madrid with a group of horny sixteen-year-olds who were having threesomes on the train, while I thought myself "un peu sophistiquée" for pounding one sangria at a Madrid nightclub and drinking my Coke sans ice like the Europeans. When I came back, Mom said I was different. That I acted too good for them. That I brushed my little brother aside when he ran to hug me at the airport. Maybe I did. I was thirteen and "world-class" now.

Mom had been happy for me to go, but anything that set me apart from them translated into a minor threat. She seemed to resent that the other side of my family lived comfortably while we suffered. It wasn't that she didn't want me to visit them or have nice things, but as we got older and Rick came around less, every August when I returned from my dad's house, it put into relief what my brother had not done—gone to science camp, gotten new summer clothes, or whatever it was.

He spent his summers with Mom, for the most part. They had a whole separate life together. When he got older, he'd play in summer all-star baseball leagues and she'd travel to games and tournaments, cheering along with other moms in the bleachers, even when she didn't know the proper lingo. "Chris, Chris, he's our man, if he can't do it, no one can!" she'd chant, to my brother's great embarrassment. Sometimes he'd travel to the Bay Area to see his dad, which slowly became seeing his brother, Rick Jr., who lived in San Jose, and had accomplished his dream of becoming a DJ. Rick Jr. was twenty years older than my brother, had kids of his own, and was always working, but Chris looked up to him and started to talk about becoming a DJ, too.

As we got older and my brother became more aware of what we had and didn't have, she became more sensitive to and protective of him. Like any mom, she wanted her kids to have equal and fair access. But she seemed to internalize it as a reflection on her motherhood or worthiness that we didn't. And that trickled down. It came out in weird ways, which after the European issue, I learned to navigate by downplaying anything extra I'd been given.

Over the years, I adapted to the financial disparity between the branches of my family by keeping quiet. If I mentioned our struggles in California to my father or his parents, I watched how quickly the subject changed. How their eyes shifted or their jaws steeled. How they distanced themselves from the moment. From *me*. I said less. Less about our moves and living conditions, about my mother's spiritual explorations or financial state. With Mom and Chris, I shared less about silly day camps and fresh lobster dinners, careful not to highlight things she couldn't afford or project an attitude that she might read as too much ease. To align with my mother, which I did, was to identify with struggle. I had many opportunities via my dad's family, and through her as well. She gave everything she could—bought the house, and was always willing to support creativity and education. Still, for a long time—far too long—I judged people's ability, including my own, to withstand hardship as a mark of "realness." So much so that later in life, when I had more chance for comfort and ease or even a decent paycheck, it would be hard to embrace. It would always feel like something of a betrayal.

But the Oldsmobile was not one of those times.

The house had been a blessing; the Oldsmobile I campaigned for.

For weeks, I'd been hassling Mom to buy a gold Cutlass that we passed in a used-car lot every day on the way to the bus stop. She was looking for a car anyway and they had no-money-down financing. I was desperate. I needed this car as much as I'd needed the house. High school was about to start and there was no margin for error. I could eke by with bargain clothes, creative fashion sense, and newly won European je ne sais quoi. And it was easy enough to keep my new, wealthier friends at the magnet school from seeing my apartment by going to theirs or suggesting we meet at the mall. But there was no way around a car. Cars were more than transportation in Southern California; they were cultural cachet.

There was a concert coming up at a local church, and I wanted to invite my friend Diane to come and to sleep over after, but I was scared we'd have to take the city bus home, something the girls I went to school with just didn't do. Mom was considering the car, I could tell. And she had steady work managing Hillside. I didn't know what else was happening moneywise, and when I say I didn't care, I mean that the week of the concert, every night before bed, I got down on my knees and literally prayed to god that she would bring it home.

When I left for school the morning of, there was no car, and Mom didn't say a word. If she didn't show up at the church to pick us up, I'd play dumb and tell Diane she forgot and we could hop the B75 home, a route I *just happened* to have memorized. That night, I white-knuckled it through whiny acoustic sets and swaying refrains. Afterward, Diane and I nibbled on stale chocolate chip cookies from Costco and lingered in the parking lot, dissecting our school crushes. A group of kids playing tag ran past and as they cleared from my vision, the gold Oldsmobile rolled into the lot and came to a stop in front of us. Mom waved from the driver's seat. Chris hung out the passenger window, hollering, "New car, Neen!" His whole face lit up.

I turned toward Diane and shrugged. "We got a new car," I said, implying that we'd had an old one to trade in.

I ran my fingers over the hood and absorbed the sensation of a prayer answered, before opening the door to let Diane into the back. I slid in after her. The velour bench seat was plush and bouncy, the windows streak-free, the radio crisp and clear. Chris sat up front, a small king, looking as buoyant as I felt.

"Hi, girls," said Mom, turning down the blasting norteño. "How was the show?"

"Oh, you know," I said. "Heartfelt."

She caught my eye in the rearview and gave a barely perceptible nod. A flicker of acknowledgment between us.

Decades later, I'd find out that my dad had sent her a chunk of money that month out of the blue to make up for meager child-support checks during the early years, when he was still cobbling together odd jobs. Just because his parents had money didn't mean he did. He'd been focused on enlightenment, not acquisition. But he'd been working with the state of Texas for a while and was comfortable.

Diane and I became BFFs, spending Saturday afternoons cutting pictures out of fashion magazines to make collages and memorizing the faces and names of the '90s supermodels. During our brief foray into Catholicism, I'd welcomed organized religion. Even if I didn't take it literally, it offered order and structure. A clear sense of this world and the other; heaven and hell; here and beyond. But the more frequent my mother's spiritual oscillations became, the more I clung to mall culture and pop stars, tempering the unknowable with the bright bubble gum of life. By the time she dragged me and Chris to an Evangelical revival, my spiritual curiosity had all but deflated.

It was an 80-degree Sunday in Oceanside. Sapphire sky. At the pier, a hundred people, maybe two, were packed into a crescent of stone bleachers that descended to an open-air stage at the water's edge. Clapping and singing, they swayed to the rhythm of crashing waves. We ducked into an open spot just as a new song started. Between the crackle of the speakers and the rush of the Pacific, I couldn't make out the lyrics, but I closed my eyes and raised my hands over my head. Along for the ride, I tried to let go and allow the energy to wash over me.

A pastor in a dark suit appeared onstage and began to pace from left to right, his voice booming through the loudspeakers. "Do you accept Jesus Christ as your lord and personal savior?" he hollered. "Do you ask him to come into your heart and wash away all sin? *If so*—if you are ready to start living, I mean REALLY

LIVING, make your way down to the stage. Our brothers and sisters are here to greet you, to bring Jesus into your lives."

Two lines formed, shuffling slowly toward the sea, where a man and woman stood in front of the stage. It looked something like a Communion line, but instead of the Eucharist, as each worshipper approached, they had hands laid on them. Some cried out or started to sing. Others crumpled and dropped to the ground. At first, I gasped, but no one else seemed bothered, so I kept swaying and humming. As the singing grew louder, more exuberant, I felt the energy rise. It was joyous and prickly, an electric current running between me and the other swaying bodies.

"Whose heart is ready?" the pastor boomed. "Whose heart is open?"

Mine *was*, I was shocked to realize. This was it. *This*, I thought, is what my mother must have been chasing. What she'd seen in Guru Dev's eyes. I was touched. Entered by the Holy Spirit. I wanted to give myself to it. To let it carry and guide me.

Part of me had always been open. I'd yearned for something to believe in. But that day, I *felt* it. I hummed louder. I still couldn't make out the lyrics. The closer I listened to the people around me, the more garbled the sounds became. It was some sort of code. A foreign language. I turned in place, squinting at the sea of heads, bobbing and weaving, their mouths open wide. Their eyes, glassy and distant. They weren't singing at all, I realized. Chanting, maybe? Decrees?

"Mom, what are they saying?" I whispered, leaning in close so no one could hear.

"What, Bird!?" she shouted over the crowd.

"*Shhhh.* Why do they look like that?"

"It's called tongues. They're speaking in tongues."

"But what is it?" I said, still swaying. At my side, Chris was watching seagulls pick apart a stale loaf of bread a couple of steps down.

"It's holy," Mom said, pantomiming the word *holy* as if it was a secret.

"Holy how?"

"It's sort of, like, well. It's like channeling, I guess. It's coming through them."

My joy started to curdle. The buzzy glow went sharp.

"*What's* coming through them?" I gripped her elbow. "Is it real?"

"Not *really*," she said conspiratorially. "But don't worry about it, babe. It's no big deal."

"Something isn't right, Mom. Look, please."

She scanned the crowd, squinting hard, as if to see them through my eyes. "All right, babe," she said finally, letting out a low chuckle. "Maybe you're right. They do look a *liiiiittle* out there."

I couldn't take it anymore. "I want to go," I hissed, starting to push my way through the crowd. "*NOW.*"

When she saw that I was serious, Mom grabbed Chris's hand and chased me up the cracked stone steps. At our backs, the rising tide smashed against the pier. The jumble of hundreds speaking in tongues turned to radio static. Back on the sidewalk, bikini-clad Rollerbladers swerved around us as if we were traffic cones. Chris shimmied and stomped the sand from his shoes.

"What freaked you out so bad, Bird?" Mom asked.

"Whatever was controlling them."

"Oh, I think it's fine," she said, flicking her wrist as if shooing away a cat. "It just makes them feel closer to god. That's all."

"But the language was like, *like, gibberish*! It was weird. Wasn't it *weird*?" I needed someone to acknowledge how weird it all was. I looked to my little brother. He shrugged. He was five.

If god could enter me at will and speak through me, then to "really start living," as the pastor had invited us, was to consent to becoming a vessel. A channel. Like Anita Two. My mother seemed content to slip in and out of the ether; my father spoke in haikus of singularity and oneness. Of merging with the collective. But how the eff would I know who I was if I merged with everyone else? As I felt the boundaries of my selfhood threatened, a primal scream let loose. "*Enough*," it said. It wasn't just the tongues. It was everything. All the churches and conspiracy theories. The constant moving. The running through ideas of god like items on a menu.

"Okay, Bird," Mom said, smiling. Her eyes crinkled with a hint of exasperation. Something no one else would have noticed, but I could read her like a sailor does the sea. "I guess this one was a little out there for you."

I could have murdered her on the spot. But as we walked toward the car, I kept silent.

In the Book of Genesis, doubt is manifest as Satan, as a snake in the garden. Doubt is the moment a woman thinks for herself. Her curiosity birthed the entire concept of sin. The bite that launched a thousand denominations. For me, doubt was more like a fever rising. It was how everything we called god covered something else.

A cracker as the body of Christ.

Mount Shasta as cosmic vortex.

Turtlenecks cloaking scarskin.

Even the feeling of temporary bliss that had washed over me in the bleachers, a sensation originating in my own body, was part of something manufactured, an agreed-upon mass hysteria. I wanted bliss, but I needed to come back afterward. To return to the mundanity of paper-bag lunches and nightly dish duty. My mother bucked hard against the very thing I craved: the warm complacency of an ordinary life. That, I think, was the part of me that she understood the least. My need for the very security that she had once had. One of us needed to tether for good; if not, I was scared that one day we might just float away.

Even though she'd just bought the Oldsmobile and Chris loved his school and I was moving up in the world; even though life was shaping up to be better for us all down south and Mom seemed happier and lighter, I was desperate to go back to the only place I'd ever felt truly settled and safe. I started begging her to go home. I don't know how long it took, and looking back I wish she would have said no, but eventually Mom agreed that when the school year was over, we could go back to Siskiyou. To Dodge. I'd go first and stay with Carra and her parents for the summer. Mom and Chris would follow later, after she'd found and trained her replacement at Hillside.

––––––––––––––––––––––––––

I said before that my mother didn't understand my desire for an ordinary life. But maybe that's not quite accurate or even fair. Maybe she did. Maybe she understood it so well that she tried to protect me. Understood it so well that she knew what it would cost us. My brother. Me. And her. What it had cost her own mother. What it cost women like us. A price that she tried everything in her power to keep me from paying.

What she didn't tell me is that we never can go back home.

Not really.

Not like I'd imagined.

XV.

For something that looks like chaos, fire is quite ordered. If you learn to read it, you can even predict what it might do. As a room burns, it seeks to equalize its own temperature. Walls and even furnishings absorb the heat, and as they heat up, they create off-gases. There's an inflection point at which so much gas is built up that every flammable surface spontaneously combusts. This is called flashover. Not all fires reach flashover, but they all have the potential. One of the warning signs is the appearance of small slithering flames in the smoke. Snakes or jellyfish, firefighters call them. If they appear, you have seven to ten seconds until the room combusts. Knowing what to look for is the only thing that will save your life.

Mom's story of the Laredos picked up right where it left off.

"Hold my coffee real quick, will you, Bird?" she said, pressing her travel mug into my hand as she downshifted.

"Nooooo," I whined. "I'm in white pants. Why don't you have a lid? Every morning it's 'hold my cup real quick.' And every morning it spills." I took the cup from her hand and wedged it crookedly into the center console, already sticky with spilled coffee of mornings past.

She laughed. "God. Everything is so tidy with you. Sometimes I wonder where you come from."

At the stop sign, she glanced in the rearview mirror. She drove like a DMV instructor—seat scooted as forward as possible, her spine erect, hands at ten and two.

"*This*," she said, gesturing to her coffee. "This is how I know you're her. My mother reincarnate."

"It's a cup of coffee, Mom," I said, deadpan. "Everything isn't a sign."

The renters had moved out, and we were living back at Morris Street, but Mom had signed district papers so I could attend Dunsmuir High instead of Weed, agreeing to drive me the twenty minutes south to school until I got my license. We rolled past the courthouse onto Main Street, where scattered patches of trees gave way to a row of washed-out, abandoned storefronts. There were Black Butte Saloon and Papa's Place, the only two bars in town, whose barstools were worn soft by the same five drinkers. The abandoned movie theater, Weed Palace, its grand marquee still intact, and the social heart of town, Cedar Lanes, where you could still bowl a game for under five dollars. Weed hadn't changed since we'd been away.

"I've been confronting people, babe," Mom said, turning past Boles Creek, a housing project where I would soon spend many drunken nights.

"As in?"

"When they're whispering in Ray's," she said. "I interrupt and give them a chance to come clean. To be human about the whole thing."

I gulped. "And?"

"They just stare at me and shrug. Like they have absolutely *no idea* what I'm talking about. If they would just cop to it, I'd let it all go. Start fresh. But they're cowards. Bullies. Liars."

It wasn't just Mount Shasta anymore, she said.

The story had spread to Dunsmuir and Weed, Yreka even, twenty miles north. The way she told it, my mother's name had made its way into every town within a forty-mile radius. It'd been almost five years since she left the note on Nathan's truck. How was it possible that they hadn't moved on? Or that she hadn't?

"Dangit, my kids want to be here and that's where they're going to be!" She pounded her fist against the steering wheel.

My chest tightened as I stared into the thicket of pines lining the road. There was a game I played. It was like those magic eye optical illusion posters at the mall. First I fixed my gaze on a single tree just ahead, staring until we got closer and at the last minute, when I could no longer see it, I let my vision spread and blur and the trees fused, hundreds flying past my peripheral in an emerald streak.

Then I'd find another and narrow in. Begin again.

"This is slander," Mom said as I let the trees focus and blur, focus and blur. "And I won't take it. I'm building my case. Ooooh, you better believe it." Her voice went husky, a drop in register that I recognized as a simmering of things unsaid, conversations on loop in her mind.

I kept quiet, bracing myself. Crisp, blur. One tree, many trees. Definition, nothingness. She flipped on the blinker and took the Central Dunsmuir exit, coasting off the freeway past Shelby's Diner.

Building my case, she'd said. Building a case meant documents.

It meant she was collecting evidence. Could I find evidence, too?

Dunsmuir High School sat at the top of a steep winding hill that ran into more forest. The entire campus was a single two-story building, a garage for shop class, a couple run-down tennis courts, and a small field where we played touch football during P.E. or walked the dirt track. Mom pulled up to the front door and I jumped out, waving as I faded into a swarm of students rushing to beat the first bell.

"Girl!" a voice shouted from behind.

It was Carra, rushing to catch up. I stopped, letting others push past. We linked arms and walked through the doors together. "Party at Isla's tonight," she reminded me as we split toward our first-period classes. In coming back to Dunsmuir, I'd been chasing childhood belonging. But what I returned to was a tsunami of teen hormones. In Oceanside, I'd spent my weekends performing to Céline Dion and toilet-papering houses for kicks, but my Siskiyou friends had already traded in sleepovers for blunt smoke and getting fingered in the woods.

First I was shocked. Then I wanted in.

That night, it was four of us. Carra, Charmaine (from our tin-roof tea parties), their friend Gloria, and me. Gloria was beautiful, with long, thick dark hair, which she braided every night before bed and her mother cut each full moon. The youngest girl in a large, strict Mexican family, she'd mastered sneaking out her window to party at night while maintaining a 4.0. She had a way of slipping around things; her broad smile and perfect teeth got her far.

We walked into the party just as "Gin and Juice" came blasting over blown-out speakers.

Isla's living room looked like almost every Siskiyou County living room. Wood-paneled walls peppered with taxidermied animal heads—bucks and ducks, raccoons. Shag carpet. Floral granny couches that had been shoved to the side to make room for dancing. The party was just getting started. A few upperclassmen swayed to the beat, but the real energy was emanating from the kitchen. Carra and I walked back to find a couple of guys stabbing cans of Coors Light with a screwdriver and chugging them in a single gulp.

"Here," said Max, a lanky sophomore with a crew cut and white-boy swagger, as he shoved a beer into my hand. Aside from that glass of sangria I'd snuck in Europe, I'd never had a drink. Dad was a teetotaler. Mom got tipsy on a single glass of pizza parlor merlot. Mimicking the guys, I hunched over the sink and pushed the screwdriver into the bottom of the can. As the aluminum buckled, I giggled nervously, then shrieked as it pushed through, spraying bitter foam into my face.

"Now like this," Max said, lifting his can quickly and placing his mouth over the hole. "Crack the top. It comes out fast. Be ready. You *ready?*"

I nodded and cracked the tab, choking as cold beer rushed into my mouth faster than I could swallow. I closed my eyes and opened my throat to let it run down. It was bitter and crisp. Foamy.

"Whoo!" I cried, throwing the can into the sink after my final gulp. The guys burst into laughter as I started to spin. I gripped the counter, crouching down to brace against a hot wave of vertigo.

"You good?" Carra asked, her hand on my back.

"I don't know."

"Wait, shit. You never shotgunned?" Max asked.

For a couple of minutes, I sat there spinning, my head against a drawer, but then the room settled, and the dizziness was replaced by a wave of euphoria.

"Another!" I said, bolting upright and flipping my hair back.

The guys cheered and Carra laughed, joining me this time, the four of us chugging in unison, while the first strains of Naughty by Nature's "Feel Me Flow" came on.

After *Another!* and *Another!* and *Another!* the world went vertical. I slunk into the living room, working my way into a tangle of bodies grinding on the dance floor. Someone passed me a joint and I took it, coughing out a huge wave of smoke after my first hit, ever. I took another, loving the feel of crackly paper between my lips and how the thick vegetal smoke became a screen between me and the world. I smoked and smoked until I was in a little glass chamber, alone, muffled voices all around, cool water streaming down my face.

Wow, I thought. Now *this* is a feeling.

When I opened my eyes, I was in the shower. Deadweight and soaked, I was naked except for my bra and underwear, and being propped up by two drunk senior girls.

"She's awake!" one cried.

"Oh, thank god," said the other.

"What? *Whaaaa?*" I slurred.

"You begged us not to take your bra off," said the first, laughing.

I was still totally flat-chested and hadn't gotten my period, which I was so ashamed of that I wore a three-inch-thick padded bra that I'd convinced Mom to buy me. An interim measure until mine came in. But I was apparently so aware of being perceived that even during the first and one of very few blackout drunks of my life, I'd convinced the girls who'd thrown me into the shower instead of calling an ambulance to keep my bra on.

The next day, I was startled to wake on Carra's couch with a fat lip and puke-streaked hair. "Rough one, huh, kiddo?" said Tom as he put on Pink Floyd and cranked up the volume. I smoothed out the blanket that someone had laid over me and flashed him a sheepish grin. Rough, it was. But also, sort of a rush. I'd never been so out of control. Underneath the thundering headache, it was a relief to not care. To not even be able to. To have nothing but the hangover to tend to. All that shitty beer swimming through my bloodstream had, for a few hours, freed me from the questions starting to knock harder at my psyche. Loosened the grip of sticky anxiety that told me there was something I could neither name nor contain happening at home. I didn't swear off drinking for weeks like most teens staring down their first brutal hangover might.

Everyone in my mother's stories drank. Her mother to the death, her father to mourn, her brother to flee. As I began to drink, it was warm and easy.

Familiar, almost. Familial.

Like some part of me already understood it was a way out.

In English class, I'd been seated next to a petite blond named Sierra. She was newish to town and wasn't close with any of my old friends, but we immediately hit it off. With an active distrust of authority and a nihilism that tempered her hippie-ish upbringing, Sierra could outwit any teacher and, to my great enjoyment, did so often. All my life, I'd been focused on being good. On maintaining peace. On fitting in. Following the rules. But Sierra didn't give a shit about arbitrary rules or those who are paid to enforce them. She demanded to be met on the terms of her own intelligence, which for a thirteen-year-old, I found ballsy. Her confidence was infectious. She was also very sad and very ready to party. We quickly became inseparable.

Mom got a job cleaning rooms at the Resort, a luxury golf resort with lakeside chalets, and managed to get Sierra and me hired as well. Most weekends, she'd drive the three of us to work, stopping by Burger King if anyone had extra money for breakfast sandwiches and coffee. Hungry for social analysis, Sierra lapped up Mom's musings on patriarchy and the New World Order, firing off burning questions about feminism and the prison-industrial complex. They debated and built together, while I rolled my eyes and leaned against the door to steal another ten minutes of sleep.

When we first started, Mom took it upon herself to train Sierra and me, and her standards were stringent. Even though our house was marginally clean, at work she was meticulous—she could spy a single hair on the floor or a bathtub ring not properly dissolved. Anything we did, me in particular, reflected on her, and she took it dead serious. Under her tutelage, we became top-notch cleaners. Even the bosses began to notice. Eventually, we started to clean without Mom, but most weekends she'd still give us a ride. We used our paychecks to pitch in for gas, and I'd pay a random bill here and there for Mom when she needed it, but mostly I spent my money on the clothes I'd always wanted but couldn't ask her for.

During the two years we worked there, Sierra and I went from being the only freshmen at senior parties, wide-eyed and giggly, to serious all-weekend partiers. And the more we partied, the worse our cleaning got. Morning pickups were less bushy-eyed debate and more hungover grumble. At first, Mom couldn't fathom why we looked so sloppy—our ponytails crooked and frizzy, our eyes still raccooned in last night's mascara. Our lack of professionalism drove her nuts, but by the time she figured out what was going on, partying had taken on a life of its own.

We had a routine for each season.

Fall was for football parties. We didn't give a shit about sports, but football was the hub of Dunsmuir's autumnal social calendar. Everyone—no matter what age—gathered at the field on Friday nights to shiver their way through four quarters of amateur battery. Sierra and I lingered outside the fence closest to the end zone, sipping on cocoa spiked with bottom-shelf peppermint schnapps, trying to secure a ride to the after-party.

Winter was for house parties: Big Pun and fat blunts in thin-walled apartment complexes.

Spring for bonfires in the woods. Country music wailing from the cab of a pickup while boys sang along drunkenly, crying some nights, fighting others. Girls in hoodies and bootcut jeans downing 40s and bottles of Boone's Farm, feeding the fire with logs chopped from nearby trees. "I hate White Rabbits!" we screamed when white smoke clouded our faces, a spell-like chant that we invoked to send it blowing in another direction. The scent of burning forest clung to our clothes and hair for days afterward.

And summers, or the parts that I was there, were for parties at the lake or the creek or the river—any body of icy water where we could drink and swim and bake like lizards on hot, sunny rocks. We just needed a ride. We always needed a ride. Boys were mostly happy to oblige as long as we kept our unspoken end of the bargain. Being cool and looking hot. We poured ourselves into jean cutoffs that barely covered our asses and strutted up and down

Dunsmuir Avenue, the main street that snaked through town. Under the blazing sun, we walked, blotting away forehead grease with chalky CoverGirl compacts that we stashed in our back pockets, dabbing our faces until we looked like bootleg eighteenth-century aristocrats, all in the hope that a hot upperclassman would drive by in their pickup, wave us into the cab, and ferry us away.

To a joint, a keg, a bonfire, *anywhere but here.*

XVI.

Mom said Pete was *in on it*. "He knows, Neen." She nodded toward the register at Pizza Y, Mountain Time's rival pizza parlor, where we were making our way through the salad bar. She was showing me how to maximize a one-trip versus all-you-can-eat. Chris was in the arcade.

I glanced over my shoulder to the counter where he was taking a phone order. "Pete Barr?" I whispered. "I seriously doubt that, Mom." A junior at Dunsmuir High, he was a stony skater who spent his weekends taking orders for extra-large pepperoni pies. We weren't close, but he'd had a crush on Sierra at one point and used to give us rides to parties. From what I knew, he wasn't the sort of teen boy who would give a shit about small-town gossip involving some forty-five-year-old woman. None of them would.

"He's in cahoots with the Laredos," she said.

"Cahoots?!"

She'd been talking like that lately. Like we were in a campy Western, where a mustachioed villain ties a princess to the train tracks and an unwitting cowpoke comes along to rescue her. And it wasn't just the Laredos. Her cosmic coffee-talks about UFOs and Lemurians were snowballing into more sinister conspiracies, like impending martial law and being forced to take something called the Mark of the Beast, wherein we would all have microchips planted in our hands that linked to our banks, and wherever we went, we'd get scanned like a cereal box at the grocery store. We'd

gone from what sounded like Nostradamus's far-off whimsical notions of California falling into the sea, to a ticking clock on the US
government turning us into human credit cards.

I fanned cucumber slices into concentric circles over a bed of
iceberg. "When we started coming here, I used to see him a lot,"
she whispered through clenched teeth. "He was always nice to
me. He knew I was your mom. Then the other day, he starts acting
all gaga out of nowhere. They've got him in on it. *No, no,* here!" She
grabbed the tongs from my hand. "Create a base at the bottom
and work the lighter items into a pyramid. Use your edges, too."

She wedged tiny crowns of broccoli around the rim of my plastic salad bowl.

"They really think I'm trying to break up his marriage," she
said, scooping a tiny hill of kidney beans onto her plate. "As if.
Puh-lease. I mean get real! I'm old enough to be his mother."

"Exactly," I said. "Is that why we stopped going to Mountain
Time?"

"You think you're moving to this spiritual place. But, really, it's
a podunk town with podunk people who'd rather shit-talk than listen to the truth for one goddamn minute."

"Everyone is in everyone's business here," I said. "There's nothing better to do."

I reached for the ranch dressing, but she batted my hand away.

"No, no. Ask for an extra plate and a separate container for the
dressing. That way, it doesn't take up room."

"God," I said, walking to the register, equal parts embarrassed
and impressed.

"All groovy?" Pete drawled as he handed me the plates.

I nodded too eagerly. "So groovy."

Mom showed me how to carefully dump the overflowing bowl
onto a plate. "And voilà!" For the price of two sides, we had meal-
size salads. She looked pleased.

"I'm building my case for slander," she said, digging in. "That's why I need to get this letter to the police chief." She pulled a tri-folded piece of paper from her tote and shook it out. I noticed the handwriting. The way it stretched out like taffy when she was mad.

I sighed. "Let's say Pete is 'in on it'; what would 'they' tell him, exactly?"

"You know, same old, same old. That I'm trying to bust up Nathan's marriage."

I was this close to screaming: *Well, are you?! Just fuck the guy already!*

"Nothing's more important to these country women than their MAN, ya know!" she said with a comic twang. And about that, I have to say, she was not wrong. I had come to learn that nowhere was the sanctity of *the man* more revered than small-town USA, where beefs were stubborn, families held grudges, and reputations were hard to overturn. High school had provided plenty of insight into the pettiness of not only my peers but their parents. At away games, I sat next to gossiping mothers who spread rumors with no qualms. I noticed how quickly people assembled into a Greek chorus, chanting the same thing from many mouths. How one rumor could bar you from a spot on the cheer squad. The non-cosmic contingent of the county seemed wary of anyone or anything that challenged the status quo. Something about the close quarters, the endless wilderness, and the lack of stimulation up north seemed to dull the imagination. The inverse of Tolstoy's families, folks in Siskiyou differed in the ways that they were happy, and were alike in the ways they were miserable.

As I got older and understood how the small-town network functioned, it was easier to see how my mother—an independent, disabled, single mother of two—could be considered a threat. For all the crystal shops on Main Street, I think Mom was still in a state of shock that we hadn't landed in a cosmic energy vortex, but in the beating heart of California's red zone. The New Age contingent was vibrant, but a minority compared to the conservative families that had lived there for generations and had voted red just as long. A place where high school days were often the glory days, and post–high school, social dynamics remained the same. Like coal country or the steel belt, Siskiyou County's economy was dependent on the extraction of natural resources. After advancements in milling technology and tightened environmental restrictions in the '80s, the timber industry deflated, and the once-important region was brushed aside by California's powerful lawmaking machine, which demonstrated little care for far-flung corners that didn't impact its economy.

Jobs were hard to come by. And many were embittered or saddened by the loss of their livelihood and what they considered their legacies. It wasn't just the logging jobs people grieved, but all the others that came with it—jobs in hospitality, real estate, construction. By the time we arrived, it was a depressed economy with no clear avenue toward revival. There was an overwhelming sense that something once abundant had been lost or, in more antagonistic terms, been taken.

With time, the feeling I'd clung to, *we're all in this together*, started to manifest in more damaging ways. Poverty was not a unifying force but a stressor that kept people so locked into survivalism it was hard for them to see where the real problems lay. That, combined with a low-grade malaise and cultural isolation from the rest of the country, could expand perceived disenfranchisement into paranoia.

We existed in the Venn diagram where the New Age and the libertarian intersect, a terrain ripe for conspiracy. These two ideologies—Duntley's spiritual prospector and the don't-tread-on-me crowd—were next-door neighbors, which created a level of tolerance, if not friendliness. Divided on core social and political principles, they were united in a general sense of outsiderism and antiestablishment attitudes.

In times of political and social uncertainty, the esoteric and its unruly cousin, conspiracy, have provided frameworks to regain power from the margins. When people have been neglected or abused by systems or individuals that they have no power over, blame must be directed away from the source of the pain. This restores agency—it shifts the locus of control from internal to external.

But oftentimes, the ideas or systems we're pinpointing are not the ones at the root of the issue. As Brian Greene, theoretical physicist and string theorist, writes in *Until the End of Time*, "Evolution did not configure our brain processes to form beliefs that align with reality. It configured them to promote beliefs that generate survival-promoting behaviors. And the two considerations need not coincide." We blame the systems or ideas or people that allow us to keep our core—our most psychologically necessary—beliefs intact.

Belief becomes stronger than truth.

Belief answers more questions.

Young children do the same. They aren't built to perceive their caretakers—the "system" they rely on—as untrustworthy. If they are neglected or abused or become unsafe, instead of pointing the finger outward, they often internalize and blame themselves. Psychologically, it's safer and more empowering to understand that you have done something wrong than that the person tasked with your care is at best unstable, at worst, malicious. When the person we are surviving is also the one who nurtures us, an unbridgeable schism emerges between true and untrue. Between impossibility and necessity. Whether out-of-work loggers under the thumb of a paternalistic company town, down-and-out mothers left to beg for more, or a child at the whim of an unstable parent, we are not meant to believe that our provider is unstable, or at worst, extractive. Our mind simply refuses it.

What cannot be true, then, simply *is*.

"I'd accept an apology, you know?" Mom said, pushing aside her salad. "That's all I'm looking for at this point."

I nodded, but I wondered if that was true.

"I'm sorry, Mom."

"Not from you, babe, it's not your fault." She sniffled and my heart quivered at the sound. Wrenching a few napkins from the dispenser, I dabbed her cheeks.

"Don't cry," I pleaded, wincing at the desperation in my voice. But I was desperate. To help. To make it stop. To rid my family of these phantoms. For my mother to be out of pain. And also for her to shut up forever about the whole damn thing. In the slurry of my own emotions, I couldn't hear it yet—how much my mother's story sounded like Raelle's.

A group of people out to get her.

People who were slowly, psychologically, torturing her.

But in that moment, watching her cry, something else hit me. *Pete FUCKING Barr*. If my peers were the ones spreading rumors, I could do something about it. Obviously, I couldn't ask him directly. But Cheryl would know. I couldn't believe I hadn't thought of it before. Charmaine's mom, Cheryl, worked at the only grocery store in Dunsmuir. Everyone passed through her checkout line, and when they did, they told her things. Cheryl knew which scratchers were going to hit, but she also knew who the real father was. I'd always sensed that she knew about our teenage parties and hookups, too, but kept it to herself. During lunch, we'd run down the hill and rush through her line, loaded down with turkey sandwiches and Snapple, and Cheryl would just smile and nod, letting out a warm raspy smoker's laugh.

"Be good now, girls."

"Yes, Cheryl. Of course!" we'd chime, running out the door and back up the hill, laughing and panting our way to the top.

At lunch the next day, Charmaine and I sat on the stage in the auditorium/lunchroom eating fluffy cafeteria rolls and I asked if she'd ever heard any rumors about my mom. She was direct. A softball player with a unflappable demeanor. I knew I could count on her for the truth.

"Will you ask your mom if she's heard anyone talking about her?"

"Saying what?" she asked, looking confused.

I waved the question away. I couldn't bring myself to say it aloud. "Will you just ask?"

"Of course," she said, her jaw firm. "And fuck them if they are!"

Gloria walked up and I changed the subject, quickly. No one knew what was going on and I planned to keep it that way.

A few days later, Charmaine reported back. Cheryl hadn't heard anything at all, positive or negative. If Cheryl knew nothing, it was unlikely the entire town, much less half the county, knew. At first, I was relieved. Maybe it was all a big misunderstanding. I thanked Charmaine and rushed off to biology. But as the *clack-clack* of my platform boots echoed through the empty halls, it hit me what that meant. What I had been trying to un-know since that night at the Alpenrose.

XVII.

The year my mother self-immolated, Sylvia Plath's *The Bell Jar* was released in the US. It elicited an uproar and a wave of devotion from young women readers who felt seen for the first time. Through the protagonist Esther Greenwood, Plath articulated a collective malaise veiled by the perfectly coiffed image of post–World War II American women. My mother's own senior portrait is emblematic of what was expected in the late 1960s and early '70s. It's a black-and-white studio shot, the frame softened at the edges. Her skin was still unscarred, then, and it looks porcelain. Her shoulder-length hair was styled in a flipped bob so buoyant and flawless it's almost sculpted. Greenwood shared the same white, mild-mannered, middle-class upbringing as my mother, groomed to wear skirt suits, get an education, and become working girls. The world was their oyster. If only they'd wanted it. If only their minds had allowed. Greenwood, a writer, wins an essay contest and shows promise, but falls into a deep depression. It's the dissonance between how things look from the outside, not just individually but collectively, and what's going on internally that is so startling.

As my mom was coming of age, people were not sick but *troubled* or *different*. In part, this was lack of scientific understanding. But in equal measure, cultural stigma around mental illness created resistance to directly name or even notice anything deemed "a problem"—loosely understood as anything, or anyone, that kept life from clicking along as usual. The nuclear family—the safekeeper of social order, or per Marxist philosopher Louis Althusser, an "ideological state apparatus"—is the system that first teaches us to be obedient, which translates to becoming a good worker and contributing to a healthy economy. Anything that threatens its implied horizon becomes a problem.

In *Madness and Civilization,* Michel Foucault's social history of madness, he writes about a period in eighteenth-century Europe called the Great Confinement, when the poor, the criminal, and the mentally ill were imprisoned together, characterized as equally animalistic and unable to engage with what was considered the primary driver of a productive society: work. There's a more domestic, private way of understanding the alienation we build around illness. It's a message passed down through generations. Its directive is wordless but firm. Simply put: we do not speak of such things. Most of us don't learn to keep quiet via Marxist theory. We learn it at the dinner table. With a glance. A disapproving look.

In many cases, those like mine, we learn through silence itself.

Silence is what keeps the engine going, even as we watch it derail.

By the time I was born, mental illness in the media, particularly in women, had become synonymous with the monstrous. In horror films like *Carrie, Sybil, Misery,* and *Mommie Dearest,* madness manifested as bloody, cruel, or violent. In the '90s and early aughts, it was portrayed as either complete unraveling or quirk. Women with mental illness were cast as damaged goods, unstable sirens, wacky bohemians. "Troubled" girls took center stage—a slew of gritty, charismatic protagonists, often gorgeous, overtly sexual, and with a singular sensational issue à la xoJane. These stories put the struggle of young women front and center. And yet. The film *Girl, Interrupted* was lauded as a no-holds-barred breakthrough in mental health representation, but during a talk at Brandeis University, the author of the memoir it was based on, Susanna Kaysen (who spent time at the same hospital as Plath), called the adaptation melodramatic. Elizabeth Wurtzel's *Prozac Nation* told the story of a hyper-intelligent, mentally ill Harvard freshman. While the book was revelatory in its raw articulation of depression, Wurtzel's pain was culturally palatable, even glamorized, because she was thin and pretty and white and super smart. Gen X media might have the first wave of taking traditionally feminized mental health disorders, like anorexia or self-harm, seriously. But it was still sensationalized and narrow.

My generation was a sliver between Gen X, who had *raised themselves* because everyone was getting divorced, and Millennials, whose elementary lives were forever imprinted by 9/11. We inherited the problems of those before us but didn't yet have the language to talk about them. We were first to the internet, and had no idea what was coming. Tupac and Too Short scored our house parties, and the pretty-girl angst of Alanis Morissette and Fiona Apple and Shirley Manson were soundtracks to cry alone to in our cars. It wasn't exactly a time of nuance. Meredith Brooks screaming "I'm a bitch, I'm a lover" felt like power. Being angry was fresh. In hip-hop, Missy Elliott, Foxy Brown, and Lil' Kim recast sexual empowerment while playing on misogynistic tropes. These were our models of dissent.

My friends and I were a group of mostly white and Latina girls coming of age during the neoliberal '90s in a poor timber town. As we struggled to beat back our demons, many of us probably wildly depressed and ignorant to how booze exacerbated that depression, the pop culture we consumed shaped who we felt we could be and told us what was acceptable. The magazines we read and the shows we watched were all about makeup and clothes and how to get the guy to like you. If you were white, the main contender was misogyny—we were still on our way to more sophisticated conversations. Mental health, as it had for generations before us, was given side billing at best.

Besides *depression, nervous breakdown* was one of the few terms you'd hear thrown around. It meant, in the lexicon of the time, you were *going to the loony bin*. By then, mental hospitals weren't even widely open or available, but the terminology of institutionalization remained in the collective in imprecise ways. Now it sounds crass and ignorant. I couldn't identify where my friends and I even learned the term *loony bin*, but the books we'd been raised on in grade school were sensationalistic and prosaic. All we had to conjure an image of mental illness was *One Flew Over the Cuckoo's Nest* or the woman we endearingly called "Crazy Lori," who lived in front of the dilapidated Travelers Hotel on Dunsmuir Avenue and talked to herself all day.

When *Benny & Joon* came out in 1993, the year before I started high school, it was lauded by critics for its humanizing portrayal of mental illness. Many mental health advocates spoke positively about how the film illustrated Joon's struggles with autonomy, but the subtext and overall tone of the film left room to interpret her—who is now widely read as having schizophrenia—as simply being misunderstood. Joon lives with and relies on her brother, Benny, and outside their relationship, she's relatively socially isolated until Sam, played by Johnny Depp, comes along and does things like stick forks in dinner rolls and make them dance and cook grilled cheese sandwiches with an iron. He's wacky! Kooky! Unconventional! And because of that, he "gets" Joon.

"I mean, except for being a little mentally ill, she's pretty normal," he tells Benny at one point. While it was a pivot away from the damaging portrayal of madness as monstrous, or as edgy and sexy, its tweeness underscored the other side of the binary, which is that people with mental illness are just misunderstood outcasts who can't conform to the rigid strictures of a small-thinking society. The subtext is that Depp's character is *actually* the weird one, which has the effect of undercutting Joon's illness. Granted, it was the

'90s—a time in which the love of Johnny Depp still seemed a cura-tive for pretty much anything. But in trying to humanize illness, it became caricature: another form of erasure.

All this to say that, for most of my life, my mother didn't present like the people whom our culture had coded as sick. She was nei-ther monstrous nor a vixen; not an Ivy League depressive or a zany loner. Even as I started to grasp that there was something serious happening, I had no way to imagine or contextualize what that might be. Even later, in college, as I went out in the world and be-gan to absorb literature and art, reading darker works like Plath's *Ariel* or singing in the chorus for a performance of *The Tempest*, even as I'd become fascinated with Carl Jung's dream analysis and Irvin Yalom's existential group-therapy novels, I would never see a mother, a woman, like the one who raised me. Maybe that's why I went looking for her, myself.

XVIII.

I never called myself a runaway because it wasn't that dramatic.

One day, I just stopped going home.

At the end of my sophomore year, Mom's aunt Fern surprised me with a $2,000 check that Grandpa Lou had left me in his will. The day I turned sixteen, I got my driver's license and used it to buy the cheapest car I could find—a 1990 Dodge Shadow. At the Resort, Sierra and I had stopped caring. We'd lie on the couch for an hour before we started cleaning a room. We ate people's cookies and took swigs of their wine. We built obstacle courses to race the golf carts. When a new manager took over the cleaning crew, we were promptly fired.

Jobless and untethered, I started to crash between a rotating cast of friends' houses, climbing through their windows late at night after their parents were asleep. My trunk became a mobile wardrobe. Every morning, I'd pop it and select my outfit of the day like a truck-stop Cher Horowitz. Black vinyl pants, lavender zip-front booty shorts, sheer tees with the belly cut out. It was 1996—the era of shimmery white Carmen Electra eye shadow and Wet n Wild 666 lip liner. I'd learned early that if you looked average enough, à la Mom in her turtlenecks, or sexy and stylish enough, like the popular girls with their boobs and brand names and boyfriends, no one would question what was going on underneath. I broke dress code every day, challenging the principal to call my mom—to do anything. But no one did. Or, maybe, they tried. I don't really remember. I was already gone.

School became little more than a place to socialize. When I did go to class, Sierra and I met in the girls' locker room before the first bell and swigged tequila straight from the bottle, peeling a lime into wedges and eating them whole with gas station salt packets to chase the sting. At first, drinking had been a novel release. Something to sand down the jagged edges of a life that felt increasingly shadowy and unfixable. But my carefree partying had become driven and nihilistic. I would smoke or chug or snort or dose anything offered to me: weed, speed, booze, psychedelics, opium.

My mother called my father in Texas on a weekly basis, crying. I was out of control, she told him. She didn't know how to get me home. I'd never been like this. I was a good girl. My father, who assumed I was "acting out" in the way hormonal, rebellious teen girls do, counseled her to try his familial modus operandi—tough love. Which basically meant calling the cops or taking away my driver's license, legal means available to the parents of wayward teens. She made empty threats but never followed through, probably aware that calling the cops on me meant calling them on herself.

Teachers pelted me with looks of disappointment and assigned me detentions, which I received like merit badges and served, unfazed, week after week. All but one, the geometry teacher whose first-period class I'd missed the most, wrote me off. None of the adults in my life sat me down and asked: *What happened? Why are you doing this?* Even Mom, after reading up on her parental rights and getting ready to "lay down the law," never directly asked me why.

By the middle of my junior year, I was in descent. I was no longer a proper noun, a name—*Nina*—but a verb. A falling. For my mother, faith had been a way to survive a life of persecution, perceived or otherwise. Belief in god, the afterlife, the underworld, the astral plane offered a more profound and timeless frame for her suffering. Because she could believe in anything, I'd believe in nothing but the corporeal. I would grind myself down into the humus of life. Elect myself a member of the church of the real—a congregation that cared only that I could piss in the woods and shotgun a beer. My god would be a stoned ride in the bed of a truck on a star-speckled night. My cosmology, a constellation of backcountry idols and booze-addled spirit guides. My ablution: cheap beer and drugstore cologne. I still swoon when I smell Gravity. Each night, I obliterated myself. Every morning, I brought myself back to life.

And that is what I called a miracle.

On the way home from parties, driving drunk down windy forested back roads, I'd turn my headlights off and Sierra would climb onto the roof of the car, lie on her belly, and grip the open window frames like a starfish. Clutching one of her hands in mine, I'd steer with the other, gunning us through the dark. She'd whoop and shout, her cries echoing through the tree-choked canyon.

We weren't suicidal, exactly.

We just didn't care whether we lived or died.

Sometime in the middle of all this, our school administrators staged a faux car crash through a nationwide program called "Every 15 Minutes" meant to scare the shit out of teens and make us stop driving drunk. The whole operation was clandestine. For a week, select students were pulled out of class to practice their roles as either drivers or victims. The day of the event, an announcement came over the loudspeaker.

There's been an accident. All students report to the field.

We spilled into the halls, moving at the rate of a fire drill, talking our shit, making weekend plans, happy for a break from class. Outside, it was a massacre. An ambulance was parked crooked in the lot, its siren blaring. Two cars were T-boned, their sides smashed in. Cops were on the scene taking reports. Kids were being loaded onto stretchers. Others lay on the ground, unmoving, covered in fake blood, while people knelt over them, wailing like they were actually dead. Rolling my eyes, I walked toward the ambulance for a better look, and was surprised to find Carra lying on a stretcher, bloody and unconscious.

Nearby, her friends from the volleyball team were crying. Not in a staged way. They were moved by the visual of their friend and teammate in crisis. I saw them imagining what it would be like if she died. Somehow I was unfazed. I'd done enough theater to know a hack job when I saw one. I thought of Gloria and Charmaine, who, a week earlier, halfway through the school day, had pulled into the lot just where the ambulance stood now, wasted on vodka and OJ, laughing and crying at the same time.

"What the fuck, you guys?" Carra and I were in P.E. walking the track and saw them pull up.

Charmaine's foot was bleeding because she'd locked herself out of her house, and wasted, she and Gloria decided to pull the air conditioner out of the window to get in and dropped it on her foot. On the way back to school, they'd driven the wrong way up the freeway off-ramp.

Later that year, three guys from our class would turn a corner at night speeding off the 800-foot bridge and slam into an overpass. The truck crumpled like a can. They were lucky to be alive. We didn't need a contrived crash to wake us up.

We were almost dying all the time.

The adults had spent all that time and money on shock-theatrics to show us how dangerous our egregious drinking and driving was, but they never stopped to ask why we were doing it in the first place. Instead, they gave us detentions. Instead, they turned to newly formed pop-sociology proclamations about the effects of the internet or violent video games or gangster rap or the break-down of the nuclear family. Social scientists studied things like the queen bee phenomenon and early online bullying. *Online* was a

Wild West to them, and we became their lab specimens—a generation whose behaviors and outcomes they could separate from themselves and blame on technology. There was a sense of fear in the adults. A sense that something was happening they couldn't name or control, something they were afraid of.

Maybe where there was more money, other things were happening. But in our rural corner of the world, where the median annual income was $26,000, people were navigating byzantine systems of paperwork just to stay housed and fed and receive the most basic social services. I'd watched how isms in the form of local gossip impacted people's ability to get apartments and jobs, to have their health or safety taken seriously. Everyone was so busy surviving that they couldn't even ask their kids why we were partying so hard.

Before every dance performance, for a split second, I would white out. It always felt infinite and like that night would be the night I'd finally choke. It happened just before the curtain opened, as we stood in formation onstage behind the heavy velvet panel. On the other side, the audience a dim, anonymous rustle. The air in the theater dusty and expansive—like history, like the ancients. The music would cue, and the curtain would part, the spotlight a crude blinding sun, the audience a sea of halos. And my mind, white. White like driving down the highway in a flash blizzard, suddenly unable to see two feet in front of you. White, of purity. White, closest to god. I couldn't remember anything. Not the steps I was supposed to perform, not first or third position, and certainly not why I was onstage in front of all those people. Panic would flood my limbs. But as the music began, every time, my body would start to move, and before I knew it, it was dancing the dance without me, executing the choreography that I'd studied for months, as I caught up to the moment.

When my parents spoke of ascension, of becoming a vessel, of leaving, of merger, this was all I could conjure.

As an adult, I'll ask my dad to explain yogic flying. His answer will be something characteristically abstract, like: "It's a state of pure consciousness that unfolds."

"Yes," I'll press. "But what do you *do*, exactly?"

"It's an urge that rises spontaneously from within."

Exasperated, I'll log on to YouTube and look it up for myself. On the screen, one meditator hops up and down in full lotus and his action sparks the others. They start to pop up left and right, hopping and bouncing in place, then they move across the mats, arranging themselves into lanes as if to avoid a traffic jam. It *does* look contagious—though more Jiffy Pop than *pure consciousness unfolding*. As I watch them, I realize yogic flying isn't levitation—it's collective joy found in bouncing on extra-springy foam mats. But if you asked my parents then, they were flying. As if the whole point of this life was to get *somewhere* other than here. Obliteration takes so many forms.

It wasn't just the drinking or the drugs. I, too, had been seeking disintegration of the self—a form of lightness that my mother found in the godly. Onstage, I remembered nothing because I was nothing. And in that, there was total freedom. Freedom from the questions and answers of embodiment. From the weight of what I'd been asked to carry.

Exploding my life had been easier than trying to put words to what was happening. Flinging my body through the dark was my attempt, I suppose, at using my limbs *as flares for help*, like the Buddhist monks—trying to show someone, anyone, with my erasing, my falling, that something was wrong. I'd reach what Bradatan, the immolation scholar, calls a limit-situation, a point at which one can no longer effect change in their surroundings with language or action. All I had left to use was the body, which became both weapon and voice. Onstage, mine knew the way not just because

I'd trained it but because the music entered me and articulated what I could not say. It spoke for me.

Or in the great choreographer Twyla Tharp's words: "Art is the only way to run away without leaving home."

Everyone should have known something was wrong when I stopped dancing.

XIX.

It was spring when my mother came looking for me. By then, I'd missed something like thirty days of geometry. A lifelong straight-A student, I'd destroyed my chance to get into a four-year university and was on the verge of not graduating. Sierra and I had ditched class to drop a tab of acid that morning. We were still coming down on the porch at Z's house when he stuck his head out the door.

"Nina, phone. Your mom."

I floated up the front stairs and into the living room. The air was choked with bong smoke. A group of guys sitting on the couch playing Spycraft shouted at the screen. Z and his older brother, who Sierra was dating, had the cool parents and house in Castella where we all hung out. Since I'd left home, I spent most of my weekends there. I walked toward the back wall, where the phone sat next to an upright piano with a cracked leg.

"Hello?"

"Nina?" My mother's voice was husky and raw.

"I'm here."

"You need to come home. You're sixteen years old. You can't just run around doing whatever you want. I'm done. This has gone on far too long."

"Okay," I mouthed, surprised at the softness in my voice. Maybe it was the fuzzy feel-good comedown, but it felt like I'd been waiting for this moment.

"You belong at home!" she continued, like I hadn't just agreed.

She had prepared a speech and was determined to deliver it. "What I say goes, you hear me? I AM the mother!"

A chorus erupted from the couches. "Oh damn! Shit! No way! That was crrrrazzzy!!"

"Nina?" Mom said. I could hear her body tightening, imagine her head cocked to one side, her lips pursed.

"Yes, Mom," I said. I was tired of running. "I heard you. Come get me."

"I'm coming. You're coming home. NOW."

I set the phone back on its cradle and slipped into the bathroom. I stuck my face under the faucet and ran cold water over it until my skin went numb. When I looked up, my reflection in the mirror was flat. My eyes hollow. Maybe this *had* been hormones—typical teenage shit, like everyone said. Maybe we could get it right. Finally tell the truth. Maybe I could tell her that I was scared and worried. That I didn't know what to do, or worse, that I had the sinking feeling there was nothing to be done.

Twenty minutes later, my skin prickled as the gold Oldsmobile rattled into the tree-lined drive.

The car I thought would save me was old now. As I slid into the passenger seat, it sagged; the once-spotless velour interior was streaked with coffee spills, crumbs, and ink stains. And for some reason that I can't remember, the entire back window was missing. Mom was curled over the steering wheel, bundled in a ratty full-length down coat and fingerless black gloves. Warm air blasted from the heater vents, and she rubbed her hands together before turning toward me, her big brown eyes peering out from underneath a dark green beanie. Her cheekbones looked more gaunt than sharp; her thin lips were cracked with cold, and makeup pooled in the crevices of her skin. Without turning away from me or saying anything, she put the car into reverse and swung out of the driveway. She shifted again and the car lurched forward. The hubcaps rattled.

"This is not okay, Nina," she said. *I know*, I thought. But we weren't talking about the same thing. "You can't just run around doing whatever you want," she said, merging onto 5 north. "You belong at home."

As she picked up speed, wind rushed in through the giant hole where the back window used to be, rattling the car and whipping our hair around our faces. My skin was raw. The space around us felt edgeless. Through the flickering light, I traced her jawbone. Her rouged cheeks glowed moist and gold. I touched my own and was surprised to find them wet with tears. I brought the wetness to my mouth. It was salty and metallic. She was saying something, speaking to me through clenched teeth. I could see her anger, her fear, but I couldn't hear it because I was looking at her chipped bottom teeth. And for a moment, I was disgusted. Ashamed. Of her. Of myself. Everything around us, decaying. And there was nothing to be done about it.

"You belong at home," she said again, this time softer.

"I know, Mom," I said, but my voice was distant. Placating. I was already outside the moment, looking back. Looking at my mother with a yearning, a nostalgia, for something we never really had. As if I already knew what was going to happen next. As if I was already mourning. *We'd tried our best, hadn't we?*

"I know. That's why I told you to come pick me up."

That night, I crawled out my bedroom window and crouched on the roof to smoke. In the distance, over the treetops, the mountain pulsed a ghostly white. Stars poked holes in the navy sky. I used to think that stars were on fire, too, but it turns out that it's just their heat that makes them glow. Wet wood pulp mixed with Marlboro. An earthy industrial musk. The wind picked up and pulled the burning cherry of my cigarette into neon strands and dots. A Morse code in fire.

A message to anyone out there.

Back in my room, I stepped over the rug that covered the hole from the very first night we slept here, together, in a cozy little row in our sleeping bags—Chris, Mom, and me. The night we woke to her rolling us away from the fire. The hole she covered with a dollar-store rug, where Chris and I sat later smoking fake paper cigarettes. Their tiny, contained danger. How we watched them burn. How natural our fascination with fire. How human the impulse.

Mom laid down a new set of "ground rules." We'd never had rules. We didn't need them. Bring home As, say *please* and *thank you*, don't talk back, write your thank-you notes—that was it. But at the breakfast table the next morning, she barked out a new bottom line. "You'll come home every day directly after school," she said, glancing at a list printed neatly in her college-ruled notebook. I wondered if she'd run it by my father, too. My delinquency seemed to bond them like nothing had since their TM years. "You'll be home by four and do your homework immediately. On the weekends your curfew is ten."

I almost choked on my Cream of Wheat. "No going out on school nights, at all." I stared at her. These were reasonable guidelines for a sixteen-year-old. But I'd been staying out till two or three in the morning, answering to no one. I didn't feel sixteen. I never really had.

"You're lucky I didn't take your father's advice," she said.

"And what, lock me up?" I laughed. "I didn't *do* anything."

"Parents can keep their kids detained." She coughed, brushing hair back from her face. "I mean, *legally*." I wondered if this was something he'd told her, too. He always seemed to be at a right angle to the problem.

That night before bed, I wrote her a letter. It was a bitter outpouring of all the resentment and grief that I'd stifled. *Mommie Dearest*, the letter began. We'd watched the movie together, horrified when Joan Crawford's character whipped her adopted daughter with a clothes hanger, or when she served rare steak for dinner and left it out for days until her daughter ate it.

I wrote all the things I'd been too afraid to say. How I resented our constant moving; the Laredos; her being a walk-in; poverty; the fire; and how she constantly talked about the world ending, which was *very fucking destabilizing.* I wrote about all the ways in which I was asked, explicitly and not, to carry things that were too heavy. It felt like I was writing for my life. Writing to get back power I never remembered giving away. Maybe that I'd never had to begin. As she herself taught me, in a battle to the death, you use everything you've got. I licked and sealed the envelope, then wrote her name on the front in block letters. Before I left for school the next morning, I set it on top of the TV.

When I got home later that day, boxes were stacked in twos and threes all over the floor of my room and on top of my bed. My clothes had been ripped from the closet and shoved into garbage bags. My toiletries all crammed into an old Easter basket next to the door. Mom was standing on her tiptoes, peeling posters from my wall.

"Mom?"

She didn't turn around. "If that's how you feel, what you wrote in that letter," she said, her voice trembling but steely, "then you can. Get. The. Fuck. Out Of My House."

My ears prickled with shame. What had I *done?* Fighting tears, I picked up the closest box and walked out to my car. As I wedged the box into the trunk, the cardboard flap caught, and atop a pile of neatly folded jeans, I saw a small paperback book with my mother's handwriting on it. It was a tattered copy of Christina Crawford's memoir. My mother had torn off the front cover and on the title page, in swooping starlet cursive, had autographed it herself:

"Love, Mommie Dearest"

Of all the roles she'd played, mother was her most beloved. The one she'd fought hardest to keep. The one—and, of course, I didn't fully grasp this then—that could have been taken from her at any moment. But I knew enough to hit her there; I knew it would hurt the most. The worst part was that I meant every single word. I rushed to get the rest of the boxes from my room and crammed as many as I could fit into the car.

As I backed out of the drive, my mother stepped onto the porch. Chris watched from the front window. He was going into third grade. I started to cry then. During that sad drunken year, I'd been so insulated by my own rage that I hadn't thought enough about my brother when I'd stopped coming home, or when I wrote that letter. They were still a package deal, and by snipping the cord with her, without realizing it, in a way, I was leaving him, too. Sometimes the margin between what we do to survive and who we become is dangerously thin.

I was carrying too much for her.

Spilling over with nowhere to go but gone.

XX.

After Mom kicked me out, I spent the rest of junior year living at Jessica's house. Jessica was a friend of a friend who had an extra room and, when she heard about my situation, asked her parents if she could offer it to me. They said I could stay if my dad sent his child-support check to them, which, surprisingly, he agreed to do. Jessica and her parents were all chain smokers. They gave me a room on the second floor, where I slept in a twin bed tucked into a narrow alcove.

Mornings before school, I'd wake up, light a Marlboro Red, and smoke it lying under the covers. It was like watching a movie of someone else's life. As if I was me and not me, lighting cigarette after cigarette, relishing the burn, watching from behind a smoky scrim, as my story unfolded on a track that started to feel automated.

There's a trajectory for poor small-town girls. We'd seen it start to play out in our class, already. First, a series of bad boyfriends. Pregnancy. Dropping out. Dead-end jobs. More children. A life spent scraping by. Regurgitating the same conversations. Trying to make something for yourself with what's left. Around town, we saw women who had once been girls like us. Their lives ahead of them. The same women my mother said haunted her. I told myself that I was not like them. That their fate would not be mine. That I was just incubating, regaining my strength.

Abe was both prophecy and antidote.

A stocky white guy with a shaved head who wore white hoodies and long white shorts over white thermals, Abe rode around town on a BMX. He had the swagger of a pit bull and had just moved north from Sacramento, where he was raised on drain-ditch fishing. One day in P.E., he asked for my number and I already knew what was going to happen. He was sturdy and stable, physically and emotionally. At first, I loved the way his thick, ruddy fingers gripped my arm. He became a fortress to shelter against. A tree to climb out of my despair. His mom started to invite me to dinner at their house, which she'd decorated in what I call Cabela's chic—matching Santa Fe–style couches, *Gone Fishin'* plaques, a country kitchen table. As I ate with them, made basic chitchat, and went for long walks with Abe down to the river to fish, my spine settled.

After getting and losing two jobs in a year, that summer I landed a competitive position with the Youth Conservation Corps, and I started to use my body productively again. After months of waking up at seven in the morning, building trails and hauling rocks for forty hours a week, I started to stabilize.

Senior year, the generosity of Jessica's parents ran out, and I humbled myself to ask Mom if I could move back to finish high school. She agreed on the condition that I pay rent if I stayed after graduation, which I said I would, though I'm sure she wouldn't have held me to it. It was her way of trying to demand I be responsible. After the summer gig at YCC, I got a job waiting tables at a local diner. I minimized my partying, started dancing again, and even got my grades up enough to make it into the National Honor Society. As I began to turn my life around, part of me receded. I started wearing sweatpants. Skipping the makeup. My Carmen Electra era, over. My friends said it was Abe. They didn't like how he treated me. He started to show up at parties uninvited when I wanted a night alone. Or get aggressive when I talked to other guys. The security he'd provided would turn out to be temporary. As Mom said, sooner or later, *they all lay their trip on you.*

I graduated with a small Bank of America scholarship and a chip on my shoulder. For the yearbook, we all chose a quote to go under our portraits. Mine read: *The best helping hand you'll ever find is at the end of your own arm.* Arrogant, but at the time, it felt like I'd pulled myself out of a dark pit. While I knew I was loved, and had support from many sides, materially—my mother taking me back, my father paying to have a roof over my head, the hospitality of Jessica and her parents, Abe's family, all my friends and their parents who'd let me crash over that terrible year, and probably so many other kindnesses that have faded with time—there were, I learned, places that people just weren't willing to go.

Life back home was *polite*—there's no better way to say it. Anger between Mom and me had fizzled on both sides, and in its place was something worse. Something I'd never felt between us: resignation. Our new dynamic was a tender, wobbly thing, which we both treated too delicately, for too long, until we could no longer reach each other. We spoke in strained platitudes. We spoke with extra care. We spoke around everything, as if our bond could no longer withstand the heat necessary to cut to the heart of things.

My mother didn't trust me. And I hadn't trusted her in a long time.

Since I'd blown my shot at a university, I stayed in the area for community college. I focused on school and work and got back into dance and community theater. Chris was going into fourth grade and spent most of his time riding bikes, eating dinner with neighborhood friends, at baseball practice, and snowboarding in winter months. When Abe was around, Chris hung closer, drawn to him as a rare male figure in the house. Craving domesticity, I started teaching myself to cook, and made us our first-ever Thanksgiving dinner. Mom bought Cornish hens and a bottle of Cook's to be fancy. Instead of pie, I balled cantaloupe and served it in chipped glass bowls with whipped cream. Chris sprayed the outline of a mountain and *Snow's Up Dude* onto the kitchen windows with fake snow from a can.

Mom had liked Abe at first. She recognized that he'd helped me when nothing else could. But as she saw more of us together, she noticed how I deferred to him. How vehemently I defended him, even as I felt increasingly trapped, which for some reason I couldn't admit to her. She tolerated him to keep me close but her advice started coming through in other ways. "Cosmic" ways. She offered to give me a tarot reading.

"See, you've got the Two of Swords here. Stuckness," she said one night, pulling a card from the Rider-Waite deck. We were sitting cross-legged on the couch. Scrunching her brow thoughtfully, she flipped over a second card. *The Tower*. She let out a long, low whistle.

"Is it bad?"

"It's not a matter of bad or good. But it's definitive. The Tower is a reckoning. Everything that doesn't serve you shall fall."

"Oh my god," I huffed, rolling my eyes. "You can just say you don't like him."

"This isn't me, girl," she laughed, holding up her hands. "The cards speak."

By the time I finally broke up with Abe, two years later, we were throwing things at each other. I'd finished junior college, gotten my associate's degree, and, in secret, had applied and was accepted to University of California San Diego as a third-year transfer student. I told him I was moving and didn't invite him to come. He asked for one last night together.

Already imagining my new unencumbered life in San Diego— finally the *real* college experience—I agreed. What could it hurt?

We drank cheap white wine and I made shrimp scampi. I thought about all the good times, because they were safe to remember on the way out the door. Because I'd just stopped taking birth control and we'd been told it took a while to leave the system, we had sex without a condom. The second he pulled out, a strange energy clamped down on me. *Fuck.* He wasn't trying to say goodbye—he was trying to keep me. Early the next morning, I drove away as fast as I could, desperate to escape the life I felt hunting me, the life I'd begged my mom to come back to. Praying I was wrong, I threw myself into the apartment hunt.

School was starting in less than a month and I had to find somewhere to live. Uncle Dan let me stay with him while I looked for a place, generously giving me his waterbed while he crashed on the couch. He was on a tight fixed income, so I bought myself a loaf of wheat bread and peanut butter to stash in the kitchen. It was all I could stomach, anyway. I was sick immediately. Every morning, I'd turn on the bathroom sink and shower while I threw up so my uncle wouldn't hear me, then I'd make a sandwich and ride the city bus an hour to La Jolla to look for a room in the endless sea of stucco buildings surrounding the university.

I ran through my list of places, tapping on paper-thin shared walls and telling overly cheerful people about my hobbies, while they asked questions to ensure that I'd join their weekly "roomie dinners" and not hide out in my room like a *weirdo*. I felt so much older than all of the bright-eyed students having their first adventures away from home, while I was pregnant with the past. And as I would soon find out—literally.

I took a test and called Mom with the results.

My voice must have cracked when she picked up.

"What's wrong?"

I paused. How could I have done this? Was I trying to fuck my life up, again?

"What, Neen?"

"Well, it's . . ."

"Shit."

"How did you know?"

"My god, I only saw it coming a mile away."

"I'm not keeping it," I said.

"Just think about it."

"MOM. You don't even like him."

"Listen. I am not telling you to keep it. I'm telling you to think about it. To make sure you really, really think about it. It's not about him. Make sure whatever you choose is what you want. Promise me. This is a choice you just can't take back."

"Exactly," I said, imagining life raising a child with a father I couldn't stand. It's not that I didn't want to be a mother. But I was too young and I didn't want her version of motherhood—a single mother, struggling, with a father that I resented. When she urged me to be sure, she was thinking about her past, too. About the babies she might have had.

Her freshman year in college, she got pregnant. She'd had a boyfriend she loved and, when they found out, they planned to marry. And then he slept with her roommate.

"A real sexpot!" she called the roommate, still seething at the memory.

She wanted to keep the baby, but in her telling, her father forbade it. In 1970, good Catholic girls were not single mothers. Many years later, after my brother was born, it would happen again, and another man would pressure her again, to do the same. That one, I wouldn't know about until much later. When she was feeling wistful, she'd talk about the babies. Randomly recite their ages. "He'd be twenty-nine now." Or "They would have been thirty and ten." She never really got over them, I don't think. Never once did she tell me that abortion was wrong, only that it hadn't been right for her. I told her I'd think about it, but I didn't need to. I booked the earliest appointment I could and flew home.

Mom drove me to the abortion clinic the day after her fiftieth birthday. Out front, a lone protestor was singing songs and playing the guitar. At first, the music sounded harmless and folksy, but when I listened closer, he was talking about the love of god for a child. Propped against his knee was a handwritten cardboard sign: *It's Not Too Late.*

Mom grabbed my hand and rushed past him, shielding me with her body. In the lobby of the freezing clinic, we sat side by side as I filled out the paperwork. I'd turned twenty a few months before, so didn't need her for anything other than moral support. There were other girls with their mothers, too. Scared, skinny teens. And one couple, just as young. Two older women, alone. When they called my name, I went into the procedure room by myself.

Afterward, Mom was waiting in the holding area when I came out crying, a bloody pad between my legs. She rubbed my back as I cried, not saying a word. I cried not because I wanted the baby, but because I'd had to make the decision at all. Because it felt like shit. I regretted being so careless with life. Both the one in me and my own. But mostly, I regretted not knowing how to let go. To say goodbye for good. Mom's touch was tender as she linked my arm in hers and guided me out of the office, down the ramp, and past the cluster of protestors. More had gathered, and as we passed, they reached toward us, garbled provocations spilling from their mouths.

Just as the man started strumming his guitar again, Mom turned and growled: "Fuck OFF!" He was startled enough to let us pass in peace. I was shocked. She did not throw the F-word around.

"Thanks, Mom," I said.

"Sure, Bird. That's what mom-peoples are here for."

She steered us out of the parking lot and toward the nearest

Wendy's, where we ordered chocolate Frosties and sat in the car to eat.

I could barely touch mine.

"I just can't believe I did that," I said.

"Well, that's the Tower moment for ya," said Mom. "The cards never lie."

The next week, on Craigslist I found three girls from Palm Desert living in a slick white condo near the university who didn't say anything about "roomie dinners." I signed a lease, sight unseen. Chris was down in the Bay Area visiting Brother Rick, so Mom decided to drive back down to San Diego with me. She would take the U-Haul, while I followed in my car, retracing the journey we'd made eight years earlier. Down California and back again. Doing what we'd been doing since we first arrived. Traversing the state, circling each other, missing and returning, as if destined to repeat the same places, the same lives in different forms, on infinite parallel loop. I think we inched toward each other again on that trip. Taking a drive always seemed to do that.

When I first arrived at UCSD, I didn't know about George Winne Jr., the twenty-three-year-old student from Detroit who lit himself on fire in a plea to end the Vietnam War. But, thirty years after his death, I sat in Revelle Plaza, where he'd self-immolated, eating a homemade lunch of rice and steamed vegetables under a cerulean sky. Usually, I was rushing past on my way to Italian class and didn't stop to look around. But that afternoon, I read the plaque:

> In honor of George Winne Jr. who immolated himself in Revelle
> Plaza in protest of the Vietnam War in 1970. He held a sign
> that read, "In the Name of God, End the War."

It would be years before I'd learn that Winne Junior covered himself in gas-soaked rags. Or that he was rushed to nearby Scripps Hospital by campus police, who found the sign lying next to his body. Or that as he lay dying, he begged his mother to write to Nixon and demand an end to the war.

It would be years before I would start thinking about my mother's fire story in relation to his and to all the stories of the others who died for a cause. Before I would start wondering how it was connected, how martyrs are birthed and constructed. Whose lives matter. How a body can be an offering.

"I believe in God and the hereafter" were Winne's last words. "I will see you there."

If he hadn't made that statement, he might have been forgotten by history. And if I hadn't chased my mother's story, hers might have, too. But that day, as I read the plaque, it was still a piece of trivia. Fire still a story from before—from once upon a time, so that no matter what I'd read or heard, what neon signs flashed before me, there were no *aha* moments. That was before I understood fire's ability to shape-shift—its capacity to smolder, then pick back up.

My mother's story was buried deep in time, its embers low and forgotten. It would take another ignition for them to emerge.

PART III

Free Burn

XXI.

Rome, New Year's Eve, 2003

A sparkling explosion flew past my face. Dad, Beth, and I were packed in a crowd of thousands on Piazza del Colosseo. Faces flashed purple, pink, green, and gold as fireworks exploded high above the ruins of the Colosseum, lighting its empty archways in strobe. Italian history flipped through my mind like a deck of cards. Facts about Rome, dates of wars, boring details that I could never manage to retain during the four months I'd been studying literature up north, in Padua, a small university town thirty miles from Venice.

But there was one story I couldn't shake: *Damnatio ad bestias.* The Roman death plays. First-century public executions that took place across the empire, the damnatio weren't typical executions but elaborate productions with costumes, settings, and props. Reenactments of myths. Eurydice, for example. They built fake forests and filled them with wild animals, mostly big cats—lions and panthers—then released people who had been sentenced to death into the arena to either fight or run for their lives as characters in a prewritten story while the crowd watched. A chill ran up my arms as I thought about them. About how archetype has been used throughout history to erase the terror we enact upon one another; it's easier to torment a character than a human being.

"Hey!" Beth nudged me back to the party on the street. "DIECI! NOVE!" I joined the crowd, counting down.

"Sette, sei, cinque, quattro. TRE, DUE, UNO!"

Bottles of prosecco popped. Corks whizzed past.

It was officially 2004. Our last night in Italy, together.

In the morning, Dad and Beth would go on to Naples, and I would be up at dawn to catch a flight home to finish my last quarter at UCSD.

"Buon anno!" Dad said, pulling me in for a hug. His frame was tight and angular against mine. He was happy. I could tell. He loosened the khaki trench he'd picked out special for their big European holiday and pecked Beth on the lips. When he first told me they wanted to fly out after my program and spend the holiday driving from Venice to Rome, I was excited to spend time away from the ordered routines of their daily life. To show them Italy. When he told me we were going to stay in convents along the way, I rolled my eyes. It felt like another dose of forced divinity. But staying with nuns, downing perfect espressos and panini at chic Italian gas stations, and translating fiery Italian masses to my dad and Beth ended up being spectacular fun. Our last stop was Casa di Santa Brigida, a Roman convent where sisters of the Bridgettine Order cooked us New Year's Eve dinner. Afterward, we'd wandered out and found ourselves at the Colosseum counting down to midnight.

The crowd parted to make way for a cab. Four young Italians tumbled out—the girls with glossy hair and stilettos, the boys in mirror-slick shoes and butt-tight acid-wash jeans.

"Come on!" Dad yelled, grabbing our hands and shouldering through the wake of the crowd. "This might be our only chance."

"Chance for what?" I cried. "What about this?" I spun in a circle bumping against sweaty arms and legs, pointing toward a sky warm and alive with fire.

"It's late, Neen," he called over the roar of the crowd. "And we're miles from the convent. Who knows if we'll find another cab tonight."

"He's right," Beth said, but even she sounded reluctant. I sighed and followed as they snaked through the crowd. My father held the back door of the cab open, and I crawled in first and scooted over for Beth.

Bodies filled the space around the car. Firecrackers popped against the cobblestones.

"Roll up your windows!" the driver barked in rough Italian.

"No way!" I cried, sticking my arm out the window. I wanted to stay this way forever. Dodging the spray of fire and Romans soapy with champagne. Soaking up a phosphorescent sea of limbs and light and noise.

"The fire is coming in my taxi!" the cabbie yelled in Italian. "I said roll up the windows, now! It's not safe."

"Neen," Dad said, glancing back. Beth gazed out the window.

"Jesus, okay." My ears pressurized as the window sealed. A firecracker popped immediately against the car. "Cazzo!" the cabbie shouted, slamming his palm against the steering wheel. Dad and Beth looked to me for a translation: *fuck*. I just shrugged. The driver grunted as he shifted the taxi into neutral and started to coast, pushed along by the sea of bodies. I closed my eyes and tried to soak in our final hours.

Every morning for the last four months, I'd walked miles to school through narrow cobblestone streets, stopping for an espresso and chocolate brioche, which I ate standing at the marble bar of Caffè Carlotta. During late-night study sessions with Liz, a sharp, sarcastic Italian from Massachusetts who spoke three languages, I'd labored through the poetry of Umberto Saba and read an entire modernist novel in Italian, *Zeno's Conscience* by Italo Svevo, in which the protagonist, Zeno, is obsessed with quitting smoking, always promising each cigarette will be his last. Most of the students in my cohort were from Brown and Fordham and Yale. For them, studying abroad was predestined, a rite of passage. But for me, learning in rooms where Galileo taught and wandering labyrinthine stone arcades of a town founded in the 1100s was a revelation.

Apart from time spent dancing, every major life choice I'd made up to that point had been reactive instead of imagined, reparative instead of creative. Untethered from the weight of others' wants or needs, Italy was less a place than a time. A time in which I experienced the breadth of my own mind. I'd been studying literature and creative writing at UCSD, and while it was interesting, I never felt like an artist. Dance had been art. After the break in high school, even though I kept dancing for years, I never recovered my momentum or dedication. All through junior college, I'd studied performance. I was in the chorus of *The Tempest*. I read the plays of Wilson and Shakespeare and Christopher Durang. I participated in dramatic readings of Gwendolyn Brooks. *They eat beans mostly, this old yellow pair. Dinner is a casual affair.* I'd transferred to UCSD as a theater major, but when my dad's family urged me to do something more practical and even Mom said I should have a backup, like *becoming an X-ray technician,* I just sort of let it go. A career onstage seemed less and less feasible. You had to want it more than anything. What I wanted most was freedom.

But I was never going to do something legitimately practical like become an accountant or a doctor. So I turned to language. Words, I understood. I'd always done well in English. Was a reader, writer, talker. Maybe I could be a journalist. Work for magazines.

I took an experimental writing class. We read Kathy Acker and Samuel Delany and created board games from fictional family narratives. It was fascinating, and strange work came out of me. But I felt like an impostor. Other students channeled familial chaos into something evocative and edgy. They smoked Nat Shermans and made chapbooks in their spare time, while I drank 40s on the weekends with a union pipe fitter who took me on unironic dates to Red Lobster. I wrote, but I wasn't *a writer* like them. I didn't even know what the fuck a chapbook was.

But, in Italy, surrounded by thousand-year-old ruins that the locals lived among casually, I'd begun to see past, present, and future not as distinct but merged into a continuous state of being. Through art history talks and courses, I learned how Renaissance painters allowed to create only religious images for centuries found ways to practice subversion. A hand here. A symbol there. The creative spirit will always emerge. While I was growing up, images of saints and martyrs were plastered around our homes. Here, where so many of their stories originated, I began to see the art in my own life. To realize that in the sacred, the profane was always present. That maybe they didn't have to be so bifurcated. I started to think that maybe I had something to add.

As I sat in the back of the cab, coasting away from the Colosseum, contemplating heady notions of art, my mother was home, in the Ring of Fire, falling to ruin.

Halfway through my semester abroad, she'd started sending me strange emails. It wasn't just the Laredos anymore. There was another man. A man I knew: David. David was the brother of Evelyn, Mom's oldest friend in Siskiyou. Evelyn had been hospitalized with cancer soon after I moved to San Diego and given just weeks to live. I'd flown home to say goodbye. Her brother, David, was there from the Midwest. He seemed like a sweet, no-nonsense guy who was shocked to find his sister's hospice room full of energy workers, self-appointed priestesses, and exuberant Taiko drummers. Mom and I took turns running to the cafeteria for watery coffee.

By day four, Evelyn was gone.

I had to fly back to school before the memorial, but Mom and David had exchanged contact information. Mom wanted the family's permission to submit Evelyn's nature poems for publication— a lifelong dream of Evelyn's. So it wasn't weird when she mentioned that David was coming back to Siskiyou to visit, or later, that he'd started acting strange about the poetry.

People get weird around death, I thought. Maybe the family had changed their minds.

Then, the summer before I left for Italy, she mentioned that David wasn't happy with his wife. Casually while stir-frying cabbage, she said that he was sticking around only to inherit his sick wife's family money after she died.

I was shocked. Then, wary.

"I'm surprised he would tell you that," I said slowly. Mom brushed the hair back from her face and fanned away a cloud of steam.

"I mean he doesn't even have to say it, really," she said. "His communication is *loud and clear.*"

"But he did . . . say it. He said those things to you?"

"Yes, Neen." Her voice was husky and strained. Impatient. "We talk all the time."

I'd been home a week and hadn't seen David call. What I had seen was her hunched over in a chair sending emails via WebTV. Balancing a keyboard on her lap, pecking away two fingers at a time.

"You do? Over phone or email?"

"Oh," she said, brushing my question away as if dusting a mantel. "We're way beyond that. We're beyond words."

A shiver ran up my spine. "What do you mean?" I asked, afraid to hear the answer.

"We're very active on the astral plane, Neen. That's the thing with these guys. They're not evolved enough to just own it. But then they come around on the astral plane all *hot for you.*"

I'd always pictured the astral plane as fourth dimensional. Not like a bar you could hang out in and chat up men. But there I was against my will, picturing Mom and David on an astral date, featureless glowing orbs communicating in boops and beeps, while at home their bodies sat stationary, propped on the couch like locust shells. It was pretty funny. Okay, it was *almost* funny.

"I just hope he's man enough to follow through," Mom said, turning off the stove.

How I wish I could say I'd stopped her there. That I'd leapt up and shook my mother, demanding to know what in the actual fuck she was talking about. That I'd been able to tell her none of this is real. That I'd known that to be true.

Instead, I ate the dinner she made. And that fall, I went to Italy.

In Padua, as the days got colder, the other students and I met in Piazza della Frutta for a nightly Aperol spritz. Men roasted chestnuts over big barrel fires and served them warm in paper cones. I scoured the city for a can of pumpkin to cook my host family a real American Thanksgiving. Meanwhile, Mom's emails, previously upbeat check-ins, grew unhinged.

She and David had planned to be together after his wife died, she wrote, but now he was chickening out. He'd started sleeping with someone else back home. A woman she called Isabelle. When she tried to confront him about it, he pretended he didn't know what she was talking about. Her calls went unanswered; his email replies, once congenial, became shorter. And eventually, curt. When I made the mistake of wondering in one of my emails to her why astral David would say such different things than *earth* David (what else to call him?), she launched again into a rant about how he wasn't evolved enough to admit the truth of what his spirit knew. It was the same thing she'd said years earlier about Nathan over salad-bar salads.

She forwarded me their communications. Reading them, it became clear that my mother was conjuring a Shakespearean-level scandal—a classic love triangle, but on the astral plane. Was Isabelle real? There was no way to know. David's responses were one-line. They sounded polite at first, then confused, then scared. But what was even scarier were my replies to my mom, the contents of which were so incongruous with what was happening that I wouldn't have believed it myself if I hadn't saved the emails.

Mom to Me, 12/04/03 at 3:56 PM

Hey Bird. Things getting weird-o with David . . . He's fucking this Isabelle chick now, and I can hear them talking about me. Some nights, I can't get any sleep. the love between he and i is unbelievable and i'm sure he is my twin ray, he talks to people there about it all the time, it blows his mind because he has been such an earthly guy, but whether you get to be with your twin ray is unknown.

Me to Mom, 12/05/03 at 1:39 PM

Love ooo Mom. Please don't stress. Did you try melatonin for sleep? Wish you were here and we could just forget that place and all the people. You'd love Italy! We took a trip out to the region where they make prosecco—sparkling wine—and got to eat fresh cheese from cows at the top of this foggy mountain. Say hi to Chrissy for me.

Later, I'll go back and read and reread the emails, deeply ashamed and shocked that I could be talking about Italian cheese when my mother was clearly experiencing a total splicing of reality.

Growing up, I thought of New Age language like a cosmic bat signal whose meaning activated only for those who already understood it. I never believed the most out-there theories, but they were a part of the language I spoke. It had informed the way I saw the world and framed the edges of what I'd considered theoretically possible, but the more distance I had from home, the more I realized that without belief to animate it, the language itself was flat. Anechoic. Faith was the air that filled out words like *twin ray, astral plane, enlightenment, collective consciousness*. Without belief, esoteric language is a hollow encasement for more complex, illusory, and in some cases, even ominous things.

If you do a cursory search online for "astral plane," you enter what I call the cosmic web: a Pandora's box of outdated websites with blinking angel GIFs and misspelled statements in ALL CAPS about interdimensional karmic ascension. Each search to define a term gets more and more abstract. The origin of the root words might be traceable, but the ways in which they have been used and reused, reincarnated into today's New Age lexicon, renders them both devoid of meaning and chameleonic.

The further we move from tangible objects or experiences, the more the meaning of a word stretches. A dog is a dog is a dog, but *an unbound sea of consciousness* is subjective and contextual. As the origin of today's New Age language is cherry-picked from disparate spiritual lineages and world religions, there's rarely a central source or meaning. Its superpower is also its danger. It's a decentralized belief system that turns the power of interpretation and execution over to the individual. A Rorschach in which you might see whatever it is you're looking for.

Most anyone else would have read my mother's emails as clear evidence of mental illness or impending breakdown, but I was numbed out. Reading them back, I see a schism, much like the moment after I heard the walk-in story, and again, after hearing her fire story—both times in which she left her body, and I had detached from my own. In my reply, I see both a daughter in denial, distancing herself via inane tales of prosecco country, and one who cares but is afraid, has no tools to address what's happening. I'd become so accultured to hearing such bizarre stories that even while I knew something wasn't right, I couldn't say for sure that the astral realm didn't exist.

It wasn't the sort of thing you could fact-check or talk to others about, not critically, anyway. The pool was self-selecting. The only people with enough information to even discuss it were those who already believed. The most plain and painful truth is that I no longer felt any desire, or even ability, to influence my mother's reality. If she'd told me she was an alien priestess, I probably would

have asked what her duties were and sent a congratulatory bouquet. But also, and this is the weirdest part, a microscopic sliver of
me still believed, and probably always had, that on some level,
everything she was saying was possible. That one reality didn't negate the other.

I'm back in the cosmic war rooms, listening closer now to her and
her friends, as they crowdsource theology and conspiracy over
cups of crappy coffee. Replaying those snippets, I hear something
that I couldn't before: stories of trauma—of abandonment, mar-
ginalization, abuse. Traumas never recognized or acknowledged
by their families or the state. Maybe they'd found language to de-
scribe their alienation, their sense of loss, of disenfranchisement.
Maybe there was meaning in their pain, after all: if they were paying their karmic dues, they weren't victims but warriors of lights—
women who had endured much on the road to enlightenment.
Tribulation as a marker of spiritual development. Picture the stations of the cross: Christ's fourteen stages of suffering rendered in
stained glass and systemized as a sort of mortality pilgrimage. At
its furthest reaches, suffering as spiritual development simply becomes martyrdom.

"Sickness is a belief," wrote Mary Baker Eddy, "which must be
annihilated by the divine Mind."

But what, I wonder, if the Mind itself is sick?

What if the divine is not impervious to disease?

XXII.

Rock Bottom Brewery always looks the same. Striped awnings. Copper vats of beer shimmering behind a glass wall. A waxed wooden bar with a hanging rack of personalized mugs for Mug Club drinkers. "How much do we have to drink to qualify, again?" Daniel asked, stroking his goatee. He wriggled closer to me in the slippery leather booth. I ducked under his arm, pressing into the hollow of his chest.

My first Christmas after moving to San Diego, I'd gone home and run into him at a bar in Mount Shasta. We embraced on a sticky dance floor, and I was fifteen again, swooning. Daniel was a high school crush I'd made out with once. That week, I went to visit him at the cabin he was renting deep in the woods, and we picked up right where we'd left off. Except, now, he had a son. A sweet little duck-haired blond boy who was almost three.

After I flew back to San Diego, we became high school sweethearts in arrears, falling into a romantic eighteenth-century love with handwritten letters and lots of pining. He was a painter, self-taught, and splashed his envelopes with vivid watercolor scenes. Some cartoonish and raunchy, others romantic and hazy.

The oldest of nine in a raven-haired Mexican-Sicilian family, he'd grown up poor in resource but rich in passion. He understood my vernacular of dysfunction innately. That is to say, he felt like home. For two years, we dated long-distance. Letters became bimonthly visits, him down south or me up north. My trips home became less about seeing Mom and Chris and more about visiting Daniel and his son, who lived with him half-time. At Morris Street, I'd count down the hours until he got off work and would come pick me up. After everything I'd done to extract myself from home, I fell for a man whose roots in the area were inextricable. Who would never be free from it. Being with him was both escape and tether. Everything about it felt so natural, and if not fated, somehow inevitable.

We hadn't seen each other when I was in Italy, and he'd surprised me at the airport when I landed back in the States. Now, two pints of IPA in, we climbed into the car to drive back to my apartment. Maybe we were just buzzed, but everything felt hypersaturated. Slowed down. His chittering laughter. The heat of his body next to mine. His hand, a heartbeat on my inner thigh. The way the steering wheel slipped through my hands like water. Or maybe I'm just remembering it that way now, the way moments that change everything slow down and grow big in our minds.

"Whoa, cowboy!" Daniel laughed as I pulled into my narrow garage, almost sideswiping my roommate's Expedition. I turned off the car and fell back against the seat, my heart tapping a strange rhythm. He leaned over and drew open my flannel, sliding his hand underneath my shirt. I play-slapped him away and jumped out of the car. He chased me through the garage, and we raced up the stairs into the kitchen. As I bent down to put the leftovers in the fridge, he was against me, hands on my hips, already hard under his shorts. I turned to kiss him, and over his shoulder, I saw a green light blinking on the answering machine.

For some reason, I pushed him aside and pressed play instead of running to the bedroom. Part of me wishes I hadn't. That I could rewind and get back into the car and never have come home at all. That instead, we had driven down to Black's Beach and swum in the sea and kissed naked while the hang gliders sailed silently toward the sunset. Or that I'd never come home from Italy.

That I was still there, wandering the cobblestones forever, stopping for espresso, reading, eating, thinking of nothing in my real life—only of art and literature, and all the glorious ways I might make a new one.

There were three messages. The first was a telemarketer, the next my roommate, Sarah, apologizing for leaving town without doing her dishes again. As she rambled on, Daniel rolled his eyes and hoisted me onto the counter, pressing his body between my legs. The marble was icy against my thighs. I peeled off his shirt and kissed his chest, breathing him in deep. Sweat and spice and pine and gesso—the chalky white paint mixture that goes on a canvas before color to prime it. All the painterly things I'd learned.

The machine beeped again, and an unmistakable voice floated into the room.

"Ohhhh, Nina," it said. "This is Marge Meyer. Your mother's friend."

I turned toward the sound.

Marge Meyer spoke like Sinatra sang, breathy. She was in her seventies—a former navy woman with an airy disposition that came packaged whole cloth from the 1940s.

"You'll need to call me right away, dear heart." My mind started to spin, spiraling through a montage of tragedies—an accident, robbery, Mom dead, Chris injured. But what Marge said was stranger and more unexpected than anything I could have imagined. "There's been a fire," she began.

She was saying something terrible, but after the message beeped and went silent, I realized I hadn't absorbed a thing she said. Her tone was so singsong, so ain't-life-grand, that I couldn't hear it.

"Holy shit," Daniel whispered, his face twisted with concern.

Panicked, I hooked an arm around his waist and pressed play again.

This time I picked up snippets. "Fire at your mother's house. Arson. Jail."

"Play it again. Again. Again," I said.

He clasped his hands over my thighs and played the message two, three more times. Mother, I heard. Fire. Burn. Mother set fire. All the Italian terms for fire, for burning the self, the home, cycled rapidly through my brain. *Ha bruciato suo corpo. Si e bruciata. Bruciato la casa.* Yes, I thought. She has. She did. She already did. I saw my mother at twenty, burning. I saw us on the couch at Morris Street as she told me the story of her burning.

"You okay?" asked Daniel.

I was somewhere else, my breathing strained as I glitched between languages, stuck in a surreal loop of translation, unable to ask in either one, *why?*

The folks from Boston University said this might happen.

Reverse culture shock, they called it. They said I might get confused about everyday things after coming back to the US—depressed even. That I might feel alienated. "Between two worlds without a sense of home" was the exact phrase on the reentry pamphlet they'd given us before the return flight. I'd just laughed. My whole life had been *between worlds without a sense of home.* That speech was for the soft kids, I'd thought. The Browns and Fordhams. But I should have paid more attention.

"I don't understand," I said finally, tears spilling over. Daniel pulled an envelope off the fridge and scribbled something on it. The scritch of pencil grated against my skin. He held up the note:

There's been a fire. Your mom is in jail. Call Marge.

I stared at him, stunned. An eerie sense of déjà vu came over me. I had time-traveled and forgotten to close the portal, and now we were living out my mother's past, in early aughts San Diego—a place with perfect weather, a place where things like this didn't happen. Where I'd moved so they wouldn't. I blinked, trying to clear the confusion. "Why would they put her in jail?"

"I'll dial," Daniel said, lifting the cordless.

Neon dots danced across his face as he punched in Marge's number.

While abroad, I'd been further from my mother than ever. All the spaces she'd once occupied were overflowing with the poetry of Saba; with Svevo and Calvino and Natalia Ginzburg; with Renaissance art; with Nero d'Avola and Gauloises chain-smoking in early morning piazzas; with paper-thin pizzas *con uovo* and perfectly al dente carbonara; with logs of burrata covered in grapefruit and balsamic.

Now I was yanked through time zones. I was home. Swimming in Daniel's skin and hair. I was tangled with him. I was in my kitchen. He was here. Holding out the phone to me. Marge's voice sang through the receiver.

"Helllooo, Nina? Dear, is that you? Yoo-hoo!"

"Marge." I swallowed a sob. "What happened?"

"Ohhhhh, Nina! I'm sorry, but they've taken your mother to jail. On charges of arson."

"Why would they put in her jail?" I repeated, my voice shaking. "She needs help. She must need help." And as I said it aloud, I finally understood it was true.

"I know," said Marge. "Have a pencil? I know a lawyer up there in Yreka. You'll need one. Take down his name and number."

I repeated the name of the lawyer and the number, aloud. Daniel wrote it down.

"But she's safe for now. And that's what matters. She got out just in time."

"In time for what, Marge?" I shrieked, on the edge of collapse.

"And your brother is safe with his rancher friends."

Chris. Shit. *Chris.* Colin was a childhood friend of my brother's. His family lived on a ranch outside of town and were direct descendants of the town founder, the one whose company built the home Mom had just lit on fire. Chris must be mortified. I imagined him shrinking as small as he could. Trying to go unnoticed in a place where everyone was really going to be watching now.

"Karl will take me up to the jail tomorrow," said Marge. "The visiting hour is from four to five thirty every day. I guess it's more like the visiting hour and a half!"

"It's *her* house," I said. I was desperate to understand why she was locked up, why no one had helped her, why I hadn't, but all I could think about was the absurdity of the charge. "I mean, can't you burn down your own fucking house?"

"Oh, dear heart," Marge clucked, letting out a little sigh. "Apparently, that's a felony."

XXIII.

Just before four o'clock the next day, I pulled into the dusty parking lot of Weed High. I thought Chris would be annoyed that I was late. Mom had always been late to pick me up from dance, and I hated being the last one waiting. The looks of pity. The offers of a ride from more punctual moms. But I didn't see my brother anywhere. It occurred to me that maybe he hadn't come to school.

A sophomore, my brother was a star shortstop, surrounded by talks of college scholarship. He'd been accepted by the real country folks, drew friends and girlfriends with ease, and had just enough swagger to be popular while still flying under the radar. A difficult and precise note to hit. Weed High was three hundred kids maximum, and the fire had been reported in the town paper. Everyone had to know. He would despise the attention. One of few biracial kids in town, and the only boy in our family, he hated sticking out.

I looked up then to see him crossing the parking lot. He wasn't thinner exactly, but his muscles, sturdy from years of sports, were leaner. Sinewy, almost. His standard uniform of a Falcons cap, baggy jeans, hoodie, and puffy black winter coat was familiar, but the backpack slung over his shoulder seemed to weigh him down. His steps were like glue. I glanced at my phone: 4:10. Visiting hours ended at 5:30 and it was a twenty-minute drive from here. All day, I'd been spiraling, oscillating between panicked fix-it mode and devastation. I was used to attending to wounds, but this was buckshot. Scattered and unmendable. And my feelings were big—too big. I knew I had to carry them appropriately.

Waving vigorously, I tried to transmit urgency, but Chris could not be rushed. No one could physically walk that slow without trying. I took a deep breath and chastised myself. The fire had destroyed all their belongings. He'd lost everything. Mom was in jail. When he got close enough, I pulled him in for a hug. He let me hold him for a few seconds longer than usual, his body limp. He smelled like teenage boy—stale clothes and drugstore cologne.

"Hey," I said.

"Hey," he mumbled.

When I stepped back to look at him, I was startled to see Mom, and Uncle Dan, in his eyes, dark and deep-set. I'd never noticed the family resemblance so clearly before. He had the longest lashes—lashes that curled naturally and were the envy of women in his life. They softened the three-day stubble growing on his boyish face. He broke eye contact first and shuffled toward the passenger door.

I climbed into the driver's side and cranked up the heater.

"Heading straight to the jail!" I chirped, cringing at the upbeat tone of my voice. I pulled out of the parking lot and swung a left at the Catholic church—the long way. Chris glanced at me sideways, wedging his hands under his legs.

"You could just go down the hill," he said.

"I know, I'm gonna take 97."

Highway 97 was the back way that would take us past the mill and around the corner from what remained of our house. I was dying to see it. I turned right at the fire station that had responded to Mom's 9-1-1 call. Smokestacks pumped thick white clouds against the snowy backdrop of Mount Shasta as we passed the mill, which still employed most of the town. Waves of wood pulp and industrial glue seeped through the heater vents. The smell of home. Nothing I had done in the world, outside of this place, mattered when that smell hit. It triggered a county-line malaise. A low-grade depressive state. Passport stamps couldn't relieve me of where I'd come from. The smallness of the place that had once held me close was cloying and claustrophobic. Sinister. The car jostled over the railroad tracks, a jarring clank-clank against the syrupy hum of Toby Keith on the radio.

If I turned right, we'd pass by what was left of the house. If I went left, we'd head to the freeway. My brother slouched against the car door, silent, but I could feel him willing me to turn left. My foot rested on the brake.

"Wanna see the house?"

"Nope."

Looking across the car, I saw him in profile and recognized myself. He was almost the same age as I'd been when I started staying out all night. When I wanted less to do with home. When I'd left him alone. I'd been so concerned with managing my mother's state of mind and building a life for myself that I hadn't stopped to talk to my brother about what was going on. To see how he was, really. Not in a long time.

I turned left.

As I drove through the backstreets of Lincoln Heights, the air in the car was raw, crackling, as if it might spontaneously combust. I faked a yawn and flipped through the radio stations. All country.

"Sooo, you weren't at the house," I said. "That's good."

"Yeah. I was at Mark's. Mom told me she wasn't feeling good and wanted me to stay with a friend."

"She told you that?" I snapped. "Why didn't you call me?"

"I don't know," he muttered, stretching his seat belt away from his chest. "I didn't know she was gonna burn the house down, Nina."

"Of course. I know. I'm sorry. I just—I'm sorry."

Why would he have called me? We barely talked.

"She was acting weird," he went on slowly, shifting in his seat. "But she'd been like that for a while, so I guess I just got used to it."

"Awhile? Like how long?" I asked. "And weird like what?"

"I don't know, just *weird*."

"Weird like mean? Or like quiet? I mean, what was she *doing*?"

"I. DON'T. KNOW. NINA. I'm just telling you what happened, okay?" He flung his backpack into the back seat. *Seven counts in, seven counts out. Change the breath, change the self.* I should be protecting my brother, not attacking him with questions, but my chest was going to explode if I didn't get some answers. My anxiety was closing in as I merged onto the I-5. For a while, I drove in silence. Chris stared out the window. Long fields of yellow grass and sagebrush and cattle flew past, blending into one-exit towns: Etna, Gazelle, Hornbrook. Halfway to Yreka, he broke the silence.

"She was doing a lot of tarot cards," he said, his voice softer. "Then she started doing it with regular playing cards, too. She had a whole bunch of them going at once. All over the house. Probably like ten decks."

"WHAT?" I exclaimed for the hundredth time.

"And she was always talking about David and how he was going to come to Weed, and I don't even think he was really her boyfriend."

"Yeah," I said. "I mean, no? I don't think he was her boyfriend."

"I just want to know if they found Pinky," said Chris. "Is my cat gone?"

Oh man. Not his cat.

"I don't know. But we'll find out, okay?"

"What about my stuff?" His voice cracked. "All my shit? Just gone? I didn't take anything with me." He trailed off. "I didn't know . . ."

I turned to see if his eyes were teary. If I could identify scared or sad, because those were emotions that I knew what to do with, but he just stared out the window. And I stared at the back of his head.

"Cool hat," I attempted. "Is that yours?"

"Yeah. This and my coat and shoes are all I have. Had to borrow the rest from Mark."

"It sort of looks like a Phoenix," I said.

"What?"

"The symbol on your hat," I said. "You know the story of the phoenix, right?" I was already spinning stories, looking for ways to make this all mean something. Seeking a triumphant end. A way we might rise above, together.

Chris turned to me, his jaw tight. "It's a Falcon. My team is the Atlanta Falcons."

"Yeah, I know. I know. Okay. I was just saying. That's cool."

Someone older or wiser should have been driving that day. A real adult chaperoning us to visit our mother in County. Someone who knew how to deal with this. To say *I'm here for you*. To say all the things that I wanted to, but for some reason could never get out.

Yreka County Jail had less security than an airport. I'd anticipated a pat-down or metal detectors, but the clerk just pushed a sign-in sheet through an opening in the bulletproof window.

"Wait here," she barked and pointed behind us, where a half dozen people stood clustered along a cement wall, teeth chattering. It was freezing. I bounced on my toes, rubbing my arms to keep warm. A few minutes later, another woman opened a thick metal door.

"Visitors! Cell D! One hour."

Chris and I let the others go first. Mothers, lovers, brothers, friends—all filed swiftly past into a long hallway. They'd clearly done this before. When we were all in, the guard shut and bolted the door behind. Her boots slapped the concrete, each thud already marking down our hour. I practically tripped over Chris as he shuffled slowly down the windowless hall. Pressing my palms to his shoulders, I tried to nudge him forward with love. He shirked my touch.

The hall opened into a windowless room with floor-to-ceiling bulletproof glass. Plastic wings partitioned off a dozen visiting areas. Chris slid into an orange shell chair in the nearest nook. I sat next to him. There were two phones on our side of the glass. I picked one up and brought it to my ear. It was dead air. I ran my hand over the receiver. It was smooth where buttons or dials should be.

"Like a soup-can phone," I said.

Chris tapped his foot. "Where is she?"

Neon orange flashed in the corner of my eye. There was a surge of motion. I pressed my face to the glass, straining to see the women at the end of the hall, walking out single file on the prisoners' side.

Three bodies remained, and then one.

For a minute, I was outside of myself, far above, looking down on us and thinking how interesting it all was—the strange, ritualized motion of the visiting hour. Then our mother was in front of us. In a Day-Glo jail suit, she was naked in a way I'd never seen in public. Without a turtleneck, the sagging burnskin of her neck fully exposed. I was embarrassed for her. For it to be forced on her like this. Her face was calm as she slid into a chair and reached for the receiver. We picked up our phones.

"Hi, guys," Mom said, her eyes wide. Her hair was greasy and matted to her forehead in stringy clumps. She looked grayer than the last time I'd seen her. But otherwise, she looked all right. Good, even. Her eyes were liquid and clear—clearer than usual.

"Hi, Mom," I said in the chipper voice I couldn't deactivate. I felt Chris rolling his eyes. "How . . . how are you?"

"I'm okay, guys. I'm doing okay." She strained toward the glass to touch us.

"What happened? We don't even know how you got here."

"Shh." She leaned as close to the partition as she could. "I haven't been able to sleep. For weeks, I hadn't been sleeping.

"I wasn't eating or sleeping. They were keeping me up at night. Then the Other voices started to mix in."

"Others? Who were the first?"

"David," she said. "David and Isabelle."

"Who's Isabelle?" Chris looked to me; the phone cradled loosely against his shoulder. I shook my head no. *Not now.*

Mom shifted in her chair and stared, blankly. "David's mistress," she said. Chris didn't respond.

"Neen, I changed my mind," she whispered. "I didn't want to die. I ran outside. Called the fire department. *I'm the one that called!* They took too long to get there. They did that on purpose, you know."

The other families in the room started to stir.

"Don't worry about me," she said quietly.

"Don't worry about you?" I spat, fiery pressure building in my temples. Clutching the receiver with both hands, I spoke with every bit of calm I could muster. "How can we not worry about you, Mom?"

She rested her good arm on the counter.

"Marge came to see me and told me she knows a lawyer."

"I know."

"Just contact him for me. Look, I'll tell you the rest later. All right, Bird? I just wanna see how you guys are doing." She looked to Chris, who was examining a splotch of mud on his shoe. He hadn't made eye contact with her the whole visit.

"Was Pinky in the house?" he muttered.

"I don't know."

He looked up, meeting her eyes.

"Chris, I know you're mad at me," she said.

"He's not mad at you, Mom." I kicked my brother's foot.

"Yes, he is, Neen," she said. "And it's okay."

"Talk to her," I hissed.

"What about my stuff?" Chris asked. He slouched farther down into his chair and exhaled noisily. "Is everything gone? I would have taken some things, you know."

"I know, Chrissy. But I didn't . . . I wasn't thinking straight."

"We'll find out," I interrupted. "We'll figure all that out. We're just glad you're okay. I'm gonna go and talk to the lawyer." We got up to leave. "He'll help us, Mom. You don't belong here. I know you don't belong here."

I stood in slow-falling drizzle outside the Texaco on the corner of Miner and Third and slid four quarters into a sticky old pay phone. I listened to the distant ringing and willed my father to pick up.

"This is Scott." His voice was formal but warm. For the first time since I'd left San Diego two days earlier, I felt a hot throb of tears.

"Dad, it's me!" It came out choked.

"Hi, Neen. A weird number came up on caller ID."

"I'm in Yreka."

"Everything okay?"

"It's not me," I said. "It's my mom."

In a single big breath, I told him everything that had happened. Marge's call, the fire, coming to Weed, the jail visit, and finally, why I was calling, which was that I needed to hire a lawyer for my mom, and for that I needed to borrow $3,000. As I spoke, I could hear him scribbling it all down and imagined him, thousands of miles away, in his tidy Texas town house, reading glasses perched on his nose, pulling a piece of paper from the small square notepad on his glossy cherrywood desk. As I talked, his notes would grow doodles and bullet points, spawn new directions for thought. He did this on all important calls, as if sketching a conversation helped him to digest it.

"Of course," he said, after I finished. "Whatever we can do."

We talked logistics, then he looked up the address of a local West-ern Union and told me to be there by seven to pick up the transfer. "And, Neen," he said before he hung up. "Give our love to Chris."

I glanced to the car where my brother was sitting, swallowed up in his coat, staring at the Air/Water machine. When he'd said he hadn't called me because he didn't think of it, I was ashamed that he didn't see me as someone to rely on. But it struck me that if I hadn't needed money, I wouldn't have called anyone, either. Re-ally, there was no one to call. We'd been part of such a closed sys-tem that while it protected and even held us together, also kept us from asking for help when we really needed it—even from one an-other.

"I'll tell him. And, Dad? Thank you."

"Not a problem," he said.

For once, I was relieved that my father wasn't the type to ask more questions.

XXIV.

After my mother is gone, my father will tell me a story about a time early in their marriage. They were fighting about something, and when he shared his frustrations with his mother, she'd sided with my mom.

Poor girl, she'd mused. *Look what she's been through with the burns.*

She did it to herself, Dad said. *Don't feel sorry for her.*

What a strange way of seeing, I thought when he'd first shared the story. As if being in a place so dark that you'd light yourself on fire to escape was somehow less noble than randomly getting caught in one. Sometimes he tells me stories like this without analysis or context. Stories that don't make him look great, and I wonder if it's a form of confession. To show me that he is human—imperfect.

To show me what he did not and still cannot understand.

Mostly, I appreciate this. It's indirect, without hiding. What he said that day didn't offend as much as enlighten me. He touched on something I'd been thinking about for a while, in trying to figure out my own reactions to and relationship with my mother. He articulated a common sentiment, which is that we need victims to be likable. A true victim wouldn't have brought it upon themselves. To receive compassion, we need hurt women to remain docile and needy.

Because a woman who is hurt and not docile is dangerous—monstrous, even.

In *Women and Violence: The Agency of Victims and Perpetrators,* Hanna Pickard, a professor of philosophy and bioethics at Johns Hopkins, writes: "Alongside the tendency to pathologize self-harm and deny the self-harmer's rational agency is a corresponding tendency to only treat her as a victim, helpless and out of control, possibly rendered hysterical by her emotions. But women who self-harm are rational agents of self-directed violence—they are not only victims."

In America, we're shown that if we are able, white, and monied, and we follow a well-trodden path, we will succeed. And that if bad things happen to those meant to succeed, it's a glitch. That glitch is a threat to the implied safety of whiteness and the moral promise of the country: work hard and be good and you will receive. But "good" is an identity one is born into. When something bad happens to a "good" person, it's a tragedy, as in, no fault of their own. They are an "ideal victim," a concept coined in the '80s by Norwegian criminologist Nils Christie, and which remains at the heart of rape culture, media representation of police violence, and respectability politics.

My mother was set up for ideal victimhood: beautiful, white, educated, able-bodied, upper middle class, from a good Catholic family, the daughter of an engineer. But when she took that match to paper, she was transformed. Maybe even transmogrified, gaining access to a higher spiritual position or power—or what Jean Baechler, in his 1979 book *Suicides,* calls "transfiguration." *A suicide motivated by gaining status of martyr.* Not only did her body change forever that day, but so did her place in the world. She emerged disabled. Turned her life to TM. Then came children, divorce, poverty, instability. While her whiteness and class background, and to an extent, her beauty, were intact, she emerged less "ideal."

The idea being that if people bring pain upon themselves, they deserve less sympathy, unless there is another qualifying factor—

mental illness, for example, which is often the first thing noted in news stories about white male mass shooters—that renders them victims, again: of mind, of circumstance. By the self-harming nature of my mother's act and a lack of understanding about its cause, she complicated the tendency to feel sympathy for a "girl like her." And post-fire, her commitment to autonomy and continued doubling down on single motherhood and radical belief left her within fringe tiers of society, both socially and economically. Because she was strong-willed and independent and free-thinking, both before the fire and after, she complicated the categories of victim, martyr, and perpetrator. But each move toward the margins of society diminished her ability to elicit empathy from people who remained at the center.

Our cultural tolerance for complexity is so low.

We want our victims to be both helpless and worthy of our assistance. Our martyrs to be godlike, yet humble.

I think my mother was so hard to understand because she didn't bow to these categories. And so those who knew her struggled to justify her actions. Many people in her life, men in particular, wanted her to be more apologetic. At first they felt connection, attraction, sympathy. They wanted to help her, or as she'd told me early and often—*eventually they all lay their trip on you*. But when she revealed herself to be independent at all costs, her actions could be viewed by whoever through a more antagonistic lens. Her agency complicated her archetype. Even for me.

When I wrote that letter and addressed it to *Mommie Dearest*, I'd been digging for the worst insult. At the time, I thought I was calling her a grade A bitch, a terrible mother, in a cutting, savvy way, but really, I was calling her "crazy." Subconsciously, I was drawing on the cultural shorthand of *Mommie Dearest* as stand-in for a truth we acknowledge intellectually but still cannot bring ourselves to accept and adapt to culturally, a truth that Sarah Schulman untangles in *Conflict Is Not Abuse*: Victims can also be perpetrators. "Perhaps because Supremacy in some produces Trauma in others," writes Schulman. "They can become mirror images."

While examples of this duality exist everywhere, in a punitive, carceral culture—one focused on punishment for anyone who perpetuates harm—it is almost impossible on a structural level, at least, to allow space for both. Being an ideal victim comes with a level of assumed goodness. People want to help you. The further you get from that center, the more that asking for help puts you at risk—struggling single mothers worried about their kids being taken away; people of color asking for police assistance; people in mental health crises who can't afford to lose their jobs, reputations, or homes. People of historically marginalized identities are afforded less understanding for the same hardships. Before determining who deserves support, we should consider what it might cost someone to ask for it.

Mom told me that once she used free government counseling in DC, or maybe San Francisco, and the next week someone from Child Protective Services stopped by for a visit. I don't know what she'd told them or how that meeting went, but she never went again. She did everything to protect her right to mother, building an alternate family structure in community with other single mothers, and when necessary, leaving, and teaching us, in ways subtle and direct, to keep quiet. At times protecting her right to a family unit meant turning away from the help that we needed.

But what if she hadn't had to?

How might we hold space for multiple overlapping yet unique identities, which our systems have categorized as conflicting?

"We are taught that our truths are disruptive, and that disruption is a negative act," writes activist Adrienne Maree Brown in *Emergent Strategy*. "Only those moving towards profit can and should create disruption, everyone else should be complacent consumers."

Complexity disrupts the black-and-white thinking that capitalism runs on, muddying the rhetoric of who deserves resource and care. What both my father and grandmother, and so many in their positions, seemed to misunderstand is that even if you don't need to be saved, you can still need support. Real structural support. The reason we didn't have it was part of a larger narrative of complacency versus disruption. Of silence over change.

XXV.

Daniel drove me to see the house. It was ten in the morning and the January sky was acid-washed. He took my hand. We walked down the driveway, burnt wood crunching into the gravel underneath our sneakers. I'd pictured a pile of charred rubble, but the exterior was mostly intact. The same peeling green paint. A few blown-out windows. Maybe Marge had exaggerated.

As we got closer, the destruction came into relief. The lawn was a boneyard, a tide line of my family's life, shattered glass and windowpanes, scorched soccer photos and charred, broken trophies. The grass turned to ash under our feet. The house was a black hole sucking us closer. It occurred to me that this had always been possible. This is what she'd been capable of all along. Daniel's pulse thumped in his palm, and I squeezed it tighter. We stepped in unison up the porch steps. It was clear now. All the front windows were blown out. Shards of glass hung like snaggleteeth in their scorched frames. I leaned forward to peek through, but I couldn't see a thing. Daniel jiggled the door handle. It was locked.

"Ready?" he asked.

He drew a deep breath and heaved his body against the door. It gave immediately and we stumbled into the living room. The smell was disorienting, familiar and foreign: the scent of home—wood pulp and glue—mingled with cold, dead ash. I pushed past him and found myself standing in the darkest dark I'd ever experienced. It was more than a quality of light or absence thereof. The darkness was tangible. Vantablack. It came off on our hands, gathered at our feet, dusted the tops of our noses. We brought it to our nostrils and coughed. It was textural, embodied; it settled on the skin. I squeezed my eyes shut and counted to five to adjust. A slow five, with halves and three-quarters like Mom counted out when we were little. I opened them. Nothing.

"Can you see?" I asked.

"Not really," he said. "Wait, hold up." He pulled a Maglite from his back pocket and flipped it on. He took my hand, and we turned a slow circle together, taking in the living room in spot-lit sections. Everything was covered in a thick layer of what looked like charcoal. There were no walls left, only charred two-by-fours exposed and hanging like stalactites. The screen on Mom's old console TV, where I'd forced my friends to watch *Flashdance*, had exploded. Shards of glass and dust hung in its hollow. The dials were melted into long plastic tears. To our left, the remains of a piece of furniture came into focus. The tweed sofa where Mom and I sat when she told me about the fire. Nothing left but a metal skeleton, tufts of charred stuffing clinging to the wires like stiff cotton candy.

Daniel moved toward the kitchen. I shuffled close behind, following the dusky ray of light.

He whistled low. When I caught up, he was poking a finger into a puddle on the counter. All of Mom's appliances had melted onto the kitchen counter—toaster, blender, coffee maker. They were magma slicks, hanging from the edge of the counter in frozen globs as if they'd been running to escape the heat and stopped halfway.

"This is some prehistoric shit," Daniel whispered.

I grabbed the flashlight and shined it around the top of the room. The frilly curtains that framed the kitchen windows were singed into stubby clumps. More jagged glass hung in their panes. The dining table where we'd eaten our first Thanksgiving was a charred pile of coals. In the corner, a pile of car batteries was stacked next to what looked like melted water jugs. Colloidal silver. Mom had been making the silver-infused water for a few years.

One of the many things she was into, late-night strokes of genius, cure-alls, side hustles she envisioned to dig herself out from the continuous grind and deficit.

"Even the ceramic smells like smoke," Daniel said.

I turned to find him sniffing a blackened coffee mug. He wiped it out with his shirt, then sniffed again. "The smell just . . . sticks."

We walked the rest of the house, me clenching his hand as he led us through a maze of blackened two-by-fours by flashlight. In Mom's prayer room, only her shattered votives were recognizable, the charred faces of Joan and Michael and Francis looking up from below as we stepped around the puddle of her chair—all that re-mained of her years at the altar, thousands of hours spent reading and crying, praying for healing, for something, anything, better than this. The things in that room had probably burned first, ephemeral as they were: books and rattan shelves, silk scarves and visions.

We started up what was left of the stairs to the attic—Chris's room now.

"Step light," Daniel said. "We don't know if it's stable."

I remember Chris counting the days until I moved out and he could have the big room. Spanning the entire top floor, it had al-ways been my sanctuary—it felt sophisticated and tucked-away, like having an apartment of your own. After Chris had waited for so many years, now that been taken from him, too. At the top of the stairs, I choked down a sob. I could hardly make myself look. The walls were covered in soot, and Chris's saggy twin bed, still half-made like he'd just jumped up to run to school, was buried un-der ash. We tiptoed through the debris to avoid crushing what was left. A decade's worth of baseball trophies lay broken and scattered across the charbroiled carpet. Team photos were Shrinky Dinked to a quarter of their original size. I stepped over the spot—you know, the one where we slept, where the space heater burned, where Mom rolled us away, where we rolled paper into long tubes and lit them, where the burn held us. All of that gone now. Even the history of fire erased. Wound under a wound.

At the end of the room, between the bed and the blown-out window that looked out on Mount Shasta, a huge chunk of roof was missing. Sunlight shot through. Shielding my eyes, I looked up. I'd completely forgotten it was light out. That I had to live through an entire day after this.

"To prevent backdraft, probably?" D pointed to the hole. "Looks like they cut it themselves."

All I knew about backdraft then was the movie poster: a firefighter in silhouette framed by a blown-out door. Behind him a warbling fire consumes a house. I pictured the Weed Fire Department sprinting across the room, my brother's trophies cracking like twigs under their heavy boots. My chest started to knot itself.

"I have to get out," I said, and yanked Daniel down the stairs, through the house, and out the front door.

───────────────────────

In "The Compulsion to Repeat the Trauma," a study on trauma reenactment, physician and trauma expert Bessel van der Kolk tells the story of a Vietnam vet who caused the accidental death of a friend via sniper by lighting his cigarette at night. For seventeen years, on the exact anniversary of the death, the vet staged a phony armed robbery, simulating a gun in his pocket with a finger so that the police might shoot.

This compulsive reenactment ceased when he came to understand its meaning.

He wanted to be punished for what he'd done. He *needed* to be punished.

That made sense to me.

But what had she done, my mother? Why did this keep repeating? In her book on walk-ins, Montgomery calls the experience a major surgery on the etheric, or energetic, level. If that was true, it wasn't the first time Mom had gone under the knife. Wasn't the first time she transformed via the body, alchemizing pain into a new form. After the first fire, my mom spent that fall into winter in the burn unit slowly recovering. Doctors grafted skin from her ass onto her arms and pumped pints of other people's blood through her veins. They tried to use as much of her own tissue as possible, but there was little to spare.

I think of her body then as a collage. Through the flesh and blood of strangers, she was resuscitated and reconstructed.

I imagine her at twenty, in a body she no longer recognized, learning to fight for a life she'd been willing to end. I'm thinking now about how she was ready to sacrifice not just her life, but her body; about yīshēn, the Chinese Buddhist concept of flesh as a portal. I'm thinking of the difference between yīshēn, "abandoning the body," or shěshēn, "giving it up."

So many layers of soot and history, all the stories we don't even know about what came before. A matryoshka doll of stories we cannot understand with our minds but that live through us compulsively. Maybe that's what past lives are. Not individual reincarnation but the endless march of the family line. Restarted, resuscitated, again, and again.

———

"What now?" asked Daniel, backing his Jeep out of the driveway.

"Just drive."

He turned down Morris and toward Highway 97, picking up speed as we passed the Mini Mart where Mom used to make calls from the pay phone when her phone got shut off for nonpayment. She'd been friendly with the couple who ran it, but near the end, she said, even they'd turned on her. Her world had become so small.

Daniel took the first Shasta exit and drove up Everitt Memorial. I rolled down my window and breathed in cold pine, remembering all the trips up the mountain with Mom. Halfway up, he pulled into a wooded clearing and killed the engine. Cappadonna was on the stereo. Daniel pulled a sandwich baggie of weed from the pocket of his parka and rolled a joint, while I got out and climbed onto the hood. Breathing in the astringent sweetness of juniper, I looked down over the valley, watching what looked like toy cars race up the I-5. Ten at a time, then nothing for a minute, then two or three more. The blare of semitrailer trucks gunning to pass echoed through the foothills. And beyond the freeway, on the far western horizon, was the soft rolling outline of Mount Eddy and the Trinity Alps, the mountain range that partitioned us from Humboldt County, where Mom and I had first landed. When California and all its possibilities were still before us. When we had all that road to cover.

Daniel climbed up next to me and draped an arm over my shoulders. "You want?" he asked, blowing out milky smoke. I grabbed the joint and hit it hard. He grinned. He was always trying to get me to smoke, but I rarely did anymore. For an hour, we sat on the hood, looking out over the forest, saying little. We were supposed to be moving to Portland after I graduated in a few months. He'd been getting by on seasonal work—painting cars in the summer, building race runs at the local ski park in the winter. But he wanted to *paint* paint. To really try to make it. Get his work into galleries. It was hard to make more than minimum wage, here.

He wanted more than he could provide for his son, who was going to stay in Mount Shasta with his mom and visit us during school breaks. The same way I'd spent my summers. I'd get a magazine job. And somehow, slowly, by making life better for us, it would become better for our families, too. The sun dipped behind the mountain, and tiny clusters of lights went on in town below. I started to shiver. Daniel slid off the hood and held me while I jumped down. Back inside the Jeep, everything was jagged and alive in a way it hadn't been in years. The feeling I'd been avoiding. Loosening my jaw, I closed my eyes. Cappadonna was serrated, scraping away all the mental plaque. *I came to the fork in the road and went straight.*

When I was little, I used to hide inside those round clothing racks at stores. While Mom hunted down deals, I incubated myself in discount fabric. I was hidden from the outside world, unfindable. My space, impenetrable. That's the way I most wanted to feel. An inversion of the Christian edict my parents indirectly followed, I wanted to be *of the world*, but not always *in it*. Eventually, my mother's arm would poke through, her bony fingers reaching to clasp mine and, with laughter and whatever she had left of the day's patience, yank me gently back into the world. It was always jarring to return to the world this way, under the bright fluorescent blare of dd's Discounts. It was all so stark. So excruciatingly clear. Her scars. The world. Its blemishes.

I'd always done better here, inside the mess. It was the anticipation of things falling apart, and the daily attention of making sure they wouldn't again, that unnerved me most.

"Damn," I whispered. "I think I really *get* Wu-Tang."

Daniel laughed softly. "I've been telling you!"

I finally started to cry—fat, quiet tears. Far off in the distance, a pack of coyotes howled their nightly mountain song.

XXVI.

People ask about my relationship with fire. You must be afraid of it, they say. *I'm so sorry*, my college roommate says after she burns toast to a smoky crisp in the kitchen, releasing plumes of smoke whose smell lingers for days. *Does this trigger you?*

It's okay, I shrug. *It's just toast.*

I have no relationship with fire, really. Relationships are cultivated. Nurtured.

This, I inherited.

In the weeks that followed the fire, Mom told me more about what had happened. David and Isabelle had become a full-blown interdimensional Boris and Natasha. Mom was convinced that not only were they plotting against her but they had somehow located and contacted the Laredos and were planning to come to Mount Shasta to meet them. A sinister town council to address the *problem of her.* She couldn't sleep. She was up all night hearing voices, was barely eating, and had been getting advice exclusively from tarot cards. At some point, the voices became more sinister. She was evil, they told her, and deserved to die. And it should be by fire.

Meanwhile, she was still going to work, I think, and maintaining enough of a life to keep my brother in school until the day before. When it became unbearable, she sent him to a friend's house, sat down in her rocking chair, and lit the curtains on fire. Whether she thought of us then or was shuttled back to the kitchen in Ann

Arbor, as the house started to burn around her, she snapped to, bolted outside, and called the fire department.

After a week up north, I'd flown back to San Diego and was scrambling to catch up in my classes and, hopefully, still graduate on time. Mom called me collect every day and ran down a list of things for me to take care of "on the outside," like some kind of mob boss. Around four in the afternoon, I'd wait near the phone and pick it up on the first ring so my roommates wouldn't answer.

"Hello?"

This is a collect call from the Yreka County correctional facility from: "MOM."

To accept this call, say yes after the tone. TONE. "Yes."

You may not use two-way or three-way calling, or this call will be disconnected.

You are connected.

"Listen, Bird," she'd launch in. "What is the status with this hearing? I need you to get on that rinky-dink lawyer. He's not telling me anything."

"Mhmm," I'd say. "I'll try him again."

She was still awaiting sentencing. After we sent the lawyer an initial retainer, he'd told us to sit tight. I assumed the legal process was slow, but weeks had gone by, and we had no more information. He evaded my questions and hers, which sent her into weekly meltdowns. Mostly, I did whatever she asked. Moved money between accounts. Canceled power bills. Filed legal papers. Made car payments. Negotiated payment plans with utility companies. I was inside her money matrix, the white hum, and understood how much time and energy she spent each day just to stay afloat. Leveraging one credit line to pay off another. Making minimum payments, forever.

When she was having a particularly anxious day, or if the list was long and no one else was waiting for the phone, she might call back three or four times. Every call cost five dollars to connect and a dollar for each additional minute. After five minutes, the phone company automatically cut off the call. To keep talking, you had to pay the connection fee all over again. But she needed it.

"I'm gonna pay for the calls," she'd say before each goodbye.

"We'll figure it out."

Even behind bars, she wanted me to know that she was the parent.

"Thanks, Bird, but I'm writing the charges down. Keeping track in my log."

Within the tight container of our calls, I began to *hear* my mother again. She was so funny and intense and tender. The pain I felt as our connection came surging back revealed to me how much I'd missed her and how emotionally severed we'd been. A part of cutting ties with her had been auditory—a form of self-preservation, of tuning her out, after years of listening and trying to understand things that were beyond my comprehension. The calls had boundaries. I knew they would end every five minutes. Maybe that's what I'd needed all those years. A go-between. A barrier to protect us both. Within set bounds, I was free to miss her. And I realized how much I did. How much I wanted us, all of us, to be okay. To be back together.

She spent three months in jail and was out just in time to see me graduate. Everyone was there. Dad and Beth, Daniel, Mom and Chris, Carra, Gloria, and Charmaine with her four-year-old daughter. The night before the ceremony, the girls and I sat with Mom on the floor of my bedroom. She handed me a present. "I know things have been hard for you," she said. "The girls helped me put it together."

It was a blue Anne Geddes photo album with little babies

dressed up like sunflowers. I flipped through slowly. On each page was a pair of photos: one of me as a girl, and one of her, at a similar age. The pairings were loosely based on something shared—in one set, we had a similar facial expression; in another, our outfits were mirror images; one captured us in a moment of adoration with our mothers.

"I didn't even know you had family pictures. How did they survive the fire?"

"Out back in the old shed."

She shrugged like she'd been surprised to find them, too.

As I flipped through the album, the similarities between her and me, and her and her mom, were uncanny. I'd never seen my mother as someone's else's daughter. As a person, a woman, who'd needed mothering she didn't receive. It sparked something I hadn't known was missing. Something deeply matriarchal. Just looking at the pictures, I started to feel less like I was floating through space and time. Then, around age thirteen, the pairings stopped. Rod was gone. After that, it was just me and her. Maybe this was her way of showing me where I'd come from. Maybe this was her way of saying all the things she couldn't herself. Tears rolled down my cheeks.

"Awwee, it's a happy day, Pice," she said, rubbing her hand across my back. Pice, short for pisces; she hadn't called me that in a long time.

"I know. It's just . . ." There was too much to say. Every word hurt. It would never be enough. "I love it."

We booked a long table at an Italian restaurant in Hillcrest for a celebratory graduation dinner. As we crowded around big bowls of pasta and bottles of red wine, the faces of my ragtag family, my friends-as-family, the motley crew that had raised me up, glowed bright, like we'd always been together. At the end of dinner, Mom slipped away, then emerged from the kitchen. She walked slowly through the crowded restaurant, making sure her grip was steady, and set down in front of me a giant custard-filled tart covered with glazed berries, slices of kiwi, and mandarin orange. In loopy white frosting, she'd written *Congratulations, Bird*. A single candle burned in the middle. I stared into the flame.

"Make your wish!" Gloria hollered from the end of the table, her cheeks raspberry from too much Chianti. A warm churn of voices enveloped me. Carra and Charmaine were deep in conversation, their foreheads pressed together, giggling quietly as Charmaine bounced her daughter on her knee. They'd driven twelve hours from Mount Shasta just to be there. Across the table, my San Diego friends were in easy conversation with Beth and Dad. Daniel squeezed my hand under the table. Chris, sitting on my other side, gave the slightest smile.

This, I thought. I had wished for this.

I closed my eyes, drew in a big breath, and blew out the past six months.

XXVII.

A cheery orange kettle whistled as I stepped into the trailer. Mom had made it cozy, turning the fold-down vinyl bed into a sitting area with an afghan and laying a silk scarf over the small dining table. I settled cross-legged on the couch. She'd been out of jail for four months, after being granted a deferred judgment, a probationary ruling that stated if she didn't get into any more legal trouble for three years, met with a county-appointed counselor, and took medication, her record would be cleared of felony arson—probation lite.

The arson investigation had found Mom temporarily insane and approved the insurance claim. Morris Street was being rebuilt. It was August, and the house was set to be done by October. In the meantime, the Manns loaned her a trailer in their front yard. Chris had a bed inside. One of the few local families Mom still trusted, the Manns were the parents of Chris's best friend. Born a week apart, they shared the same chill. Like Carra and me, they were as close to siblings as you could get without blood.

When Mom first got out, she'd gone to live with some New Age guy who had a ranch outside of town, a newer friend I didn't know. "That guy? He was great at first," she said, pouring me a cup of Lemon Zinger. "He was really good to me, actually. Bought me some new outfits from Walmart." She twirled to show off a crisp pair of elastic-band slacks and navy Keds, an oddly preppy sight after years of eclectic thrift-store getups.

"I noticed!" I said.

"I was super grateful. Then he started in on his spiel."

"Which was?" My eyebrows knitted together. I felt a familiar itch creeping up.

"Oh, you know, same old shit. Tried to put all his religious stuff on me. Wanted me to pray with him or whatever."

"You already do that, though," I said. "*Pray?*"

She scoffed. "He wanted to 'help me find a better way.' Like this heehaw was going to be the one to save *me*?! Ha! I've been saved and *then some*. I'll save your ass, buddy. How about that? These men, they all get around to it sooner or later, babe—telling you what to do. The counselor says I can stop the antipsychotic soon, but to stay on the antidepressants," she said casually, sipping her tea as if we'd talked about this a hundred times. "She doesn't think I'm schizo." I flinched, leaning closer. It was the first time she'd ever alluded to any sort of diagnosis. If her therapist was saying she wasn't *schizo*, it implied that schizo was on the table. But the way she said it—*she doesn't think I'm schizo*—made it sound like something we'd already talked about. Something she'd been considering, which maybe she had? But never with me.

"She agrees with my theory."

"Which is?"

"That the breakdown was depression and a lifetime of unprocessed issues. A lot of fear. I've got an issue with fear."

"An ISSUE WITH FEAR? That might be understating . . ."

Was the therapist a hack or was Mom downplaying it, framing the fire as a blip in her mental health with no relation to the one she'd started thirty years earlier? Did the therapist know about the first one? The counselor had prescribed a pill for depression, she said, and Haldol, which I'd look up later and find out was an antipsychotic. She was still working out her dosages, sometimes halving them to "remain in her own power."

"They make me feel sort of dull, like fuzzy or gluey," Mom said. "Not myself."

Maybe that's not the worst thing, I wanted to say, but kept quiet.

We were just starting to get along.

I'd never been to therapy or taken meds or been around people that talked about them. Because I had been raised around people who believed more in ascension and homeopathy than medication, my mother's underdosing or self-diagnosing didn't ring alarms. It made sense. She wasn't anti–Western medicine, but gave us antibiotics only when absolutely necessary. While I was growing up, she took me to the local health food store for weekly wheatgrass shots; made her own goldenseal capsules from bulk; and brewed batches of mullein tea when we were sick.

In the burn unit, she'd been on morphine for six months, and said that after she was released, she'd never wanted to see another drug. Substance made you suspectable to entities, she said. Even drinking, she said, rendered you spiritually porous. More vulnerable for dark spirits or low-level energies to attach to you. Whether out of weariness or denial, I hadn't yet stepped outside of my mother's orbit. As in, I was still letting her define the bounds of reality— of what was and was not an issue. At least there was a professional who was aware of her. That was reassuring.

Leaning back on a pile of throw pillows, she sipped her tea and casually changed the subject. "So, what's the plan with you guys?" Daniel and I were technically on our way to Portland. We'd left San Diego three weeks earlier, everything I owned packed into the trunk of my car. We'd stopped at home to say goodbye to his son and check on my family. Daniel was supposed to do some work with his dad to make fast money. Down south, I'd been working a student job with the county of San Diego and had saved about $1,200. After graduation gifts, I had maybe $2,000. We'd been talking about the move for a year, but he had nothing saved. Summer was passing, and we hadn't even been to Portland to look for apartments.

"Every day since we've been back, D says he's going to work?" I said, sipping my tea. "And every day he just doesn't. It's the weirdest thing. But he doesn't acknowledge it. He's just *not doing anything.*"

"Do you have money?" Mom asked.

"Enough for one month, maybe a deposit? But I don't have a job."

"Girlfriend," she said. "Can I be real with you?"

"When are you not?"

"You go," she said, grabbing my hand and squeezing tight. "Get the apartment. Or you might be waiting forever. If you want to move to Portland, you move. If he's worth his salt, he'll get his butt up there."

I thought of all the times she'd left. In the early days before memory, just taken me without waiting for permission. Her words were a splash of cold water. She'd made her share of questionable choices, but waiting around for a man was certainly not one of them. Not on the physical plane, anyway.

"You shouldn't be stuck here, Neen," she said. "Take it from your old mom." She chuckled, but the "here" stung. *Here,* as if to say *with her.* I shouldn't be stuck with her. Which in that moment I didn't feel, but overall did feel, and felt bad about feeling. The guilt was so heavy. I didn't know how to fix things, but I didn't know how to live with things as they were.

"Lemme get Chris." She jumped up and ran down the trailer steps and across the yard to the Manns' living room window, where Chris was inside playing a video game. I followed and found her tapping at the glass, waving excitedly. *Neen-y's here!* she mouthed. He paused the game and came out looking drained. I gave him a big hug and he squeezed back reluctantly.

"The Manns said you can come in for dinner," he said quietly to Mom. "Ribs."

"Oh no," she said. "I don't want to impose! That's so sweet of them, though. Tell them I said so, Chrissy."

He nodded. "I'm gonna go in now."

"You don't want to have *teatime in the trailer?*" I joked, trying to throw some dark humor at the situation.

He just stared at me, his eyes pooled, before he walked back into the house. As the screen door thwacked shut, I felt a deep sense of dread. An unsettling, irrevocable division in my family. Mom and Chris were back together but living separate lives. A split-screen mother and son. I was embarrassed and sad for him—it sucked to have your mom living in a trailer in front of your friend's house—and equally shocked to see my mother rendered an appendage, a figurehead in Chris's life, demoted from the role she cherished most. The weirdest part was that she seemed at peace with it. Maybe that was the medication.

Or she trusted that he would be held, no matter what. He had been playing baseball since he was a kid, so his coaches, many local cops or friends' dads, treated him with love. And being a polite and funny, intelligent sweet guy, he'd won the hearts of many local families. Over the years, he'd grown an amalgam second family from many others, much like I had with the Dunsmuir friends I'd clung to. A native to the area, really, Chris's home was Siskiyou in ways it never had been for me.

The next day, I took her advice and told Daniel I was going to Portland with or without him. He came, and after a frantic week of viewing apartments, we settled on a one-bedroom in Northwest, a leafy, comfortable neighborhood. It felt like a place where things were taken care of. Not aspirational, exactly, but as if the people who cooked in these kitchens, who dreamt and fought and fucked in these bedrooms, had sitcom problems.

That's what we needed: problems with a laugh track.

I put down every dollar I had to get the apartment and spent the next several weeks firing off dozens of résumés a day until I landed a job at an investment consulting firm looking for someone to write short articles like "The Fascinating History of the Penny" for 401(k) newsletters. Relieved to have a salary, I figured I'd write creatively on the side and build connections in the industry. For the first few months, we had no furniture and ate all our meals on folding camping chairs, until one day Daniel's gave out and he fell through, his ass slapping against the slick hardwood. At night, we zipped two sleeping bags together and cuddled on the bare floor, groping each other like teenagers. It was like sleepaway camp. It was a wreck, but it was ours and that, for me, was all that mattered. I was away. And *we* were beginning.

XXVIII.

Morris Street was rebuilt and Mom and Chris moved back in that October. Mom had started a cleaning business with her friend Gayle a couple of years earlier. After the fire, they lost most of their clients, but they'd scored a new nightly gig cleaning the Stage Door, a combination coffee shop and live-music venue in Mount Shasta. A morning person, Mom was usually asleep by nine thirty or ten p.m. But the only time they could clean the Stage Door was between three and seven a.m. I'd never seen her work hours like that, but she and Gayle were excited to rebuild their clientele.

I went home that Christmas. Walking into the house was surreal. It was a soundstage—a new home in an old skin. The grungy house that I'd cherished in my youth, and come to resent as a teen, had been gutted and rebirthed as a generic tract-style, three-bed, one-bath home with gray siding and teal trim. Its hotel-ization was complete with Home Depot ceiling fans, a slippery new bathtub, and corny oversize light fixtures. Mom's prayer room was full-size. And the attic bedroom had been split into two smaller rooms. As I explored the new layout, breathing in the plasticky smell of fresh paint and carpet, I couldn't shake what I'd seen with Daniel. I pictured workers scooping out its blackened insides like melon. Grafting fresh wood and paint onto its charred bones. I wondered how deep they'd had to dig to clear out the dead and swore I could detect whiffs of ash—a lingering stench impossible to clear away. The inverse of a perfume or a stew wafting through the kitchen recalling a special person or warm memory, the fire remained—*phantom smells*, they call them.

I was grateful that my family was secure and safe again and that they'd gotten an objective upgrade, but still a familiar sense of dinge and doom closed in on me. My urge to escape, to run, was dissonant with the pristine cookie-cutter setting. This was the sort of house I'd always wanted. Clean, new, basic. The sort of house where things should be fine. But new drywall and fixtures couldn't erase history. Even having new rooms cut into old, changing the walkways and movement of the home, didn't change what had happened there.

I shook it off. We were starting from scratch, I told myself. Of course it was going to feel weird. Even our typically gaudy Christmas tree, the centerpiece of the season, had been replaced by an artificial white mini pre-decorated exclusively in red mirror-ball ornaments. There was nothing for us to do, no boxes of tinsel to throw over it in chaotic handfuls. Perched on a pair of newly thrifted floral couches, we exchanged gifts with the primness of strangers. If the photos from that year are a proper record, our joy was precarious—our smiles are tight, our eyes weary. In one photo, Chris and I hold up identical copies of the movie *Elf*, which we'd gifted each other without knowing, laughing as we realized. In another, Mom shows off a leather photo album I gifted her to start collecting new memories—a recall of her graduation gift, of saying we can start over, again. As per tradition, we opened stockings last. But gone were the familiar mismatched ones of our childhood.

"Here, guys, I got us new ones," she said, as if the idea had simply occurred to her, as if they were a refresh instead of a replacement for what had gone up in flames. She handed us bright felt stockings embroidered with golden angels, stuffed with her signature dollar-store knickknacks: body wash, pieces of loose Starburst, recipe cards, mini salt and pepper shakers. After presents, as Mom and I prepared dinner, Chris napped under the ruby glow of the artificial tree. We spread out on the couches and ate while watching *Elf*, laughing a little too hard at the familiar lines, letting the sound lubricate what felt like a gathering of strangers. Our holiday cheer was strained with the desperate need for it to last.

But it didn't. Those photos of us smiling tightly, clustered close enough to feel each other's warmth, but each in our own chamber, would be the only ones to make it into the new album. After them, the pages would remain blank. We wouldn't get the chance to re-thread our lives together. To have the conversations with our mother that could have changed things.

Our first Christmas back together would be our last.

PART IV

Decay

XXIX.

I could tell you a lot about leaving. About how flight is inherited. How some departures leave scars that heal, while others cut so deep, they birth whole landscapes, frontiers to attend to. New terrain to settle and build life from scratch—*as if we could*. That Western illusion. The New Age. The cosmic portal. As if by leaving, we could remake ourselves, again and again. I could tell you that after all the fires were extinguished, I did the only thing there was left to do. I rode the train back to Iowa. To Detroit. Looking for my mother. Myself. My brother. A place for us. Somewhere not to start anew, but to pick up the thread she dropped. But first, I have to tell you the worst part. The part that requires me to stay. In my body. In this moment. This memory.

It was nine thirty on a Monday the week before my twenty-fourth birthday. When I returned to my desk from the break room, clutching a mug of coffee, there was a message from my brother, who never left a message.

"Hi, Nina. Can you just call me back as soon as you get this?" He sounded watery and weird. I rushed outside and leaned against the building. He picked up on the first ring.

"Chris?"

"Nina." His voice wobbled and I knew. It was inevitable and impossible, and I knew. Silently, I begged him not to say it.

"Mom died," he whispered.

I screamed, but it slipped down my throat and came out instead as a silent froggy gasp. The stone wall raked against my spine as I slid to the ground.

Later, I'd find out that she fell to the ground, too.

That at three o'clock that morning, after she had finished cleaning the Stage Door, our mother had collapsed on the sidewalk out front. Someone walking by called 9-1-1 and an ambulance rushed her to Mercy, the hospital where Chris had been born, where Kim sang in the waiting room, where Evelyn died, where Mom first met David, where everything began and ended and, eventually, went to shit. The hospital was just a mile away, but she didn't make it. The paramedic said she died almost instantly. Pulmonary embolism, they said. Blood clots in her lungs.

She was never awake at that time.

She'd never have been awake if not for that job.

I can't remember anything else my brother said, but I sat on the ground, looking at my hands, scanning my delicate fingers, long rounded nails, and the bluish tributary of veins running through them, all my blood running free and clear—unclotted. And I pictured my mother's hands, clutching mine as she navigated us through the streets of San Francisco; gripped around her lidless gas station coffees as they sloshed and spilled; kneading my sore feet on late winter nights after long weeks at dance. Even after everything had come crashing down in the last year, I'd somehow never imagined an earth without my mother. As hard as I'd tried to create boundaries, as much as I wanted and didn't want to be with her at the same time, it felt impossible that she could die, and I would go on living.

But there I was, crumpled against the wall of the office building, my heart pounding, my throat a desert. My brother was still on the phone, waiting, I realized. "I'll be there as soon as I can," I managed to squeak out. "Love you."

I booked a wildly expensive seat on the first flight I could find into Medford, Oregon, a tiny airport an hour north of Weed, threw clothes into a suitcase, and tried to keep myself upright. The Manns were waiting, when I landed, in their big black SUV. Chris was sitting alone in the back seat. I slid in next to him. There was so much I wanted to say, but words meant nothing. My brother was sixteen, the same age I'd been when I left home. I clutched his hand. It was clammy, but for some reason, I was afraid to squeeze it—to hold on to him for dear life. Maybe I was scared to fall apart. If I could have, I would have readily eaten my brother's portion of pain. But the distance between us was so acute that I couldn't muster a simple "I'm here, we'll get through this." The intimacy of the moment, the stark realization of what we'd lost, that it was just us now, was too much to bear. I let his hand slip away and we rode side by side in silence, looking out the tinted windows at the rocky hillsides covered in bleached-yellow grass.

By the time she died, Mom had lived in Siskiyou County off and on for almost twenty years. At the news of her death, a strange mix of friends emerged, many of whom Chris and I had never met. There were the New Age folks, but also social workers, teachers, ranchers, activists, even cops. We planned a small family ceremony for her at the local Buddhist abbey, but her eclectic band of local friends decided to hold a community memorial at the Stage Door as well. They ran an ad in the local paper inviting anyone who'd known and loved her. Secretly, I was relieved someone had taken charge. Even if I didn't know who the hell these people were. She'd left no will or directives other than mentioning years earlier that she wanted to be cremated. Despite her eleventh-hour nostalgia for the church, a Catholic funeral seemed inauthentic. How could we all properly honor a woman whose life was devoted to the divine, but via so many different channels?

When I walked into the Stage Door, a gnarl-faced man with high-water jeans and scuffed cowboy boots handed me a program. At the front of the room, there was a small stage with a podium flanked by dramatic white flower arrangements. Dozens of people stood at the back of the room. More filled rows of banquet-hall chairs. Some I hadn't seen in years. Marge Meyer, the singsongy harbinger of bad news; and Kim, the vocalist, draped in plum-colored shawls, sat in the center aisle. Charmaine's mom, Cheryl, and Carra and her parents were there. Gloria and Sierra were there. Dad and Beth had flown in and were sitting in the front row next to me and Chris. Daniel's mom and a few of his sisters slipped in late and stood against the back wall, their long silky black hair cascading into somber black dresses like something from *The God-father.* The rest of the room looked quirky and colorful, a combination of aged hicks and white ladies in flowy scarves and linen pants. But Daniel's family looked appropriately widowed; they looked the most like I felt.

Presiding over the service was a gray-haired white lady in a violet cassock, who beamed as she introduced herself to the room as Edith, a minister of the Church Universal and Triumphant. Mom had been recently dabbling with their teachings. I didn't know much about it and was beyond asking or caring, but as I watched Minister Edith prepare to speak, I remembered a vague conversation with Mom about attending a seminar at their Montana head-quarters. Church Universal was a cultish congregation that mashed together tenets of Buddhism, Christianity, nature spirits, alchemy, and esoteric mysticism. They self-published mystical texts like *Violet Flame to Heal Body, Mind & Soul.* It was the most famous and successful offshoot of the I AM movement, Guy Ballard's Shasta-born religion. Full-circle shit.

"We're here today to honor Sister Anita," Minister Edith began, lifting her hands as if to the heavens. Apparently, Mom had been more involved than I realized. "She was a bright light whose works and selfless deeds touched the lives of many of you in this room. I'm sure of it." As she dug around for a passage to read from her church's version of the Bible, I numbly scanned the program. There was a loud shuffle in the back of the room, and I turned to see Chris's entire varsity baseball team file in, hands clasped at their waists like altar boys or soldiers reporting for duty.

"To begin," Edith was saying, "I'd like to hear from you. The community. Her spiritual kin. The lifeblood of Anita's time here on the earthly plane."

A sea of heads dipped in feigned reverence, hoping they wouldn't be expected to speak, while others perked up and looked around to see who might volunteer. I wondered what these people had to say about my mother. I could feel their eyes boring down on Chris and me, waiting for us to perform grief. But I couldn't even feel my face and I was sure my brother wasn't ready to stand up in front of a room full of people we hardly knew. You know who was, though? *Kim.*

She took her time rearranging her shawls while everyone waited. "Anita, Anita, what can I say?" she began, holding her hands over her diaphragm like an opera singer. "Every rose has its *thorns* . . ." At that, I whited out, coming to only when my dad surprised me by jerking up out of his chair. He scanned the crowd and seemed bewildered to find himself standing. "I'm Anita's ex-husband, Nina's father, though I didn't have much to do with it," he said to a slow rumble of laughter. "Anita wanted a baby, and I just happened to be there. She had nothing if not will . . ."

Many nodded, letting out grunts of agreement. It was clear my mother had left behind a string of complicated relationships. After an hour of rambling speeches and derivative hacked-together scriptures, the ceremony ended and we all milled around as I did my best to "host," which meant accepting the condolences of strangers, like the wacky local rancher who offered to take Chris in and raise him on his farm. "Very generous," my brother said diplomatically, shaking the man's hand. "Thanks. Appreciate that." We locked eyes and stifled a laugh. Kim swooped in from behind to hug us both and slipped a note into my hand: *Call me, sweetie.*

I met a group who said they got to know Mom while she was campaigning for Dennis Kucinich, the Cleveland congressman who, she'd become convinced, was the nation's last hope—a socialist who believed in health care for all and same-sex marriage long before the DNC openly endorsed them. The group flitted around me like excited bees. While the house on Morris was being rebuilt, they told me, Mom had attended all the Kucinich rallies she could, driving three hours to the state capitol in Sacramento and back in the same day, even canvassing door to door. In that year between being released from jail and her death, she'd become politically active in a way she hadn't been since her twenties. I'd had no idea.

"Anita was so passionate," they chirped. "Committed. She knew Kucinich was the only honest way forward and went to bat."

"She was a true believer!" one said, and they all nodded in unison.

"She never could resist a good campaign," I said, genuinely charmed.

Chris didn't want to come back to Morris Street. Ever. I couldn't blame him. It was no longer a home for him, I imagined, but the site of all the worst shit that had ever happened. He stayed with the Manns. My old Dunsmuir friends who'd come to town for the service stayed at the house with me, while I set up a center of operations to figure out what to do next. Dad and Beth were nearby at a local hotel.

The day after the service, my father came to the house and waved me into a small room; it was a new room that had been created by splitting the former downstairs bedroom in two—so that it was touching the edge of Mom's old prayer room. My father sat on the floor, legs tucked under him, knees touching. I mirrored him. From his pocket, he pulled out a small picture of Guru Dev, the same photo my TM teacher had propped up during my initiation ceremony twelve years earlier. The same one my mother had been struck by in the hospital chapel thirty-three years ago. The face that held what she'd been *looking for all her life*.

Dad set the picture up on a milk-crate filing cabinet and started to chant. A long string of Sanskrit sounds filled the room with all the resonance of a humming crystal bowl. As he chanted, his body started to quiver. I closed my eyes and let the sounds wash over and through me. When he finished, he bowed his forehead to the floor and sobbed. His body racked with waves of emotion. I'd never seen my father cry like that, and it overwhelmed me. I started to sob, too. We lay in child's pose, side by side, our bodies like tiny walnuts notched into themselves, and wailed—separate, but together in our grief.

My father's lessons could be ill-timed or heavy-handed. He could come across as if a pure lifestyle was the only avenue toward lasting bliss. But that day, when what I needed more than anything was to break all the way down, it was my father's tears that made room for mine. I'd need him more than ever, now. And he'd be there, for weeks, by my side. Afterward, he stuffed all the funeral flowers into a garbage bag and drove us to the Mount Shasta City Park, where the headwaters of the Sacramento River sprang from a patch of mossy rocks. People from all over the world came to fill their bottles at the headwaters—*Best Water on Earth* was our proud local motto. We carried the bag of flowers to a tiny footbridge over a creek that would become the river.

"Always throw funeral flowers into moving water," Dad said. "You want to release them. Don't hold on. On three."

"One, two . . ." we chanted. On three, we tipped the bag over together. A rainbow of iris and daffodil, lily and rose and sun-flower, tumbled out and swirled down the river. They were bouquets from Mom's funeral, arrangements sent from my dad's family and my boss, batches of blooms dropped on the front porch by neighbors. There were pinks and yellows, the colors of spring, of Easter eggs; there were whites. Winter whites, mourning whites. White of snow and god and purity. I thought of her turtlenecks. As we watched the flowers become tiny specks on the creek, I was skinned with grief.

"Maybe if I'd been there for her," I cried. "If I'd been able to help her, to listen, she'd still be here."

"Oh, Neen," Dad said softly, resting his hand on my shoulder. "I don't think so. Without you and Chris, your mother would have been gone a long time ago."

XXX.

Just before she died, I had started feeling like a person again. Like things were taken care of. Like they might work out. But that had been a dress rehearsal. In the months following Mom's death, the logistics of our grief further divided Chris and me. I was devastated, but beyond the breakdown with Dad, there was no time or energy to attend to anyone's feelings. Not my brother's or my own. I slipped back into damage-control mode, plowing through the weeks before, during, and after the memorial service. That would go on for another year, then two, until I no longer knew the difference between getting by and living, and everything I did became the least of what I felt.

Fueled by adrenaline and disbelief, I had to visit the morgue, get her body cremated, collect the ashes, figure out what to do with her house, her money, or lack thereof, and most important, what was going to happen to my brother. Because she'd died intestate, everything, including the guardianship of Chris, was now a legal case. He was a minor, and I was the only adult next of kin, so by default, at twenty-three, I inherited all her assets. Using the word "assets" is an inflated way of saying: the house on Morris Street, a brokedown pickup, and about $312 in a savings account, all of which went into a freeze during an indeterminate amount of time called probate. When you die without a will, anyone you owe money to takes first claim.

I asked Chris if he wanted to come to Portland to live with Daniel and me, but he really wanted to stay in Weed and finish high school, which I understood. I would have wanted the same. Weed was his home. And as he grieved, it held him in a way I couldn't. The Manns, who'd been so good to my family over the last year, generously offered to become his legal guardians until he turned eighteen. A local lawyer, the father of one of Chris's friends, took our cases on pro bono and negotiated with Rick, who was living in New York then and eventually agreed that it was in his son's best interests to sign the papers.

We couldn't rent the house until probate was over. To keep it, I had to pay the mortgage and my rent. I'd been hoping to quit my office job and take a chance on something more creative but was now supremely grateful to have something steady. My boss was generous with leave, and coworkers donated PTO when mine ran out. Drowned in grief and paperwork, I pushed through an endless checklist of tasks. We had support from friends, family, townspeople, and even strangers, but ultimately, I was responsible. On my own to sweep up the detritus and take its accounting. And somewhere in the fog of the weeks, it became clear that I always had been alone in this.

Uncle Dan was too sick or sad to come to the service. He didn't clarify, but emailed heartbroken condolences. I could tell he cared, but he never offered to *do anything*. There were no other adults to include in decisions about my mom's intimate affairs. Because her life had been fragmented, it was impossible to fully share her death.

Memorial Day, I went back to the house. It'd been a few months since she died and I needed to get the house cleared out to prepare it for rental. I walked to the shed out back, looking for a missive—a scrap of paper with last wishes, a plan, something, anything my mother left behind that might tell me what to do next. It was startling to be alone and in charge, with no blueprint.

Planks of rotted wood bowed under my feet as I stepped into the decrepit shed. Dusty shafts of light shot through the cracked filmy windows. Lining the far wall was a row of blue milk crates stuffed with manila folders. Mom's filing system. I squatted down and started to dig through them, waving away plumes of dust. One folder was labeled *New Ears*. She'd talked often about a plastic surgeon in Maryland who, every year, gave away a few free pairs of reconstructed ears. She'd been determined to get on his list. She wrote letters, she'd said. But when I opened the file, it was empty.

Next to the milk crates was a mildewed cardboard box with her handwriting in purple Sharpie. I couldn't make out the words, but stuck my hand inside and pulled out a stack of files. There were copies of letters she'd written to the Laredos, a loose-leaf journal, and an entire screenplay she'd written for a class at the College of the Siskiyous. I scanned it quickly, recognizing a fictionalized account of her life story set in the Amazonian jungle, starring a gritty truth-seeking investigative reporter and a dashing dark-haired man equally committed to justice. The script was mostly them deep in existential conversation while flying over the jungle in a chopper, scanning for bad guys. I set it aside for later.

I dug deeper, and my fingers grazed something hard and rectangular. I pulled out a lime-green book with faded gold lettering that read JOURNAL. Flipping quickly through the yellowed pages, I recognized the handwriting, but it was too linear and sharp to be hers. I read aloud from a random page: *First, I was born in Canada in a little town not far from here. My mother was the innkeeper's daughter. She married a farmer 10 years older than she. Drinking is in the earliest of my memories.* My skin prickled. Grandpa Lou. It had to be. I hadn't known about the inn. About the early drinking. I read the passage again, in what I imagined was my grandfather's voice. Warm and low. Fatherly. Skipping ahead several pages, I scanned for any names I might recognize, stopping suddenly as I stumbled upon his record of that day. The first fire. *I had to attend a seminar at our works in Illinois. As I was having breakfast that morning, I got a long-distance call from my son from Ann Arbor, Mich. He informed me that Anita and another girl (the older one of the original group) had set themselves on fire in a house in Ann Arbor in a suicide pact.*

I'd never heard anyone else talk about the fire. I kept reading, hungry to connect across time and space with my own blood, and hear how they'd been impacted. After Lou received the news, he left his conference and flew immediately to Ann Arbor on a company plane. Uncle Dan met him at the hospital. At that time, the University of Michigan's burn unit, which would later become one of the world's best, held only ten patients. My mother and Raelle were the newest. Still unconscious, they were wrapped in heavy bandages from head to toe, only their nostrils showing. The doctors told Lou that if the shock could be controlled and infection kept to a minimum, there was a slim chance that his daughter would survive. My grandfather and uncle went downstairs to the hospital cafeteria to absorb what had happened.

"I don't think I can go back into that room again," Lou said, shaking his head.

"You can," Dan replied. "You can, you will, *you must.*"

It was moving to read about my uncle pushing their father. Making sure he didn't shut down in the time she would need them most. Mom was twenty, Dan, twenty-eight.

Years later, after Mom had left Michigan for good, my grandfather would admit himself to Brighton Hospital, one of the oldest rehab centers in the country, equidistant between Detroit and Ann Arbor. In an undated entry from his time there, he wrote: *In March 1972, I visited the burn unit and got the greatest shock of my life. They had moved Anita to a private little area. I saw her for the first time without her head bandages. "She had no ears." I could hardly contain myself. I called for all of the doctors and accused them of cutting off her ears. They gently told me that her ears had been burned off in the fire. I went home that night and drank myself into a stupor. I felt tremendous guilt and remorse. I blamed myself for the whole episode. I think that night I passed from the problem stage to the acute stage.*

Dropping to a seat in the dusty shed, I had full-body goose

bumps. For most of our lives, fire had been a phantom, a prologue, an eerie legend that we formed ourselves around. Any conversation about that night had been imagined—reconstituted and one-sided. But for Lou and Dan, fire had never been a metaphor. Holding my grandfather's worn leather journal in my hands and reading about it in his words, I felt for the first time the devastation my family must have felt, a family I'd hardly known, but that mirrored my own. A single father—two kids, almost eight years apart. My mother died at almost the exact age her mother had.

Thinking about those two men, in the hospital cafeteria, trying to navigate such a bizarre, profound grief together, filled me with deep longing to be in the room. To be there, together, through it all with them. Maybe that's overly romantic—the fire might have pushed whatever was left of their family apart, the way grief can, the way her death threatened to do now to my brother and me. I saw how the cycles of disconnection, of alienation and aloneness, can be passed on from generation to generation, even if you never knew the people—even if they were dead long before you were born. Maybe especially then. Maybe I just wanted to be there with them, in that hospital cafeteria, so that they would be here, now. So that there was some continuity of tragedy. Some togetherness in the loss. I'd come to the shed looking for a missive from my mother, but what I found made me realize how small and sad that wish was. How there was something much bigger missing, a whole other entity I'd yearned for but hadn't named: Family. Her family. It's hard to miss what you've never had. Maybe this is why people go looking for a self, a god, a land, anything to remake themselves whole. I wished Dan and Lou had been there. I wished they could have told me what to do next.

Shortly after I found the journal, Uncle Dan died. After Mom died, I'd reconnected with his kids, our cousins back in Michigan, who were all grown now with kids of their own. *Aunt Nita*, they called Mom, remembering fondly my parents' visits back to Michigan, when they'd slept in the basement, meditated, and ate *their own weird foods.* They were *different,* my cousins thought. Weird in the cool way. Cool aunt: another role I'd never seen her in.

Chris had no memory of our cousins at all. I remembered going right after my grandpa died, but had little connection to my cousins. I'd planned a trip out there to meet them over Christmas. To do what I could to close the loop. Connect Chris and me to our family. When they left a message saying their dad was sick, right after Mom's death, we were so deep in the chaos that we could barely take in the news. When they said he died a few months later, and that in the end he'd cried out for his mother and sister, we were crushed, but with no capacity to say or do much about it. For me, it got filed away as one more loss in the litany of loss that had been the last couple years. I was grateful we'd gotten to know him at all. That he took Chris to games. That Mom got her brother back in the end, however tenuous their bond.

They were all gone now. Their family of four.

Brother and sister dead within months of each other.

My grandfather's journal was a portal. Back in Portland, I was electrified with the sudden need to fact-check my mother's story. To hunt down every detail I could. Google didn't exist when Mom first told me about Ann Arbor, and in the years after, it had never occurred to me to look it up. But now it was urgent. Gripping a mini jelly jar of red wine in one hand, my face flushed with nerves, I keyed in Anita McQueen+Michigan+fire.

Dozens of results popped up, but most were locked behind the paywall of a newspaper archive. I grabbed my purse from the couch, dumped its contents to the floor, and pulled my credit card from a pile of loose tobacco and dirty pieces of Trident. I created an account and ran the search again, holding my breath as I typed in her name. And there, in their original columned newspaper form, wedged between ads for dishwashers from the 1970s and bridge club benefits, appeared a series of headlines that flattened me.

Your search for Anita McQueen yielded the following 16 results:

Holland Evening Sentinel **Two Women Burn Selves**
Fergus Falls Daily Journal **Two Girls Seek Death by Burning**
Oakland Tribune **Two Attempt Suicide by Using Fire**
Lowell Sun **Two Women Try Double Suicide by Fire**
Tucson Daily Citizen **Two Badly Burned in Suicide Attempt**
Traverse City Record Eagle **"Lovely to Die Together"**
Panama City News Herald **Human Torches Still Critical**
Ironwood Daily Globe **Woman Dies of Burns**
The Hayward Daily Review **Two Young Women Critical after Suicide Try**

THE HAYWARD DAILY REVIEW

November 10, 1971

ANN ARBOR, Mich. (UPI)—Two young women who thought it would be "lovely to die together" were in critical condition today from extensive burns suffered in a double suicide attempt. The two women, described as drifters, wrapped themselves in gift paper and set themselves on fire Wednesday. They still were burning when police discovered them sitting Indian style on the kitchen floor of a duplex near the University of Michigan. "Two officers saw flames coming from the area of the kitchen floor and heard the girls screaming," Police Chief Walter Krasny said. "They were not doing anything to put this fire out. They were on the floor, legs crossed, facing each other."

The officers took the women to the burn unit of the University of Michigan Medical Center after firemen smothered the flames by wrapping them in heavy blankets. The victims were identified as Anita McQueen, 20, of Livonia, Mich., and Raelle Weinstein, 26, of Skokie, Ill. Krasny said that in the ambulance, one victim placed her "burned hand on the hand of the other and said, 'It's lovely to die together.'" "We have no idea why they would do something like this," Krasny said. "They didn't use gasoline or anything. We presume they were fully clothed in street clothing and just set themselves on fire."

I moved backward through the results, devouring each story, clocking small differences. One article called them "drifters." Another mentioned that Raelle's parents were window blinds salespeople in Chicago. Another that the firemen wrapped them in heavy blankets and used knives to cut smoldering clothing from their bodies. "Human Torches Still Critical" came a follow-up piece weeks later. It was shocking to see my mother's secret history, something that until that moment I'd imagined was between us, recorded for anyone to search online. That night had been printed and archived for over thirty years. Photos and official police statements lying dormant for decades.

"Hey, babe!" Daniel's voice jolted me back to the present. The clock read after nine. I blinked to adjust my eyes and spun around slowly in my desk chair, bare toes scratching the woolly southwestern rug my dad had sent as a housewarming gift. We'd been so excited. So ready to build something bright and stable.

"What're you working on out there?" he asked as I shuffled into the kitchen.

"Oh, nothing," I said, steadying myself against his chest.

I wasn't ready to tell him what was happening, or that I was going to have to follow wherever it took me. I wasn't ready to admit that a part of me was already gone. I didn't know yet that I would spend the next several years seeking answers to questions birthed that night. Or that our work is always there waiting for us. That nothing—and no one—can shield us from the work of untangling our inheritance. Instead, I burrowed into his chest where it was warm.

Every morning for the next six months, I went to the office and edited 401(k) newsletters, struggling to make small talk over dry bagels and coffee. At five o'clock, I climbed into my car and navigated back home over the wide, muddy Willamette River. Back home, I stripped off my work clothes, pulled on the same ratty pajamas, filled my jelly jar with wine, and climbed into bed with the journals and papers I'd found in the shed. I started with the more coherent ones, mundane tables tallying her monthly expenses and to-do lists, and quickly moved to the later entries, the ones right before her breakdown—mangled sheets of loose-leaf scrawled with disjointed narratives, words climbing a crooked trail off the page like she'd fallen asleep while writing. There were several copies of the same letters. To Nathan. To the police chief. To someone named Barry. All handwritten, with slight tweaks to the language, a new detail added or a phrase she didn't like crossed out. I didn't need much sleep during that time. Food became an afterthought. I was both dead to the world and ultra-alive, high on the energy potential of revelation. Something was churning up in me.

One night, Daniel pulled the journals gently from my hands.

"Maybe don't read those *every single* night, babe. I'm not sure it's good for you."

I smiled politely and nodded but had no intention of stopping. I had to read every single page, every word, every crossed-out line. For within them was the key, the legend. I didn't know what I was looking for. Just that I would know when I found it.

XXXI.

As I'd started talking more openly about the past, sharing snippets of my mom's story with friends, one of them insisted that I watch *Heavenly Creatures*.

Based on the true story of two teen girls growing up in New Zealand, Juliet and Pauline, the film paints a portrait of friendship bordering on obsession. Social outcasts who bond over childhood medical maladies, Juliet and Pauline spend all their time together. From the outside, everything looks giddy and frenetic as only teen girl friendships can. But in private, they are world-building. Juliet invents a place called Fourth World, an alternate heaven without Christians. She invites Pauline to Fourth World, and it turns out that Pauline can see the same things Juliet does—as if they have shared imagination. They start to spend more time together there. So much that it becomes more real to them than the actual world. Their parents don't realize how dysfunctional the friendship is until too late.

When Juliet's parents split up and decide Juliet will go to South Africa, Pauline begs to go along. Pauline's mother says no, sending her into a rage. Pauline decides to kill her mother and convinces Juliet to help her. Later, police find a diary entry describing the murder. The girls are arrested and sentenced to five years in prison. Upon release, they're forbidden from ever seeing each other. Separated, neither of them has another incident, and both go on to live eerily normal lives.

Watching the girls interact onscreen was uncanny. Their intimacy was deeper than romantic love. It was total enmeshment, in which their identities became so intertwined that they became unable to distinguish one from the other, reality from unreality, right from wrong. I imagined Mom and Raelle inhabiting a reality—actual or imagined—where a group of unnamed men were hunting them. Feeding off each other in a sort of frenzied bonding that no one else could understand. Which, from the outside, must have looked insane. Most reviews of *Heavenly Creatures* billed the girls as having a "unique bond," which is an extremely gentle, even euphemistic way of putting it. One, though, mentioned something more intriguing. A rare diagnosis: folie à deux.

The madness of two. Or in literal translation, the *folly of two.*

I fell down a rabbit hole, reading everything I could about it. The simplest way to think of folie à deux is as a contagion of thought that incites a temporary shared psychosis. Or mental illness as a temporarily transmittable virus. There are several different subtypes, and each has what's called an inducer, or a primary person—the one with mental illness—and a secondary, whom the illness rubs off on. How it gets passed between them is largely unknown, but to thrive, it requires two primary ingredients: intense intimacy and social isolation of the pair. The passive person often has a genetic predisposition to psychosis. Folie à deux is commonly co-morbid, meaning it's present with another mental illness.

In my mother's telling, Raelle's fear had overpowered and consumed her ability to choose for herself. But she left some things out that I read about later. She didn't tell me that the night before they lit themselves on fire, they stood at the intersection of East State and Market Streets in Ann Arbor and were taken in by the police. Pedestrians reported them for standing on the corner, silently staring at the moon for hours. They were in "some sort of trance," said the 9-1-1 caller. Down at the station, they must have pulled it together, because they revealed nothing to police, and with no evidence of suicidal or homicidal risk—the burden of proof necessary to place someone under involuntary psych hold in Michigan in 1971—the cops had to release them. One local news story even mentioned that their case would later bring Michigan's 5150 law into question. The next night, they lit their bodies like candles.

"We are still in complete darkness as to the matter," Chief Krasny reported in follow-up articles, while the women were still fighting to recover in the hospital. Everyone wanted to know *why*, wanted to know *how* this could happen to two nice girls like that. But Krasny had nothing to tell them. "Neither woman would ever communicate to us about it."

Some say the dead come to them. That their energy lingers. But after she died, my mother was out. Gone-gone-gone. I could tell because there was a vacuum in my consciousness, a hole torn in the sky fabric that I could look clear through. I could never do that before. Even when I was thousands of miles from her and we were barely talking, part of me was always with Mom or, in later years, bracing for what-next. While she was alive, I'd kept the darkest parts of her at a distance. The best parts of her, tucked inside of me.

But now I could see it all. Raelle. The Laredos. David. For the first time, I saw how similar the stories were. The paranoia. The obsession. And there were other things—smaller things. Tics and patterns of Mom's—not finishing sentences, calling herself different names—that I had clocked and registered in my subconscious over the years. I was flooded with memories, a running tally that I didn't even realize I'd been archiving for *someday*, for *just in case*. During coffee breaks at work, I scribbled in my notebooks—notebooks that started to mirror my mother's own with their wild tangents and spiraling margin notes. Individually, the things I remembered could be written off as spacey or eccentric, but against the backdrop of everything that had happened, the things that I'd always considered quirks started to look like symptoms. I thought back to the conversation with Charmaine in the cafeteria, I thought about the Laredos and David and the emails in Italy, about all that I'd shoved down or become desensitized to over the years. Then, one morning at work, from deep in the recesses of my mind sprang the memory of a hot senior guy I'd gone to school with. He'd had some kind of breakdown right before graduation, and afterward everyone said he was *permafried*. We'd all done a lot of acid, so that tracked. But when I ran into his sister years later and mentioned it, she'd looked at me in surprise.

"Oh no," she'd said. "You didn't know? He has schizophrenia. That was his first break."

The first break usually comes between ages eighteen and twenty, she'd told me. I remembered then what Mom said about the county therapist—"She says I'm not schizo." The realization landed with a soft, obvious thud. Both a shock and a feeling of *oh yes, there it is*. It was so clear and fully formed that I looked around to see if anyone else had noticed. But they were gossiping about the new hire and planning what to order for lunch. It was just me, alone with this startling moment, that changed both everything and nothing. I couldn't believe it had taken so long to emerge.

The next morning was Saturday. Pumped full of French press, I rode my bike to Powell's Books and took the stairs two at a time up to the Purple Room, where the mental health books were shelved. There, as I crouched alone on the cold linoleum, surrounded by a puddle of texts I'd pulled frantically from the shelves, my suspicion was confirmed.

My mother was practically textbook.

A schizophrenic break can look like many things. From the outside, it can resemble a nervous breakdown, but it's much more complex. The first fracture between interior and exterior reality, a break can lead to disordered, dissociative thinking, paranoid delusions, psychosis, hallucination, and even self-harm or violence against others. It's both a genetic and an environmental condition, meaning that while some people are predisposed to it, whether it manifests or not depends on environmental triggers. Many things Mom had been through—parental death, emotional abuse, substance abuse, and isolation—increase the chances of the illness firing.

A study by a group of British psychiatrists uncovered what they called a second peak of schizophrenic breaks in perimenopausal women around age forty-five, believed to be triggered by hormonal fluctuation. Mom was fifty-four when she died, and she'd been carrying around a jar of progesterone cream in her tote that she slathered on her arms after showers. Two psychotic breaks, triggered in part by hormones and exacerbated by underlying childhood stressors. It felt like letting out a breath I'd been holding all my life.

It was a term, a diagnosis, a container.

Schizophrenia settled over our story like a ruby filter.

For weeks, I visited the Purple Room whenever I could. This new reality was easier to absorb in the sterile anonymity of an air-conditioned bookstore. A wild fever rose in me every time I sprinted up the stairs and pulled books from their shelves greedily: *Surviving Schizophrenia. An Unquiet Mind.* Ravenous for anything to steady my churning grief, I became a researcher, an excavator, collecting facts, each one an edge piece to the puzzle. I read random passages about schizophrenia and madness, about its relationship to spirituality and martyrdom and persecution. I scoured the annals of literature, psychology, science, and religion. Plumbed the *Diagnostic and Statistical Manual*, mainstream psychiatry's bible. I learned about schizophrenia from psychiatrists' perspectives and from those who lived with it. Later, I'd dissect academic studies about self-immolation and trawl forums on astral travelers and walk-ins, spending long, dark days in the corner of the internet that is rife with sparkly, mispunctuated websites. I'd slog through as much as I could of Foucault's *Madness and Civilization.*

Slowly, I was building a new lexicon and, from that, a new lens for understanding my childhood. But it wasn't until I finally started to see a therapist that I understood a major part of why I'd been confused and silent for so long. Over a year of Wednesday afternoon sessions, a kind brunette woman named Molly listened to my story and provided one-to-one psychological terminology for the spiritual phenomena I'd come to take for granted.

Astral travel could be dissociation.

Channeling, hallucination.

Past-life regressions, trauma flashbacks.

But one term really changed everything. *Delusion.* The hallmark of a delusion is its imperviousness to debunking, Molly explained. No matter what facts or information are presented to the deluded person, what they believe and experience is the absolute truth. To disagree only agitates them and can render you irrelevant, or worse, cast you as an antagonist in their story. When delusions are clearly unreal—dreams of being married to a celebrity or seeing dragons, for example—they're easier to distinguish.

"But your mother's stories were harder to pinpoint," she said.

Because they were about real people and tracked with the culture and environment that we'd lived in, Mom's stories were actually plausible—at least, the earlier ones. And in the realm of the cosmic, the unbound, the astral, the later ones as well. While my adult reality no longer aligned with my mother's, as a child, what she had believed possible formed the bounds of my own imagination. Much of what she shared, I took at face value, not doubting it the way that someone raised in a more traditional or conservative mindset might. Even if something smelled off, I didn't disbelieve that it was true to her and that, theoretically, it was possible. In Texas and Florida, I'd been exposed to different lifestyles and values, but no one actively talked to me about what I was learning at home in California. I could either believe or reject my mother's ideas, but there was nowhere to work through them. To sort through and assess what might be valuable and what was unhelpful, even dangerous. Because my family was so decentralized, there were no checks and balances, leaving me on my own to puzzle through heady, esoteric ideas. At some point, I'd simply opted out.

Months passed as I meditated on delusion. How much of her persecution and struggle was real, and how much was potential illness talking? How might those states have been closer than they seemed? What I was really asking wasn't *why*, but *how*—how did we miss it?

How did I miss it?

XXXII.

I flew to Texas for the first time since college. Spring teased the air as we walked off our lunch of roasted squash and quinoa. Dad walked in the middle, always the intermediary between me and Beth. We stepped in unison, following the dip and rise of the two-lane asphalt road as it snaked toward Texas Highway 29. Baseball-size hunks of limestone dotted the shoulder of the Hill Country road. A foot below the rocky soil was a network of limestone mounds. When the flash floods of spring came, the landscape peeled off the earth like a sticker.

"I have this theory about my mom," I said.

"Oh?" said Dad, pushing his hands into the pockets of his puffy L.L.Bean vest. A brown wool scarf circled his neck like a languid rattlesnake. Even in Texas, he got cold. At five feet ten, he had maybe ten pounds on me, and what Beth and I had calculated was exactly zero percent body fat.

"I found a bunch of her journals," I said. "They were pretty wild. Got into this whole thing she had with this guy David." Even after I'd called them to ask for money to get Mom a lawyer, I'd never explained what led up to that night. And they'd never really asked.

"Was David a boyfriend?" asked Beth.

"No. I don't think so. I mean. I don't really know." As I spoke, my hands ironed the air, trying to smooth it into something cohesive. Something they could digest.

"I think she had schizophrenia," I blurted out.

The air soured. It was the first time I'd said it aloud, and immediately, I wanted to take it back. It felt too dramatic, too impossibly big to share in retrospect. It was disorienting, embarrassing almost, to be presenting the findings of my life with my own family. Something about it felt silly, vulnerable, wanting. But I forced myself not to explain more. To let them come to me. As I understood it, TM was used to cultivate a sense of unity, of bliss, of *we-are-oneness*, but it seemed to me that it could only be expressed sedately. *Take it easy*, Dad would say if I got too worked up. Too passionate. As if fervor was a bad thing, as if it might be contagious. Part of me hoped this would be it. That with this blatant declaration, we would finally have a real conversation about everything that had happened. That it was stark enough not to be brushed aside with transcendent truisms. That we could speak. It was time to speak.

"Really?" Dad nodded slowly, as if mulling over the possibility.

"Her symptoms matched what I've read about it word for word. A therapist confirmed—well, she can't unless she treated her. But said it seemed pretty clear. And the fires—who starts two fires?"

"I was never sure what you knew about the first," Dad said.

"She told me the *entire* story when I was *twelve*," I snapped, wincing at the fragile arrogance of my voice, my attempt to appear jaded. I think part of me yearned to see my father shocked. Not just that I knew the whole story but the fact that I'd heard it so young. Maybe I wanted to trigger his protective instinct. To see if he had one. Crossing his hands at the wrists, he continued slowly, methodically, up the hill.

"You probably know more about it than I do," he said.

"Maybe." I shrugged. "Probably."

"You know . . ." he said. "Once, your mom's father came to visit when we lived in Fairfield. She was upset with me then. Your grandpa Lou asked me if our relationship was okay, and I honestly didn't know what to say. Just then, the president of the university came walking by. He was sort of a big shot. And I remember your mom pulled her father aside, pointed to him, and said, 'See him there? That's my boyfriend.' Lou just looked at me like, 'What's going on here?' But I had no idea. I'd never heard her say anything like that before."

"And this man was not and had never been her boyfriend?" I asked.

"No," he said, tilting his head as he thought back to it. "I did see them talking in his office once. He looked a bit scared of her, now that I think of it."

Dad looked thoughtful, as if connecting the dots in real time. As if my story tapped strange instances he'd also stored but never had a larger narrative for. Had she been doing this for years? Was this guy the original Nathan, the first David? Why hadn't Dad told me about it? But then, why would he? He didn't know about the others.

At the bottom of the hill, we turned to start the walk back. Friday Mountain, where Dad and Beth had been married twenty-something years earlier, flashed in and out of view. A low, scrubby hill choked with brush and dried grass, it passed for a mountain in Texas. Beth looked expectant, as if waiting for me to say more.

"Were you . . ." I hesitated. "I don't know, ever concerned?"

I was talking about my mother, but also about me. I wanted to know if they'd spent nights wondering about my life. If they were concerned as we moved from town to town, swapping out homes, schools, spiritual practices, several times a year.

"You always had a special bond with your mom," Dad said. "I never thought it would be right, or wise, to take that away." He was right. About our bond. About keeping me with her. But I wanted to know what he *felt*. I wanted engagement, reaction, feedback, empathy, curiosity. His belief in TM as a panacea was so calcified that it was hard to elicit emotional responses from him besides *Have you been doing your program?* Trying to talk to him directly felt like solving a looping riddle whose only answer was *do more TM*.

We passed a wooden sign to the right of the road. Painted with a metallic golden sun, it marked the official entrance to their neighborhood: *Welcome to Radiance, Est. 1984. First and oldest Transcendental Meditation intentional community built from the ground up in the U.S.*

I thought of all those years I'd visited. In practical and at times existential ways, he had been there for me. I knew he loved me. He brought me to Texas in the summers. Gave me a real bedtime. Read me *The Hobbit* aloud and took me tubing and to Schlitterbahn and to Zilker Park to watch summer musicals. He taught me to ride a bike and got me a mantra. He paid my mom's overdue phone bills so we could still talk. He endeavored to bring stability and structure into my life that he knew I wasn't getting back home. He probably did many things I didn't know about. But there was little curiosity about the life I inhabited the rest of the year.

Anything I shared that invoked emotional turmoil or struggle was acknowledged with a polite nod or an even-keeled inquiry, soon to be swept away by that evening's meditation or a hot plate of whole-wheat pasta. Around Dad and Beth, I felt less evolved. As if my reality was too messy. Too base. Too human. As if I was always making a big deal about nothing. What they didn't seem to understand, and what I was struggling to tell them now, was that for the last fifteen years, I had said next to nothing about some things that were a very big fucking deal.

"She really was a believer," Dad muttered, almost to himself, as we started down the stone path back to their house.

"Who?"

"Your mom," he said, the corners of his mouth turning up just slightly, as if remembering something alive. Something that once burned between my parents, something that, in him, still did. Not romance or sex or desire, but spiritual devotion—belief. The belief that we can change the world with a simple vibration. If I could have asked my father for anything that day, it would have been to stay with me, in this moment on this earth. To react to what I'd said. To ask what it was like. To wonder.

I'd thought that sharing my revelation might bring him in. That I could puzzle through it with him. That maybe since the worst had already come to fruition, we could finally talk about what led up to it.

———————————————————————

Philosopher Jonathan Glover says belief systems are less like houses and more like Neurath's boat. We cannot change what we believe all at once. "We are like a sailor having to rebuild a boat at sea. The whole boat may need rebuilding, but at any one time we must keep enough of it afloat to enable us to reconstruct other parts." Motivational speakers and self-help gurus sell out stadiums to shout about how belief is the back door to getting what you want: redemption, nice hair, the perfect partner. Everything is for sale, but for those without money and power, *belief* is the most potent currency.

"Didn't he know something was wrong?" friends asked about my father. "What did your family think?"

The truth is, I really don't know.

Eventually, I ran out of ways to ask.

XXXIII.

I n her essay collection *The Collected Schizophrenias*, writer and scholar Esmé Weijun Wang, who has schizoaffective disorder, writes about how Western society has perceived the trajectory of "the schizophrenic":

> *The story of schizophrenia is one with a protagonist, "the schizo-phrenic," who is first a fine and good vessel with fine and good things inside of it, and then becomes misshapen through the ravages of psychosis; the vessel becomes prone to being filled with nasty things. Finally, the wicked thoughts and behaviors that may ensue become inseparable from the person, who is now un-recognizable from what they once were.*

The binary of one person who is pure and good and one who is soiled by illness prevents us from embracing a whole self. It assumes that somewhere inside exists an un-sick self, and if one could just be "free" of it, they would become themselves. But maybe they are not separate, says Wang. Maybe there is no inner unblemished self, say "mad activists," who reject the term *mentally ill* as a construct based in colonial capitalistic standards. In reclaiming the term *mad*, which was once used freely across cultures and became stigmatized by the Western psychiatric industry, they insist that madness is not "other," or outlying, or deficient, but another variation on human experience.

Simply put, there is nothing to "fix" in the individual. Instead, the work lies with society. Both how we think about, and the ways in which we accommodate or do not, varying degrees of experience. Some people choose to use psychiatric services like therapy or to take medications, and it is a choice like any other. Some don't call themselves patients, but consumers, like anyone going to CVS to buy vitamins or having elective surgeries. This not only returns agency to the people using those services but highlights that psychiatry is an industry, not a foundational facet of human experience.

While initially revelatory, without Mom there to discuss what I'd learned or to answer questions, the label of schizophrenia lost some of its air. Most of my life, she'd set the terms of her own existence and, by default, of mine. After she died, understanding her through a lens of mental illness was helpful because it offered concrete data to explain certain behaviors and events. But in a straightforward clinical interpretation, there was no room for other possibilities. No room for faith. As I began to reconsider my own capacity for belief, I had a hard time seeing her as a diagnosis.

The week before Mom lit Morris Street on fire, Dad, Beth, and I spent a night in Assisi, Italy, on our way to Rome. A bone-white village built into an Umbrian hillside, Assisi was the hometown of Saint Francis, whose relics were entombed in a crypt underneath the central basilica. In the church, relics are body parts or sometimes belongings of Catholic saints, which are found intact years, even decades, after their burial. The lack of decay, or what the church refers to as *corruption*, is seen as evidence of godliness. The relics are often representative of qualities the saint embodied— pieces of a heart or hands—as if those parts had been so enlarged and superhuman that they achieved immortality.

Flowers in hand, we descended the steps of the crypt, walking single file into a cold, brightly lit stone cavern. In the center of the room, a box housing the relics sat on a floodlit dais. Francis had been born rich, but after he was jailed in the Battle of Collestrada, God appeared to him and commanded him to forgo all worldly attachments, live a life of extreme poverty, and rebuild the church according to austere Christlike values. When Francis's release was negotiated, he set out to do just that. On his way back to Assisi, he encountered a man with leprosy, and leapt up to hug and kiss him.

Years later, Francis claimed the stigmata. Some speculated that it was leprosy, but by then he'd adopted such a pious lifestyle that he seemed a rightful recipient of stigmata. There was no way to be closer than to share twin wounds—stigmata as the ultimate trauma bond.

Because Francis was a priest, his experience was translated through the theology of the church, but what if he'd been a civilian claiming to share Jesus's crucifixion marks? What if he'd been that leper, doing the same work? Would he have been recognized, much less canonized? What made one group's wounds sanctioned and another's self-harm?

Most major world religions have a mystic offshoot for outliers, misfits, and renegades. People who felt too much, who *saw* too much. People whose boundaries were too porous. Like self-immolation, martyrdom is contextual. It reflects a particular time and ethos. I wonder how many churches and belief systems have expanded their theologies to explain the catatonic and the ecstatic—the mental states of their outliers. I wonder what work they've done, what categories they've created, to deem them sacred instead of insane.

⎯⎯⎯⎯⎯⎯⎯⎯⎯⎯⎯⎯⎯⎯⎯⎯⎯⎯⎯⎯⎯⎯⎯⎯

Three years had passed since my mom died, and whatever bohemian dream I'd imagined with Daniel was not panning out. I wasn't happy and I kept trying to tell him. Our mid-twenties had been a blur of loss and grief, work and recovery. Now we were creeping toward thirty and stuck—him waiting tables at the same restaurant, and painting on the side; me, grieving the lack of progress in my own career and second-guessing the choices I'd made. I'd left my office job and was working nights in a Peruvian restaurant so that I could pitch stories for magazines and newspapers during the day. I'd gotten some local reporting gigs and applied for every full-time position that came up on the job boards, but Portland was a small market. People with real writing jobs never left them.

One night on my way home from the restaurant, I stopped at the corner store to get a six-pack. At the register, a shiny pink five-dollar scratcher caught my eye. It felt just extravagant enough to be lucky.

"Two, please," I said to the clerk. "The pink ones."

Back home, Daniel and I sat on the couch, flecking away silver foil with dimes.

"I got nothing. You?" I glanced over his shoulder. He'd scratched off a pair of $100s and $10,000s. There was one number left to uncover. "Holy shit," I said. He held a finger to his lips before slowly rubbing away the silver film: *$5*.

"Ugggghhh." I clutched my side in mock pain and fell to the floor.

He shrugged. "Better luck next time."

"What would you do if you won the lottery?" I asked, cracking a beer.

"Hmm . . . probably build a house in Castella. Live by the river. Paint all day."

I chuckled and took a swig.

"*Nooo*. I'm talking about *money, honey*. The real deal. Thirty million bucks."

"I'd buy a house in Castella," he said firmly. "Maybe Sweetbriar."

"You're telling me that if you won THIRTY MILLION DOLLARS, you would move back to Castella?"

He bristled. "I love Castella. It's my home."

"Me too. That doesn't mean I'd want to live there, like, forever."

"You're not stuck. You're a millionaire. You can travel wherever you want. People come from all over the world to visit where we grew up, you know."

"I know," I said. "You don't have to sell me on it. What's keeping you from living there now, then?"

"Money, I guess? A way to make a living."

"Hmm," I said, more to myself than to him.

"What?" His face flushed.

"Nothing," I said. "I just never realized that."

What I did realize, lying there on the hardwood floor, gripping a sweaty beer, was that we'd never asked each other those sorts of questions. We had survived, but we'd never considered what thriving might look like.

As a kid, I'd dreamt of dance, of the stage, of costume and choreography, and the international art-filled life I'd imagined came along with it. But as things got darker at home, my commitment to normalcy, which in my kid-brain translated to security, had stunted my imagination and, at some point, stopped me from taking real risks. Daniel wanted a simple life—a life of early morning painting and baseball games on the radio. And so, I'd thought, did I. But once upon a time, I'd wanted more.

I was coming to terms with what denial had cost me and my family. I tried to talk to Daniel about this. About vague dreams stifled. But he swerved me every time. Brushing the conversation aside, he'd act like he didn't know what I meant. He didn't want to talk about discontent. About dysfunctional lineages. Not his, not mine. And I couldn't even fault him for it. That had been part of our unspoken deal. When you want things to remain unspoken, you find someone who knows the rules. Someone who recognizes you with the slightest nod across the bar. Who will keep your secrets without your ever asking. And who will expect the same in return. "Lying is done with words, and also with silence," writes poet Adrienne Rich in *Women and Honor.*

To call ours a trauma bond would be reductive and unsexy, and it would negate the fact that sex itself can drive the trauma—that passion is not a pathology but a complex system of triggers and desires, most hardly known to us. If he didn't want to talk, I gave him time. I waited for him to come to me. Instead of pushing, I dropped into the silence I knew well. For another year, we did this. It really doesn't make sense, but I guess I was waiting for him to agree with me. To tell me that we were indeed unhappy. To give me permission to leave. After a blowout fight, I reached my breaking point, wrote him an impassioned ten-page letter spilling all the feelings I hadn't gotten to talk through with him. I left it on his desk before work one day. When I came home, it was gone, but he never replied. He never even acknowledged the letter. We'd been together almost seven years. I kept waiting, and waiting, for something like permission.

It was time to let go. To learn how to say goodbye.

To blow this joint.

XXXIV.

For the next year, I oscillated between domestic goddess and party girl—between a woman desperate to make a home and one who no longer believed in the concept. I got my own apartment and constructed systems of cleanliness and order: early bedtime, boot-camp workouts, green juices, home cooking, and to-do lists with sweeping bullet-point directives like *get shit together* underlined in double red. A week later, I'd unravel it all by smoking and drinking, staying out all night, missing deadlines, isolating myself, and going through a series of short-term relationships and hookups. Build break build break build break. Home flight home flight. I lived in a state of continuous undoing. Of coming and going. I was parent and child. Structure and chaos. I was the man with the lighter holding up the convenience store. Burning the same house down, hoping to find something new in the rubble. It was a strange, almost psychedelic cycling through time, in which past, present, and future collapsed in on each other, as I attempted to gather pieces of myself that I'd lost along the way.

I was trying to get at what was under the grief. Some days, I was twelve and looking for what I'd lost at the Alpenrose; sixteen and shuttling my body through the dark to say *help*; twenty-two and daydreaming in Italian; twenty-four and buried under paperwork and grief. Ancient and newborn, ingenue and divorcée, I ran through the narrative possibilities of who I might be, but instead of doctor, teacher, engineer, I was trying on archetypes. The ones I'd seen modeled for me. I was still thinking I had to choose.

I was the virgin, pristine and brand-new.

The martyr, always suffering.

The whore, running through men like a night train.

The seer, who'd always known.

The savior, here to save myself.

To my friends, it must have looked chaotic. They were starting to get married, having kids, building companies and careers. Some days, I felt ashamed of the spiral. Like I was too old to be doing such sprawling, jumbled work on myself. *I should be more together*, I'd berate myself, on slow, sagging mornings after a weekend of backpedaling. It felt like I was regressing, but also like there was no other way to move forward. There was another voice, too—a different one. Steadier, less thrashing. *Trust me*, it said. *There's no other way.*

I see now that there was an element of controlled breakdown at play. A carefully mitigated identity destruction, *deconstruction*, that no one could have intervened or medicated or even counseled me out of. I was attempting to disintegrate and reconstitute a new self with only the parts I wanted to keep. To emerge anew, free of the past. I was in descent. Rowing the River Styx of my own psyche. No longer a noun, but a verb. A body in descent. But this time the goal wasn't the annihilation I'd chased at sixteen. It was integration. Starting over. Reparenting. Reinvention. All synonyms for how we might make ourselves whole. In a yoga class with a teacher I loved, I finally got it. *If you were never fifteen*, she said, *at some point you have to be fifteen. There's no way around it. And it's okay.* Just like I didn't feel thirty now, I hadn't felt fifteen when I was fifteen. I was older when I was young; now I had to be young again, to arrive, hopefully, in the present.

I did more yoga and started to dabble in kirtan, a form of ritual singing. For the first time in my life, I started a daily TM practice. And next to my bed, the stack of self-help books grew, the sort of reading I'd always avoided. Titles that might have made it to the back stacks of my mother's prayer room. *Women Who Run with the Wolves* and *The Artist's Way*. Even the men I dated morphed from rugged commercial fishermen and bartenders with neck tattoos to more spiritual types. There was the long-haired barista with a passion for butoh. The yogi who biked around town wine-drunk and draped in a dozen woolen shawls. They were men who talked about mother wounds and healing the womb, about the inner child and shadow work.

"The best thing that could happen to you," said the barista when I broke up with him, "is to lose total control." *Fuck you,* I'd thought, then, still clinging desperately to control. But he was onto something. Yes, I was healing and growing, but I kept hitting a wall. By letting myself fall apart and then immediately tidying the mess, I remained hidden. Some part of me didn't believe I deserved true stability. Or maybe I just couldn't stomach it yet. The only way I knew to be at home was in motion. I think what butoh barista meant was that to come out the other side, I had to let go completely. Of course, the other side of control is faith.

Gloria, my old friend from Dunsmuir, saw what was happening. We'd moved to Portland around the same time, and she had a five-year-old son now, whom I babysat often. When she came to pick him up one day, he was napping on my bed. We lay down by his side, and as she stroked his silky hair, I rambled on about the profound life lessons I was extracting from my latest romantic intrigue. She listened, then quietly, so as not to wake her boy, asked, "Is it spirituality, maybe? Is that what you're looking for?"

I sat up, primed to argue—the same knee-jerk reaction I had

when my father pushed TM as the answer to every problem. But instead, I started to cry. Gloria's eyes crinkled gently at the corners, and she placed her hand over mine.

So much of my identity had been formed around *not* believing. It was embarrassing to admit that I might need it. Faith was flimsy, mutable; it left you open for manipulation. For my mother, faith was a way to survive. But I'd seen how easy it was to slip away when you devoted yourself to anything so wholly. For me, letting go completely had never been safe. Like a pearl diver, even as I plunged deep, I had to remain tethered to land.

I wasn't like my parents—I didn't want my breath to become a slip. I didn't want to ascend. I didn't know how to live for the beyond and still care about life on earth. I had to fight to stay grounded—to not give in to nihilistic, addictive, escapist tendencies. For me, letting go would have looked less like transcendence and more like annihilation. It would have been the burn of tequila with gas station salt, the soft balloon of opium smoke. Without control, I'd still be dancing by the fire while the boys howled.

In a way, my mother's beliefs stole faith from me. It wasn't her fault and it's not what she meant, but mystical language was the original silencing force in my life. The way she'd used it to articulate her experiences—experiences that had grave outcomes—had so fucked up my ability to discern truth that somewhere along the way I'd conflated *believing* with being gone. I'd associated god with leaving. Gloria wasn't wrong. Butoh boy wasn't, either, if I'm honest. But I was defensive and wounded, most of all because I couldn't imagine what a faith of my own might look like. Certainly not my mother's mash-up of Christian Science meets Church Universal. And not my father's TM zealotry or practice as a Bahá'í. It was hard to stomach the growing wave of online yogis and tarot readers telling me to manifest my ideal life when I'd seen firsthand how the language of belief, of the divine, had been used to whitewash real-world problems. The misfits of the Tenderloin, the grubby

SRO kids, the single moms on the run, the small-town folks getting by on gossip and food stamps. So many people needed concrete things like food, shelter, jobs, medicine, and therapy. They
needed help, but what they got was god. If the etheric couldn't address people's most basic needs, what was it but a layaway plan that
never paid off?

In one of Mom's letters to me from jail, on coffee-stained paper
with thick purple marker, she wrote of the women in her cellblock.
During weekly craft sessions, they made paper flowers with Poli-
dent and turned toilet paper inserts into hair rollers. Most were in
on petty drugs and money crimes, she'd said, while the "real crim-
inals," politicians and DAs, ran free. "It's quite a life experience, all
right," she wrote. "Everybody shares and cares and I think that's
interesting. I've done about five tarot readings for the women. Just
using regular playing cards. I think they've gone well and been
helpful."

I imagined her holding court in the common room of Cellblock
D, no silk scarves to pretty up the industrial plastic tables, no candles to set the mood for ritual. There, just as she had in the Michigan burn unit thirty-three years earlier, she found a way to render
the space sacred, to make an offering. To move beyond circumstance, if not in body, then in spirit. In that letter and others like it,
I recognized a ghost of a mother I'd known. One at ease in smoky
pool halls, who spoke freely with people the rest of the world had
written off. An unlikely shapeshifter, she understood the disordered
mind.

In the cosmic terrain, she and her friends had more agency. If
they were working out their karma or moving through Spangler's
New Age levels or Maharishi's seven states of consciousness, they
didn't have to tussle directly with the systems—family, political, or
otherwise—that had failed them. Seeing themselves as lightworkers

lent gravitas and power to parts of their identities that capital-
ist America had tossed aside.

Before, I'd seen this cynically or as a cop-out, but in my own
spiraling, I was starting to understand that by refusing to align herself with any one source, such as the omniscient god of her Catholic
upbringing or even the diffuse ascended masters of the I AM movement, she'd decentralized the locus of wisdom, making it mobile
and flexible versus static; accumulative instead of all-knowing. She
did not have to belong to a group. To follow the rules. Or even stay
in one place. She could hit the road at will. Become her own traveling congregation. Do whatever she needed to keep her family
together. A freedom not afforded to generations of women before her.

It was true that she had never modeled careerism or shown me
how to organize a home or generate wealth or even wash my face
before bed at night. Sometimes I told myself that I had no role
model for a life that I'd want. But I began to understand that,
through small moments of reclamation and improvisation, she had
demonstrated what she thought most important—the right to live
a self-determined life. There had been a survival logic to her spiritual dabbling, an act of reclaiming power, one that could be read
in some lights as appropriative, in others feminist, even queer.

Maybe all those years, in defining her illness via spiritual imagery, she was claiming her vessel, rendering it—as Esmé Weijun Wang
writes—"fine and good." While my father's spiritual practice demanded devotion, my mother's practice demonstrated that deconstruction was an active part of belief—that faith was an action, not
an end point.

Whether throwing jailhouse tarot in a county-issued jumpsuit
or receiving a mantra under the fluorescent glare of hospital lights,
you could reach god anywhere, she seemed to say.

In the asylum as well as in the ashram.

Maybe the stigma of schizophrenia as split mind has been so

persistent because it's easier to say goodbye to one part of a person you love than to accept that they could be, that they *are*, terror and beauty in one. But maybe this is our work. To allow it all to exist at once. Maybe every complicated story, every contradictory, impossible, uncapturable, untellable story, is our chance at god. Every time we let many things be true at once, maybe that is god.

XXXV.

In the creation of *Schizophrene*, an exploration on the traumatic splitting of migration, British Indian poet Bhanu Kapil left the original version outside "in a dark garden" where it was buried under snowfall for months. When she retrieved it two seasons later, she reassembled the story with only the parts she could still make out. "I unstuck [the pages] to see. To read. I transcribe what I can, then throw the dirty book into the bin."

In my grief, I'd been searching and striving, leaving, and cleansing, loving and fucking, but really, I was trawling the depths for that one piece of information. Like Kapil, I'd hoped that by moving the information around, by letting the seasons make chaos then order of it, a life-changing truth would be revealed to me. I'd looked to systems like psychology and religion, history, and philosophy to explain my mother to me.

But after all the taxonomies and charts and internet deep dives and midnight revelations, I was left with little more than a pile of hypotheses and potential half-truths. Parts. Relics. They didn't bring my mother back to life or offer any cohesive resolution. No one field or theory, no excerpt or statistic or data set could encapsulate her or my experience of her. And nothing that I'd read or learned could turn back time or make my lived reality more stable. The edges and boundaries I'd needed as a kid couldn't be applied retroactively. Even naming—paranoid schizophrenia, delusion, hallucination, folie à deux, self-immolation—helped until it didn't.

And that's because the ultimate friction wasn't between the two of us. It was between her truth and the one allowed her by the outside world, a relationship for which I'd become, or elected myself, a conduit—a translator.

To live a self-determined life means not only being in charge of its logistics—what you eat, where you live, whom you work for— but also having the freedom to define those experiences for your-self. It means dignity is available to you no matter your bank account or state of mind. I needed my mother's life to be more than a statis-tic. To mean more than the flattened stories or possibilities we'd been served about women like her. About women who do not cleave to society's idea of the maternal, of the worthy; those forced to fight for dignity while struggling to keep their heads above water.

Women wandering the desert, *women*.

Women who need medication but who find god instead, *women*. Women who ask too much of their children. Women who are judged for having them at all.

To try and understand her, I'd been looking to the very systems that would have truncated her. Systems that are, by nature, reduc-tive. They rely on data and dogma. They pathologize and catego-rize. Until a certain age, I'd held all the possibilities of my mother, of woman, of person, at once, but in the outside world, they were in contradiction.

When there was nothing left to do, I began to write. For a year, every morning, I wrote. Snippets of memories and scenes emerged fully formed. I didn't craft them or worry about typos or overthink. I was a faucet and I let story flow through me until it ran dry. One day, it stopped just as abruptly as it had begun. *The End*, I wrote, laughing at the self-seriousness of it. At the impossibility of that be-ing the end. If only it was that easy. I sat on the couch and read what I'd written—300 pages—in one sitting. It was surreal. Like reading the story of someone else's life. On paper, the madness was undeniable.

"Writing is how I attempt to repair myself, stitching back former selves, sentences," writes Kate Zambreno in *Book of Mutter*, which she calls her impossible mother book. The book it took her thirteen years to write and never felt finished. The book that ate its own tail. "When I am brave enough I am never brave enough I unravel the tapestry of my life, my childhood."

In writing, I could make something matter by focusing on it. I could tell you *this is important* by giving it time. I could say *don't look away now, look closer now*. In writing, I could tell myself the things I'd been waiting for others to say: *You are here. I hear you. This matters, this meant something, she meant something, you mean something*.

I'd been waiting for others—family, friends, anonymous experts—to reflect some core truth back to me, but no analogous off-the-shelf story or data set could synthesize my life. Because that's how she made it. By taking what she liked from each practice, my mother had recentered *herself* as the source of knowledge. Of her own story.

So, then, could I. Could we all.

Like her, I would have to stitch together my own meaning.

I can see my mother writing. Hunched over the dining table, she scribbles away. In the car long after we've pulled into the driveway, notebook in lap, she waves Chris and me inside. "Be in soon, guys." Her hair is half down, one side a dark curtain veiling her face, the rest twisted into a small bun, held in a place with a Bic pen. Black. Round. She never used a dictionary or thesaurus. She didn't need them. Her vocabulary was expansive. She often used words that sounded unnatural when spoken. Too precise. Pretentious, almost.

But she never gave up the right to narrate life in her own words. She wrote obsessively, as if trying to record it. Maybe I was carrying that forward.

Maybe I could write what I couldn't find in any book. If I could envision all possible versions of her, locating her in the canons of psychology, literature, history, and art—if I could turn her into a psychological study, a treatise on fire, an anomaly, an esoteric priestess, a wounded healer, a motherless daughter, a firebrand, a martyr, a saint, a witch, an iconoclast, an individualist, a renegade, a mystic, a madwoman—then she would always be there in some form or another, the possibilities of her coursing through my veins, driving down the I-5 of my dreams. Not only could I render her immortal via narration, but if I could assign her suffering to some larger symbology or phenomenon, then no one could ever shrink her, people like her, or us, their children. My mother had the Laredos, and now I had her: my never-ending story.

Obsession as an antidote to death. Attention as a preservative to life.

Maybe that's why she wrote so many iterations of the same letters. To keep herself alive. To keep her story intact. "Schizophrenia is rhythmic," writes Kapil, "touching something lightly many times."

This is the ongoingness of madness.

XXXVI.

Over the next couple of years, I kept writing and rewriting. With near-religious fervor, I shaped and molded the initial outpouring of pages, understanding what had happened more and more with each revision. In a way writing became a conversation that I never got to have with her. But I could never capture the nuance I needed. My language wasn't refined enough. My thoughts clunky and rambling. I took workshops to improve my skill. I learned what a chapbook was. I learned how to write like an artist. I learned that I had always been one. Then a teacher encouraged me to apply to graduate school for creative writing. At first, I brushed off the idea. I'd already spent enough time pursuing a creative life and was looking into clinical psych programs, had even started taking prereqs at Portland State. It was time for a real job. *No*, she'd said. *You've got to see how far you can take this.* But her call to action stuck with me, and over a few weeks' time, it started to hum. Low and resonant at first, and then a great, clashing gong, until I broke down sobbing in a parking lot, certain that she was right. That for some reason I was supposed to tell this story. I started researching MFAs.

By then, Chris was living in Sacramento and working his way up in retail. He'd been through his own arc, the late teens and early twenties, a series of descents and rebirths. His story isn't mine to tell, but I walked alongside him as closely as I could, slowly getting to know each other as siblings, forming our relationship anew without our mother. As I was applying to MFA programs, we found ourselves at similar turning points in life. This would happen again and again, this syncing. Full system update, we'd call it.

A few years after Mom died, Chris got a huge tattoo that covered his whole calf to memorialize her and our uncle. It was a sacred heart with the words *RIP MOM AND DAN* floating above. When he first showed me, I was surprised. He'd never talked much about it, but there it was, inked on his skin, forever. That's how my brother was. Who he'd grown into. Quietly observant, internal, even-keeled. So unflappable that you sometimes wondered if he was paying attention. Then, out of nowhere, he'd say something so astute and you'd realize he was always watching, taking it in. Everything mattered even if he didn't say so. I wished I'd been able to remember that sooner, and more often.

After Mom died, and we rented out the house, we didn't have a place to be a family. He'd spent most Christmases with the Manns, and me, with my dad. But as we got older, we'd started spending occasional holidays together. The year I left for grad school, we were together for Christmas. We went to the bar and drank too much, and at some point started talking about the night Mom died. He told what he'd remembered and what he didn't.

He'd woken up suddenly at three a.m.

"Mom wasn't there," he said. "She was always home by then. I knew something was wrong." He told me how headlights had shone through the front window of Morris Street. He'd rushed to the door, nerves flaring, and pushed the blinds aside to see Jay Mann walking toward the house in full uniform. "I knew," he said, his voice cracking. "I knew before he even said it."

I could barely listen, my tears spilling over.

I remembered his message at work. How underwater he sounded. How I fell to the ground when he said the words. Looking across the shadowy bar at him, I wondered if he'd fallen, too. How many times he'd fallen since that he didn't tell me about. I'd wished I'd been there to catch him.

"I don't remember a lot of my childhood," he said.

"That's trauma, Chris," I said softly. "I think that's what it does."

I'd always had this idea of siblings, probably from the TGIF sitcoms we'd watched growing up, that you are bonded in a way no one else is. That it's you against your parents. You are each other's ride or die. But in our family, it was Mom who glued us together. And I'd tried to keep her together. I'd taken on roles that weren't mine, and missed out on the ones that were. More sheepdog than sister, I'd internalized my number one job as steering my brother away from the cliff. My contribution was keeping everything intact. I thought I had to guide him toward the life that Mom couldn't. But there was so little room for softness in that casting— no space for the camaraderie and care he might have needed most. As with Daniel, what had helped us survive would not help us thrive. Things had to change. And they would. Slowly and with friction and care. I wasn't going to lose my brother.

At thirty-three, I left for grad school on the East Coast. Chris volunteered to drive the U-Haul from Portland to Philadelphia, and Gloria decided to come along. The three of us set off, crammed into the bench seat of the truck, thousands of miles ahead of us. We were happy on the road. We stopped at a roadside clown museum. Detoured into Chicago for a hot dog. Crashed in cheap motels. Visited national parks. Saw a bear. Drank lots of tequila. Chris and Gloria saw their first fireflies. They teased me about my slow driving. I told my brother all about my string of eccentric boyfriends in Portland, and we laughed about our childhood—we'd come out with the same dark sense of humor. Chris taught us about World War II, which apparently, I'd never properly understood. He knew so much about science and history trivia and he doled it out as the landscape became corn and more corn. Whole days of nothing but corn. Mom would have been happy to see us like this, on the road again, doing what we'd done best together—*getting out of Dodge*. As we barreled toward Iowa, toward the skies under which I'd been born thirty-three years earlier, where my parents flew toward enlightenment, I was unsure if I'd ever come back west.

One night, we wound up in rural Nebraska past midnight with nowhere to sleep. The road was pitch-dark and super narrow, with no cars in sight. At the wheel, Chris was anxious and hyper-focused. We were all exhausted. Someone snapped over something petty and he pulled the truck over.

"Fuck this," he said. "I need a break." We got out to shake it off, and as my brother lit a cigarette, I climbed onto the roof of the U-Haul, lay down, and gasped. The sky was a dome, like the nights back in Shasta but even darker. Shooting stars fell at random, long bright tails streaking the sky. "Guys!" I called. Chris and Gloria climbed up, and we lay head to head, shouting and pointing at each star, as the truck's roof buckled and creaked underneath us. The night was warm and quiet, and by the time we crawled back down, the tension had dissolved.

"What if we'd never seen that?" I asked, wide-eyed as Chris pulled back onto the road.

If we'd never taken that road, poorly planned our hotels, if Chris hadn't been tired, if we weren't annoyed, we would have never seen those stars. But also, everything that came before. Everything that led us to a moment of sacred awe under a dark night sky in Nebraska.

Images of my possible lives surfaced like cutouts from magazines, aspirational collages from future and past. It was hard to tell anymore, which one was which. If my mother had been around, she might have balked at how little I'd learned. Future and past were not mutually exclusive, she might say. Didn't I finally get it? Our lineage was not just the blood in our veins but the chain of women before and after us who knew passion and effervescence, who'd seen the limits of their light and been disintegrated and re-made by their dark.

There are these moments I still can't get right. Moments where the record skips. The glitch in the matrix. The déjà vu. The *this already happened*. She already burned. *I know that.* She burned it all. *Bruci-ato tutto.* They are moments of fracture. Of trauma. Of the schism between what my mother told me and what I knew or saw. I trace their flight paths—those points of departure—endlessly in my dreams, trying to repair them, to make them whole enough to travel, again. But there is no beginning to return to. Nor an end. These stories are loops. Inherited. Ancient. Collective. Self-help gurus talk about finding your voice like it's a sweater you retrieve from the lost and found. But I don't think it happens that way. Voice is accumula-tive. Accretive. At times, porous. Everything that has rained through me is part of me. But I don't have to catch it all anymore.

Maybe those of us compelled to tell fractured family stories are the ones who feel unfinished. Maybe we take the ancestors into us and live out all possible lives, wandering down alleyways not ours, just to tie up storylines. In the gap left by my mother's family, the Detroit people, the Canadians, the Catholics and Québécois, the hockey lovers and Crown Royals, the Labatt Blues, I emerge as mother, father, brother, sister. I am the metallurgist, transforming alloy into cars. The alchemist rendering mercury to gold. I am per-fection and its destruction. I am flashover. The whole damn room combusting. I am splitting this town. I am blowing this joint. I am a woman on the run. A neon flash if you blink.

We carry all of the story, see.

We are the whole thing.

EPILOGUE

The Embers, or *Holy Fucking Shit*

Philadelphia, 2014

A month into a grueling grad school schedule, I'm running on caffeine and delirium, my nights spent drinking cheap beers and smoking cigarettes with old men in a Rittenhouse dive bar that serves 49-cent hot dogs from a lukewarm vat in the back. Naps and baths are my salve. I wake one afternoon to a text from my brother:

Weed is Burning.

What, lol.

It's gone, he writes.

What are you talking about?

Check the news.

The wind was strong the day that a man named Ronald started a fire behind Boles Creek. It was the kind of day that drew Abner Weed to settle the area. To build his milling empire. The fire went from ignition to free burn fast, tearing across town, up the hillside, and funneling into Angel Valley, where it destroyed the entire neighborhood within hours. A hundred and fifty-seven homes were gone. Morris Street was one of them.

Our home had burned down, again.

Shell-shocked, later that night in class, I try to explain the fire to my cohort. They're sympathetic enough, but can't possibly grasp what it means. And I have no way to tell them. How do you express that no fire will ever be just a fire again. That every fire will forever be all of them. Endless. Accruing. *The compulsion to repeat trauma.*

―――――――――――――――――――

It's New Year's Day, a few months after the fire, and I'm standing alone in front of Morris Street. I've flown home to see it one last time. This time, there's no burnt frame or shattered glass, no burnt grass full of charred photos, or poles for the fence we'd never built. The lot has been returned to the earth—wiped clean of us. There's no evidence that we'd ever lived there. Not a single remnant. As if it had all been a dream.

I look toward Mount Shasta. There's less snow now than when we were growing up. Her ridges are marbled with brown earth. She seems less mystical, unsheathed like this—more real.

"Whenever I look at a mountain, I always expect it to turn into a volcano," writes Italo Svevo in *Further Confessions of Zeno,* his sequel to the book I'd toiled through in Padua. Growing up, I'd thought the same. I dreamt of lava flows and eruption, of earthquakes and fires and aftershocks—of all the ways the earth might split open and swallow us. And while I'd been looking outward, it was happening all around me. For so long, I'd clung to the belief that home, that four walls, that normalcy, and acceptance, would save me. Mom tried to tell me it wouldn't. We have figured out how to harness a flame, to bring the wildness of fire into the home, to cook and warm ourselves with it. But it remains impervious to true domestication. I understand now. Maybe we were always going to arrive here.

Standing at the lot, I call Chris and tell him about a conversation Mom and I had many years ago. A conversation in which she'd told me that she wanted to leave him the house. I'd been renting it out for years, managing it until he was older, and might want to sell it.

When Mom first told me her wishes, the house had been a dump. But since the first fire and the rebuild, its value had tripled.

I tell my brother what Mom wanted, and that when the insurance check comes through from this fire, it's his. I hear the surprise and relief in his voice. *It's a cosmic middle finger from Mom,* I say. We joke that she somehow set this fire to get a return on her investment.

Talk about playing the long game, we say.

I hope this will give my brother space to breath. To imagine, what next?

With the final burning of Morris Street, we got something that many never do. A true ending. A full stop. A chance to arrest the repetition of our family story—the ongoingness of madness, of loss. Our histories speak through us. If we are lucky, we get to transmute their broken bits into something complete. To fuse the fragments into a whole.

Sometimes saying goodbye means burning it all down.

And then we work, begin again, with the charred bones left behind.

Mom and me, c. 1985. Trinidad, Humboldt County, California

Mom, me, and Chris, c. 2000, beach road trip, Humboldt County

ACKNOWLEDGMENTS

Thank you to the Dutton leadership for believing in my story and giving it a home: Amanda Walker, Stephanie Cooper, John Parsley, and Christine Ball.

Special thanks to Lauren Morrow and Isabel DaSilva for working so hard to introduce this book to the world.

To the Dutton production, editorial, and design teams—the GOATs! Thank you for your skill, vision, collaborative spirit, and endless patience for my perfectionistic eleventh-hour requests: LeeAnn Pemberton, Joy Simpkins, Catherine Mallette, Nancy Inglis, Lisa Silverman, Gaelyn Galbreath, Shannon Plunkett, Jason Booher, and Rachel Willey.

To my editor, Pilar Garcia-Brown. It was you or no one. Your vision helped me finish the never-ending story. Look what we made. Our little Frankenstein.

And to my agent, Nicki Richesin. You never doubted the potential and value of my story. You did this. I cannot thank you enough.

I have so much gratitude for everyone in the publishing world who was generous with their time and knowledge. Sharing information with young writers is one of the most equalizing things you can do. I will always pay it forward. Thank you to the institutions and communities who have supported my writing: The Attic, Rutgers-Camden MFA, Corporeal Writing, Sarah Lawrence, New York State Writers, Religion and Environment Story Project,

Banff Centre for the Arts, NYSCA-NYFA, the Writers Room, and all the editors who have published me over the years.

To the teachers that got me here, thank you. Mr. Simpson. Instead of brushing me off, you gave me a job. Anna Joy Springer. Your class was the first place that I felt like an artist. Cheryl Strayed. You said, "This is a big story. Write it all. Take your time." I'm not sure you meant a decade, but it was and I did. Jennifer Lauck, you taught me to write scenes. Lee Montgomery pooh-poohed my plans to become a psychologist and demanded I see how far I could take this writing thing. Lidia Yuknavitch, who told me never to call this story "my personal writing." That was part of the permission I needed. To the Rutgers MFA for supporting my work. Special thanks to Paul Lisicky, whose precision, musicality, and grace continue to guide me. And to Patrick Rosal, whose intellect and spirit solidified that *we can* be a whole self in all spaces. You helped me crystallize and claim my poetics. You asked, *Where is the anger?* To my MFA cohort. Your laughter, tears, and cheers got me through a strange time. Long live Dark Room. To Cherita Harrell, Shelby Vittek, and Micaiah Johnson, for reading many clunky versions of this manuscript with such ferocity of care. Special eleventh-hour shout-out to Micaiah for real-time editing and pushing me to write the drama, always. You are *the bar.*

To SAVOR. Our work was the foundation of it all. Kari Luna and Claudia Savage and Alissa Bohling, who read what this would become so many years ago and went through the living of much of it. Your support in both work and life has gotten me here. To the first writers I met in New York: Zaina Arafat, Meredith Talusan, Lewis Raven Wallace, Tim Manley, Kaye Toal, Kaitlin Ugolik Phillips, Voichita Nachescu. Finding you was my dose of *beginner's luck* in the city—everyone gets one.

To Angela Chen, Lilly Dancyger, Deena ElGenaidi, and Jeanna Kadlec, my New York writing earth-moon gang. The creative trust we've built is rare and I cherish it. I want the world for you all. Special thanks to Lilly, who has supported this project and my career through all its New York iterations.

To Siskiyou County. To my friends and neighbors and the land, all that beautiful earth. To the mountain, the rivers, the endless forest. To Castle Creek. You stamped me in ways I will never untether from. Which, I think, is mostly what people mean when they say *home*. Daniel. For holding my hand and feeding me during the darkest time of my life. To E$ and the DeLeons: Much love. RIP Lencho. RIP Nonni. My sisters, Carra, Gloria, Charmaine, Sierra. Without you I would have withered on the stem lifetimes ago. When my mother died, we didn't know what to do, but we did it together.

To my Detroit family, I wish we'd had more time together. RIP Dan, Rod, Lou, Louise, Fern, Fred. Thank you to my grandmother and grandad, RIP, for your support. To Liz, my number one fan and cousinsister. To my father. It's a rare and special thing to have a parent that cares more for the world than for their individual experience of it. Thank you for accepting this story with grace. To Chris. Of all the brothers I could have gotten, I'm so grateful it was you. Thank you for understanding why I needed to tell this story. To "Rick" and "Rick Jr." Thank you for holding it down in the early days and for bringing us Chris. RIP Rick. To Colleen, who held me down in the final legs of this book. Thank you for everything you did and for believing in me.

To my mother. Thank you for radicalizing me before I knew what the word meant. When I wanted to throw your ashes into the tongue of the ocean, Chris said you'd had enough depth for one lifetime and thought you'd be happier floating along on the surface, maybe stopping for a rum punch. I hope you're living pain-free. To my maternal ancestors: This book is a love letter and a spell to break a long line of sadness and disconnection. Let it heal and restore us, forward and back.

Finally, in the words of West Coast doggfather himself, Snoop

D-O-double-g, whose eponymous album got me through the gnarly teen years at the heart of this book: "I wanna thank me for believing in me / I wanna thank me for doing all this hard work / I wanna thank me for having no days off / I wanna thank me for . . . for never quitting." Till the wheels fall off.

WORKS CONSULTED

CHAPTER I

Doughty, Caitlin. *Smoke Gets in Your Eyes: And Other Lessons from the Crematory.* New York: W. W. Norton & Company, 2015.

Ettling, B. V. "Colors of Smoke and Flame." *Fire and Arson Investigator* 30, no. 4 (April–June 1980): 39–41. National Criminal Justice Reference Service.

Geddes, Linda. "Body Burners: The Forensics of Fire." *New Scientist*, May 20, 2009. https://www.newscientist.com/article/mg20227091 -300-body-burners-the-forensics-of-fire/.

"Lovely to Die Together." *St. Joseph (Michigan), Herald-Press*, November 11, 1971.

Ouellette, Jennifer. "Burn, Baby, Burn: Understanding the Wick Effect." *Scientific American*, October 12, 2011. https://blogs .scientificamerican.com/cocktail-party-physics/burn-baby-burn -understanding-the-wick-effect/.

Than, Ker. "In Space Flames Behave in Ways Nobody Thought Possible." *Smithsonian*, December 2012. https://www.smithsonianmag .com/science-nature/in-space-flames-behave-in-ways-nobody-thought -possible-132637810/.

CHAPTER II

Anderson, David E. "Maharishi Promises 'Taste of Utopia.'" UPI, December 17, 1983.

Bryant, Edwin F. "The Metaphysical Logic of the Siddhis, Mystic Powers, in Patañjali's Yoga Sūtra." *Journal of Dharma Studies* 3, no. 1 (2020): 3–15.

Hartlaub, Peter. "100 Years of Headlines in the Tenderloin: A Century of Stories from San Francisco's Tenderloin." *San Francisco Chronicle*, February 4, 2022. https://www.sfchronicle.com/projects /2022/san-francisco-tenderloin-history/.

Hatchard, Guy D., Ashley J. Deans, Kenneth L. Cavanaugh, and David W. Orme-Johnson. "The Maharishi Effect: A Model for Social Improvement. Time Series Analysis of a Phase Transition to Reduced Crime in Merseyside Metropolitan Area." *Psychology, Crime & Law* 2, no. 3 (1996): 165–74. https://doi.org/10.1080/10683169 608409775.

Hudson, Wade, and Rob Waters. "The Tenderloin: What Makes a Neighborhood." In *Reclaiming San Francisco: History, Politics, Culture*, edited by James Brook, Chris Carlsson, and Nancy J. Peters, 301–16. San Francisco: City Lights, 1998. https://archive.org/details /reclaimingsanfra00.

Iowa State Data Center. n.d. "Total Population for Iowa's Incorporated Places: 1850–2000."

Satchidananda, Sri Swami. *The Yoga Sutras of Patanjali*. Virginia: Integral Yoga Publications, 2012.

Sufismreoriented.org. n.d. "Meher Baba." https://www.sufismre oriented.org/avatarmeherbaba.

CHAPTER III

Reeves, Mosi. "How Bay Area Hip-Hop Found Its Sound in the 1980s." KQED, April 5, 2023. https://www.kqed.org/arts/13927349 /bay-area-hip-hop-1980s.

CHAPTER IV

California Regional Economic Analysis Project. "Siskiyou County vs. California Comparative Trends Analysis: Population Growth &

Change, 1969–2021." https://california.reaproject.org/analysis/comparative-trends-analysis/population/tools/60093/60000/.

Du Bois, Cora. *Wintu Ethnography.* Berkeley: University of California Press, 1935.

Maynor, Malinda, and Christopher McLeod. *In the Light of Reverence.* Independent Television Service & Native American Public Telecommunications, 2001.

Miesse, William. "Mount Shasta Fact Sheet with References." June 21, 2005. College of the Siskiyou's Library, Mount Shasta Collection. http://www.siskiyous.edu/library/shasta/factsheet/.

Oregon History Project. *In the State of Jefferson.* Brochure, 1959. https://www.oregonhistoryproject.org/articles/historical-records/state-of-jefferson-brochure/.

Towendolly, Grant, as told to Marcelle Masson. *A Bag of Bones: The Wintu Myths of a Trinity River Indian.* Naturegraph Press, 1966.

Winnemem Wintu Tribe. n.d. "Who Are We." http://www.winnememwintu.us/who-we-are/.

CHAPTER V

Duntley, M. "Spiritual Tourism and Frontier Esotericism at Mount Shasta, California." *International Journal for the Study of New Religions* 5, no. 2 (2015): 123–50. https://doi.org/10.1558/ijsnr.v5i2.26233.

Faivre, Antoine. *Theosophy, Imagination, Tradition: Studies in Western Esotericism,* translated by Christine Rhone. New York: SUNY Press, 2000.

Gecewicz, Claire. "'New Age' Beliefs Common Among Both Religious and Nonreligious Americans." Pew Research Center, Washington, DC, October 1, 2018. https://www.pewresearch.org/short-reads/2018/10/01/new-age-beliefs-common-among-both-religious-and-nonreligious-americans/.

Harvey, Sarah, and Suzanne Newcombe, eds. *Prophecy in the New Millennium: When Prophecies Persist.* Burlington, VT: Ashgate, 2013.

Kadlec, Jeanna. *Heretic*. New York: Harper, 2022.

Meltzer, Marisa. "QAnon's Unexpected Roots in New Age Spirituality." *Washington Post*, March 29, 2021. https://www.washingtonpost.com /magazine/2021/03/29/qanon-new-age-spirituality/.

Pew Research Center. *Beyond Distrust: How Americans View Their Government*. Report, November 23, 2015, Washington, DC. https:// www.pewresearch.org/politics/2015/11/23/beyond-distrust-how -americans-view-their-government/.

Rudbøg, Tim. "H. P. Blavatsky's 'Wisdom-Religion' and the Quest for Ancient Wisdom in Western Culture." In *Innovation in Esotericism from the Renaissance to the Present*, edited by Georgiana D. Hedesan and Tim Rudbøg, 201–28. London: Palgrave Macmillan, 2021. https:// doi.org/10.1007/978-3-030-67906-4_8.

Rudbøg, Tim. "I AM Activity." World Religions and Spirituality Project, August 9, 2016. https://wrldrels.org/2016/10/08/i-am.-activity/.

Spangler, David. *Revelation: The Birth of a New Age*. San Francisco: Rainbow Bridge, 1976.

Ward, Charlotte, and David Voas. "The Emergence of Conspirituality." *Journal of Contemporary Religion* 26, no. 1 (2011): 103–21. https://doi.org/10.1080/13537903.2011.539846.

Washuta, Elissa. *White Magic*. New York: Tin House, 2021.

CHAPTER VII

Baker Eddy, Mary. *Science and Health with Key to the Scriptures*. Boston: Christian Science Publishing Society, 1934.

City of Weed. n.d. "About Weed." https://www.ci.weed.ca.us/about.

De Botton, Alain. *The Architecture of Happiness*. New York: Vintage Books, 2006.

Fire Safety and *Logging for Lumber*. Exhibits at Weed Historic Lumber Town Museum. Weed, California: Ongoing.

Kuzui, Fran Rubel, dir. *Buffy the Vampire Slayer*. California: Kuzui Enterprises, 1992.

LaLande, Jeff. "The State of Jefferson: A Disaffected Region's 160-Year Search for Identity." *Oregon Historical Quarterly* 118, no. 1 (Spring 2017): 14–41. Project MUSE.

Langford, James. "African Americans in the Shadow of Mount Shasta: The Black Community of Weed, California." Blackpast.com, March 15, 2010. https://www.blackpast.org/african-american -history/african-americans-shadow-mt-shasta-black-community-weed -california/.

Maté, Gabor, MD. *The Myth of Normal: Trauma, Illness & Healing in a Toxic Culture.* New York: Avery, 2022.

Montgomery, Ruth. *Strangers Among Us: Enlightened Beings from a World to Come.* New York: Coward, McCann & Geoghegan, 1979.

Newberger, Devra. *The Magic of Paula Abdul: From Straight Up to Spellbound.* New York: Scholastic Point, 1991.

Schucman, Helen. *A Course in Miracles.* New York: Viking: Foundation for Inner Peace, 1976.

CHAPTER VIII

Tanzer, Michal, George Salaminios, Larisa Morosan, Chloe Campbell, and Martin Debbané. "Self-Blame Mediates the Link Between Childhood Neglect Experiences and Internalizing Symptoms in Low-Risk Adolescents." *Journal of Child & Adolescent Trauma* 14 (March 2021): 267–77. DOI: 10.1007/s40653-020-00307-z.

United States Geological Survey, Mount Shasta Eruption History. https://www.usgs.gov/volcanoes/mount-shasta/eruption-history.

CHAPTER IX

Kirkland, Gelsey, with Greg Lawrence. *Dancing on My Grave.* New York: Doubleday, 1986.

CHAPTER X

Greene, Brian. *Until the End of Time.* New York: Knopf, 2020.

CHAPTER XI

Benn, James A. *Burning for the Buddha: Self-Immolation in Chinese Buddhism.* Honolulu: University of Hawaii Press, 2007.

Bradatan, Costica. "The Political Psychology of Self-Immolation." *The New Statesman*, September 17, 2012.

Central Tibetan Administration. n.d. "Self-Immolation Archives." https://tibet.net/tag/self-immolation/.

Hạnh, Thích Nhất. "In Search of the Enemy of Man." Letter to Martin Luther King Jr. *Dialogue.* Vietnam: La Boi Press, 1965.

Oppedahl, John, and Jim Neubacher. "2 Women Set Selves Afire in Ann Arbor." *Detroit Free Press*, November 11, 1971.

Ryan, Cheyney. "The One Who Burns Herself for Peace." *Hypatia* 9, no. 2 (Spring 1994): 21–39.

Sanburn, Josh. "A Brief History of Self-Immolation." *Time*, January 20, 2011.

Veselka, Vanessa. *Zazen.* Brooklyn, NY: Red Lemonade, 2011.

Yang, Michelle Murray. "Still Burning: Self-Immolation as Photographic Protest." *Quarterly Journal of Speech* 97, no. 1 (2011): 1–25. https://doi.org/10.1080/00335630.2010.536565.

CHAPTER XV

U.S. Fire Administration. "Recognizing Flashover Conditions Can Save Your Life." May 5, 2020. https://www.usfa.fema.gov/blog /cb-050520.html.

CHAPTER XVII

Althusser, Louis. *On the Reproduction of Capitalism.* New York: Verso Books, 2014.

Danker, Jared. "Susanna Kaysen, Without Interruptions." *The Justice*, February 4, 2003. https://www.thejustice.org/article/2003/02 /susanna-kaysen-without-interruptions.

DeMare, Nikita. "Exaggerations and Stereotypes of Schizophrenia in Contemporary Films." *Elon Journal* 7, no. 1 (2016). http://www.inquiriesjournal.com/articles/1474/exaggerations-and-stereotypes-of-schizophrenia-in-contemporary-films.

Foucault, Michel. *Madness and Civilization: A History of Insanity in the Age of Reason,* translated by Richard Howard. New York: Pantheon Books, 1965.

Plath, Sylvia. *The Bell Jar.* London: Heinemann, 1963.

U.S. Census Bureau retrieved from FRED, Federal Reserve Bank of St. Louis. "Estimate of Median Household Income for Siskiyou County, CA." September 7, 2023. https://fred.stlouisfed.org/series/MHICA06093A052NCEN.

Wedding, Danny, Mary Ann Boyd, and Ryan M. Niemiec, *Movies and Mental Illness: Using Films to Understand Psychopathology,* 2nd ed. Cambridge, MA: Hogrefe & Huber, 2005.

CHAPTER XVIII

Black, J. A., G. Cunningham, E. Fluckiger-Hawker, E. Robson, and G. Zólyomi. *"Inanna's Descent to the Nether World* (translation)." The Electronic Text Corpus of Sumerian Literature at Oxford, 1998.

Grahn, Judy. *Eruptions of Inanna: Justice, Gender, and Erotic Power.* New York: Nightboat Books, 2021.

Tharp, Twyla. *The Creative Habit.* New York: Simon & Schuster, 2006.

CHAPTER XIX

Joyner, Owen. "Student Sets Self Afire; Dies to Protest War." *Triton Times,* May 12, 1970.

CHAPTER XXIV

Baechler, Jean. *Suicides,* with a foreword by Raymond Aron; translated by Barry Cooper. New York: Basic Books, 1979.

Brown, Adrienne Maree. *Emergent Strategy: Shaping Change, Changing Worlds.* Chico, CA: AK Press, 2017.

Duggan, Marian, ed. *Revisiting the "Ideal Victim": Developments in Critical Victimology*, 1st ed. Bristol, UK: Bristol University Press, 2018. https://doi.org/10.2307/j.ctv301ds5.

Pickard, Hanna. "Self-Harm as Violence: When Victim and Perpetrator Are One." In *Women and Violence: The Agency of Victims and Perpetrators*, edited by H. Widdows and H. Marway. London: Palgrave Macmillan, 2015.

Schulman, Sarah. *Conflict IsNot Abuse: Overstating Harm, Community, Responsibility, and the Duty of Repair.* Vancouver: Arsenal Pulp Press, 2016.

CHAPTER XXV

Cappadonna, "Slang Editorial." Track 1 on *The Pillage*. Razor Sharp and Epic Street, 1998, compact disc.

Van der Kolk, Bessel A. "The Compulsion to Repeat the Trauma: Re-enactment, Revictimization, and Masochism." *Psychiatric Clinics of North America* 12, no. 2 (1989): 389–411. https://doi.org/10.1016/S0193-953X(18)30439-8.

CHAPTER XXVIII

Desmond, Matthew. *Poverty, by America*. New York: Crown, 2023.

Karger, H. J. "The 'Poverty Tax' and America's Low-Income Households." *Families in Society* 88, no. 3 (July 2007): 413–17. https://doi.org/10.1606/1044-3894.3650.

CHAPTER XXIX

Whitsel, Bradley C. *The Church Universal and Triumphant: Elizabeth Clare Prophet's Apocalyptic Movement*. New York: Syracuse University Press, 2003.

CHAPTER XXX

Newspapers.com. Archive of all articles from the night of the fire. https://www.newspapers.com/search/?query=anita%20mcqueen&ymd-start=1971-11-01&ymd-end=1972-12-31.

CHAPTER XXXI

Culbert, Kristin, Katherine N. Thakkar, and Kelly L. Klump. "Risk for Midlife Psychosis in Women: Critical Gaps and Opportunities in Exploring Perimenopause and Ovarian Hormones as Mechanisms of Risk." *Psychological Medicine* 52, no. 9 (July 2022): 1612–20. https://doi.org/10.1017/s0033291722001143.

Dewhurst, Kenneth, and John Todd. "The Psychosis of Association—Folie à Deux." *Journal of Nervous and Mental Disease* 124, no. 5 (November 1956): 451–59.

Hochman, Karen M., and Richard R. Lewine. "Age of Menarche and Schizophrenia Onset in Women." *Schizophrenia Research* 69, no. 2–3 (August 2004): 183–88. https://doi.org/10.1016/S0920-9964(03)00176-2.

Shimizu, Mitsue, Yasutaka Kubota, Motomi Toichi, and Hisamitsu Baba. "Folie à Deux and Shared Psychotic Disorder." *Current Psychiatry Reports* 9, no. 3 (July 2007): 200–205. https://doi.org/10.1007/s11920-007-0019-5.

Torrey, E. Fuller. *Surviving Schizophrenia: A Manual for Families, Consumers, and Providers,* 4th ed. New York: Harper, 2001.

CHAPTER XXXII

Glover, Jonathan. "Ideological Conflict, Philosophy and Dialogue." Opening address, Royal Irish Academy conference. JonathanGlover.co.uk. (Originally the opening address at a conference of the Royal Irish Academy.)

CHAPTER XXXIII

Acocella, Joan. "Rich Man, Poor Man." *The New Yorker,* January 6, 2013.

LeFrançois, Brenda A., Robert Menzies, and Geoffrey Reaume, eds. *Mad Matters: A Critical Reader in Canadian Mad Studies.* Toronto: Canadian Scholar's Press, 2013.

Rich, Adrienne. *Women and Honor: Some Notes on Lying.* London: Only Women Press, 1979.

Wang, Esmé Weijun. *The Collected Schizophrenias*. Minneapolis, MN: Graywolf Press, 2019.

CHAPTER XXXV

Kapil, Bhanu. *Schizophrene*. New York: Nightboat Books, 2011.

Zambreno, Kate. *Book of Mutter*. South Pasadena, CA: Semiotext(e), 2017.

EPILOGUE

Svevo, Italo. *La coscienza di Zeno* or *Zeno's Conscience*. Milan: Mondadori, 1998 (originally Rocca San Casciano: Cappelli, 1923).

ABOUT THE AUTHOR

NINA ST. PIERRE is a queer essayist and culture writer whose work has appeared in *Elle, GQ, Harper's Bazaar, The Cut, Gossamer, Nylon, Outside,* and more. Nina is a 2023 NYSCA/NYFA Artist Fellow in Nonfiction Literature. She holds an MFA from Rutgers and lives in New York City.